DATE			

. 1-94

BAKER & TAYLOR

SEA SOLDIERS IN THE COLD WAR

SEA SOLDIERS
IN THE COLD WAR
Amphibious Warfare, 1945-1991

Joseph H. Alexander
and Merrill L. Bartlett

Naval Institute Press
Annapolis, Maryland

Library of Congress Cataloging-in-Publication Data

Alexander, Joseph H., 1938–
    Sea soldiers in the Cold War : amphibious warfare, 1945–1991 /
Joseph H. Alexander and Merrill L. Bartlett.
        p.   cm.
    Includes bibliographical references and index.
    ISBN 1-55750-055-X (acid-free paper)
        1. Amphibious warfare—History—20th century.   2. Combined
operations (Military science)—History—20th century.   3. Unified
operations (Military science)—History—20th century.   I. Bartlett,
Merrill L.   II. Title.
    U261.A44   1995
    355.4'6—dc20   94-20845

Printed in the United States of America on acid-free paper ∞

9 8 7 6 5 4 3 2
First printing

*To the Fleet Marines and the "Gator Navy,"
who sailed in harm's way throughout
the four decades of the Cold War*

Contents

Foreword

Amphibious operations had their heyday in World War II. The technique of assault from the sea was as innovative to mid–twentieth century warfare as the blitzkrieg and aerial bombardment were to air and land warfare. Amphibious operations allowed the democratic nations in the wartime forties to compensate for their peacetime unpreparedness of the thirties by speeding up the clock of victory over totalitarian Germany and Japan.

Seaborne landings in North Africa, Sicily, Italy, and finally Normandy allowed the Allies to regain the initiative in the war against Hitler. In the Pacific, Nimitz's island-hopping campaign and MacArthur's bypass amphibious strategy along the Southeast Asian archipelagoes brought defeat to the doors of a stunned Japan. The noted military analyst B. H. Liddell Hart considered amphibious operations the most innovative tactical advance of the war.

Upon the conclusion of World War II, however, American military experts worshiped not at the shrine of amphibious operations but at the altar of armored warfare and air power. Soldiers and airmen dismissed the amphibious art as a one-time thing, valuable to the peculiar circumstances of the late war but irrelevant on the nuclear battlefields of the future, where "pentomic" divisions and nuclear bombers would dominate.

The Korean War in 1950 showed otherwise. The spectacular amphibious landing at Inchon illustrated that even in the atomic age, bare-knuckled warfare still had a place, and the amphibious assault was still a powerful punch. But even with the validation of "amphib ops" at Inchon, this unique form of warfare never regained favor among postwar defense intellectuals who became mesmerized by the prospect of continental warfare against the Soviet Union. Even the U.S. Navy focused all its attention on ways it could deal with the

Soviets. Deep-blue-water operations and undersea warfare came to dominate Navy thinking and investments.

It is at this point that Joseph H. Alexander and Merrill L. Bartlett take up the story of amphibious operations, tracing its role throughout the Cold War through the Persian Gulf War. It is a little-known and -understood story, but one that serves to certify the importance of the amphibious option for any nation that claims to be a maritime power. This includes not only traditional sea-power nations like Britain and the United States but also the former Soviet Union, which had maritime pretensions during the period.

Amphibious advocates had good and bad days in the half century since the high-water mark of World War II. Because the intellectual attacks against their form of warfare were virulent and unceasing, their faith grew stronger. To each argument denigrating their convictions, the soldiers of the sea produced counterarguments based on technology and innovative operational techniques.

The 1950s argument that atomic warfare wrote *finis* to amphibious operations prompted the marriage of helicopters to surface assault to produce the "vertical envelopment" that permitted wide dispersion while allowing rapid concentration of forces. The threat of guided missiles and long-range precision weaponry of the sixties and seventies gave birth to "maneuver warfare from the sea," with amphibious attacks launched from over the horizon by a combination of tilt-rotor aircraft and high-speed air-cushioned vehicles.

By the nineties, amphibious operations resembled their antecedents of World War II only in the sense that they gave those who possessed the capability the means of making a forcible entry on any hostile shore around the world. Thanks to the U.S. Marines, a handful of Navy advocates, and a small band of British Marines, amphibious techniques kept pace with the demands of modern warfare. Throughout the Cold War, it remained an ace in the hole.

The big war in Europe, for which so much intellectual and material capital was expended, never came. But throughout the Cold War, the utility of amphibious operations was proven again and again, sometimes at an operational level as with Britain in the Falklands and sometimes on the strategic level as with the United States in the Gulf War. At the same time, U.S. amphibious forces served as political and diplomatic levers on the international scene as well as angels of mercy in dozens of humanitarian tragedies.

It is important to chronicle the tortuous path of the amphibious art through the maze of events that mark the latter half of the twentieth century. It serves as an introduction for what may be its golden age. With the demise of the Soviet Union, widespread, though less potentially lethal, conflicts plague the world. Those of direct concern to the United States are invariably in the coastal regions bordering on the seven seas. "Littoral warfare" has thus replaced continentally oriented warfare in the lexicon of today's strategists. The Army, Navy, and Air Force are wrestling intellectually and culturally to identify their role in the emerging scene. Way ahead of them is that small band of brothers within the naval service who kept the amphibious art alive and well over the past fifty years and are now in a position to show them the way. Their story is what follows in *Sea Soldiers in the Cold War*.

Bernard E. Trainor

Lt. Gen., USMC (Ret.)

Lexington, Massachusetts

4 July 1994

SEA SOLDIERS IN THE COLD WAR

Introduction

To students of naval history, and especially practitioners of amphibious warfare, the testimony of the Chief of Staff, U.S. Army, before a congressional committee examining America's defense requirements at the onset of the Cold War, was fraught with irony. In an alarming admission on 25 March 1949, General Omar N. Bradley opined, "I am wondering whether we shall ever have another large-scale amphibious operation. Frankly, the atomic bomb, properly delivered, about precludes such a possibility." Ten years before General Bradley's somber prophecy, an eminent British strategist, Sir Basil Henry Liddell Hart, proclaimed gravely that "a landing on a foreign shore in the face of hostile troops has always been one of the most difficult operations of the war. It has now become almost impossible."[1]

Between those prophetic disclaimers, the world witnessed what naval historians have rightly called the Golden Age of Amphibious Warfare. Many of the combatants conducted amphibious landings in every theater throughout World War II. In the West, the Golden Age culminated with the largest amphibious operation in modern history. On 6 June 1944, Allied forces landed at Normandy on the coast of France; more than four thousand ships transported 176,000 British, Canadian, and American troops across the English Channel, and six hundred warships escorted them to provide naval gunfire support as the men stormed across the beaches. Three divisions of airborne troops jumped ahead of the amphibious invasion. The daring maneuver succeeded despite the availability of several Panzer divisions that might have thwarted Operation Overlord. In the Pacific, naval forces conducted a series of amphibious assaults through Japanese-held islands until American and British fleets pressed hard on the enemy homeland. In the Eastern littoral, Soviet Navy Infantry landed in support of the Arctic Fleet at Petsamo in 1941, operated with the Black

Sea Fleet at Novorossisk in 1942, and participated in operations with the Siberian Fleet at Paramushiro and Shimushu in the Kuriles in 1945.[2]

Given that General Bradley had commanded the U.S. First Army at Normandy, his startling utterance just five years after Operation Overlord fueled further analysis of postwar defense planning. To Bradley and many other strategic planners, the advent of the nuclear age and the polarization of the two emerging superpowers—the United States and the Union of Soviet Socialist Republics—suggested strongly that conventional warfare had become obsolete. But barely eighteen months after Bradley's statement, during which time much of America's amphibious capability atrophied and withered, U.S. forces joined in a free-world coalition in a "limited," conventional war on the Korean peninsula. A brilliant amphibious assault at Inchon, an important port city servicing the capital of South Korea, prevented a catastrophic communist victory and provided political-military benefits disproportionate to the forces involved. In subsequent years, the superpowers began to reconstitute their amphibious capabilities, although progress was uneven. Simultaneously, lesser powers and even Third World nations developed and maintained limited amphibious capabilities.

This book is an operational history of amphibious warfare in the Cold War, principally as refined and executed by the two superpowers, their allies, and surrogates. The U.S. Navy and Marine Corps receive most of the coverage (especially in the initial chapters) because their postwar amphibious forces evolved earlier, attained credibility sooner, grew larger, and deployed in more distant seas than their counterparts in the Soviet Union and other major powers. Nevertheless, this study examines each superpower's amphibious doctrine, organization, specialized ships and landing craft, and force deployments as part of the naval prosecution of political objectives during the Cold War.

During that forty-five-year epoch following World War II, in which the United States and the Soviet Union engaged in an extensive rivalry for power and influence throughout the world, the military forces of the rivals never faced each other in open combat. Still, the interminable war of nerves placed great stress on the ready-alert forces of both powers. The threat of nuclear Armageddon emerged quickly as the Cold War's dominant feature. Throughout the era, this omnipresent threat escalated to unnerving levels during crises in Berlin, Cuba, and the Middle East. Especially on those occasions, the superpowers and their surrogates gambled with high stakes at enormous risk. Gradually, however, an uneasy nuclear stalemate prevailed. Conventional forces conducted most confrontations, usually involving forward-deployed fleets that commonly included amphibious forces.

General Bradley's prediction about future amphibious warfare proved unduly pessimistic. Several times in the Cold War, those nations with the capability for maritime forcible entry used that expertise—or threatened it—to gain political advantage. *Perception* was critical during the Cold War. In that regard, while the Soviet Navy never launched a landing on the scale of Inchon or the Falklands, the very presence of its increasingly impressive amphibious forces in troubled waters carried significant impact in its own right.

Cold War rhetoric on both sides tended to blur certain military realities. For that reason, we consider it important at this point to provide certain unadorned definitions as a basis for this historical account of amphibious force developments. Amphibious warfare is defined as that dimension of naval warfare in which an attack is launched from the sea by naval and landing forces, embarked in specialized ships and craft, against a hostile shore. It is essentially naval in character, integrates all elements of military force (air, land, naval, logistics, command and control), and is useful in application across the spectrum of political conflict. Amphibious warfare is also risky and complex, and therefore requires an extraordinary degree of coordination.

Amphibious warfare is distinguished from other forms of warfare by three primary requirements that shape its organizational and doctrinal priorities: (1) the necessity for rapid buildup of combat power ashore from an initial zero capability to full striking strength to enable seizure of amphibious task-force objectives; (2) the prerequisite to maintain unity of command between naval and landing force commanders throughout the transition of the assault from sea to land; (3) the precondition to minimize the inherent vulnerability of the landing force to natural obstacles and hostile fire during the ship-to-shore movement. To be successful, the amphibious task force should therefore be assured of at least temporary naval supremacy against enemy surface and submarine forces, preponderant air superiority, and a substantial superiority over enemy forces ashore. Because these conditions are uncommon, amphibious forces seek to maximize tactical surprise and reduce vulnerability by means of mobility, deception and audacity. Not surprisingly, amphibious warfare has been described as the most difficult of all military operations.[3]

The tremendous escalation in the range, accuracy, and proliferation of weaponry in the post-World War II era—especially long-range, precision-guided missiles—compounded the difficulty with which amphibious operations might achieve success. The political and economic impact of the cycle of crises and detente that characterized much of the Cold War exacerbated the confrontations.

A naval component of national strategy, amphibious warfare played a significant role throughout the decades of "violent peace." Both superpowers used amphibious forces consistently in pursuit of political objectives, as did several of their key allies. The emphasis on *naval* warfare is intentional. U.S. Marines deployed in full partnership with U.S. Navy amphibious task forces. So did the Soviet Navy and its naval infantry, and the Royal Navy and Royal Marines. In America, both of the naval services recognized that their peculiar military expertise required sustained teamwork and the common sharing of missions and visions, dangers and discomforts. The element of teamwork, so critical to this military capability, was not always forthcoming. At times, both services found themselves at loggerheads rather than in joint pursuit of operational or systems-acquisition goals. Traditional naval interdependence atrophied during the later years of the Vietnam War, and American amphibious capabilities reached a dangerously low ebb. Ominously, this untoward situation coincided with the emergence of the Soviet Navy's "blue-water" amphibious capability.[4]

Similarly, both superpowers made sharp reductions in naval forces following World War II, partly for economic reasons, but mainly due to the early fixation on nuclear weapons as the sole arbiter of national security issues. In the United States, those amphibious forces surviving postwar retrenchment struggled to establish a more relevant mission and force structure. Early evidence of Soviet expansionist policy objectives swayed American defense planners to retain modest levels of maritime power projection forces. This waxing and waning of amphibious capability characterized the naval establishments of both the United States and the Soviet Union during the first decade of the of the Cold war.

In the USSR, the Soviet Navy resumed its historical role of coastal defense of the motherland and disbanded its naval infantry altogether.

Indeed, the Soviet Navy lacked sufficient seagoing amphibious ships and a dedicated landing force until after the crisis in Lebanon in 1958. By that time, in comparison, the U.S. Sixth Fleet had deployed an amphibious ready group in the Mediterranean for the past ten years. The Lebanon crisis was a turning point for the Kremlin. Embarrassed by their lack of military credibility in distant waters, the Soviet leadership unleashed a significant overhaul of naval roles and missions. By the time of the 1973 Yom Kippur War, the Soviet Fifth Eskadra, including resurgent naval infantry troops, provided an effective and dangerous countervailing force against the Sixth Fleet in the eastern Mediterranean. Increasingly thereafter, both superpowers placed a premium on credible, forward-deployed, ready amphibious forces as one factor in the arsenal of military, political, and psychological weapons available to national decisionmakers.

Notwithstanding their proven utility, amphibious-force capabilities in the United States never evolved in a linear path. Protracted commitment of the Fleet Marine Forces to land campaigns in Korea and Vietnam threatened the continued existence of amphibious forces. The increasing capital expense and long lead times involved in constructing specialized amphibious ships and landing craft caused sequential administrations to look askance at the requirement. As amphibious ships grew larger and more sophisticated, many analysts began to "think about the unthinkable": the undeniably adverse political effect of such a ship being sunk with its full complement of sailors and Marines.

Despite these valid concerns, American amphibious forces proved their worth in a seemingly endless litany of flash points throughout the world: Inchon, Quemoy and Matsu Islands in the Straits of Formosa, the Cuban missile crisis, the Dominican Republic, the initial buildup in Vietnam and the final evacuations from that dying country and nearby Cambodia, the *Mayaguez* incident, Grenada, Lebanon, and the Gulf War. Hundreds of "presence" missions, contingency deployments, and humanitarian rescue operations punctuated the time frame between the better-known deployments. Commonly, amphibious forces provided a welcome "force multiplier" to influence a particular crisis or gain an operational advantage.

We have chosen not to limit the focus of this book to the amphibious force projections of the superpowers during the Cold War. Other power-projection incidents, which evolved external to the initiatives and imperatives of American or Soviet patron-client relationships with surrogates, are examined. British naval retrenchment in the immediate post–World War II era, most noticeably evident in the Suez Crisis of 1956, failed to correct itself by the time of the crisis in the Falklands in 1982. The armed confrontations in the Middle East since the emergence of Israel as a nation-state in 1947 have all witnessed sizable naval presence with inherent amphibious capabilities. These potentially dangerous scenarios provided a useful test of amphibious doctrine and assault/counterlanding weapons systems, evolutions monitored closely by the superpowers.

External events and internal realities caused changes to American and Soviet amphibious doctrine during the Cold War. The Kremlin ordered naval *spetsnaz* (special operations) units organized to conduct unconventional warfare along the maritime littorals of target countries. Similarly, American SEAL (Sea, Air, Land) teams developed a maritime unconventional warfare capability of their own, and U.S. amphibious forces acquired a proficiency in special warfare operations. Both rivals learned to integrate amphibious operations with their sizable army airborne forces for enhanced power projection. The Soviet Naval Infantry came to focus on advance seizure of maritime chokepoints, Sir Julian Corbett's critical "narrow seas."[5]

American amphibious doctrine remained centered on similar objectives (war games often featured both sides racing to seize, for example, the Straits of Malacca), plus the traditional mission of forcible seizure and defense of advance bases in support of a naval campaign. Amphibious force structure, task organization, and weapons systems acquisitions supported a worst-case scenario: a seaborne assault against sophisticated Soviet defense. Such a daunting requirement eventually produced a lethal but very heavy landing force.

The sudden need for increased sealift in the late 1970s could not have come at a worse time. America's overseas commitments, heightened by the Carter administration's acknowledgment of the strategic importance of Mideast oil to the national interests of the United States, coincided with an alarming decrease in the nation's airlift and sealift capabilities. A worrisome reduction in the availability of reliable overseas base facilities also followed. The American public questioned existing claims of rapid deployability and sustainability of the nation's armed forces. In response, the sea services developed the concept of maritime prepositioning, and certain amphibious missions changed accordingly. In a throwback to the advance base concept of more than a century ago, naval and amphibious objectives often became the seizure of ports, airfields, and assembly areas in order to facilitate the arrival of follow-on reinforcements and prepositioned war supplies.

Despite the dangers, the Cold War never degenerated into open combat between the two superpowers, whether with nuclear or conventional weapons. The Soviet Navy, for all its vaunted submarines, strike aircraft, sophisticated missiles, and amphibious capabilities, disintegrated without ever firing a shot in anger. In the U.S. military establishment, a generation of Navy and Marine officers "grew gray in service" while training for the ultimate opposed landing against their Soviet counterparts in some critical maritime objective area, a D-Day that never appeared. Instead, these officers of the sea services spent decade after decade in lengthy seaborne deployments to the ends of the earth—or bled in protracted, limited wars against perceived Soviet surrogates in East Asia and the Middle East.

No single military capability by itself—certainly not amphibious warfare—accounted for the downfall of the USSR and the successful conclusion of the Cold War. Nuclear deterrence by the "triad" of American strategic forces was instrumental, as was the more political policy of containment by coalition forces. Economic, political, and moral pressures from within the Soviet Union applied themselves to societal fracturing. As much as anything, it was America's willingness to match Soviet expansionism and threats with counterforce at each point of contention, around the world, year after year, which ultimately prevailed. American amphibious forces played a meaningful part within the overall role of the U.S. Department of the Navy in the scenario as it evolved between 1945 and 1991.

Unlike World War II, the Cold War spawned no Golden Age of Amphibious Warfare. The capability demonstrated its abiding usefulness, even in a highly political context, as well as its growing cost and potential vulnerability. It is difficult to imagine any major maritime nation without some form of amphibious capability in its defense arsenal. The lessons of 1982 are instructive: the United Kingdom came perilously close to rendering itself impotent just before the Falklands crisis with the announcement of plans to divest much of the Crown's amphibious capability. In America, the role of future amphibious capability is once again highly conjectural. One reasoned forecast came from Gen. Carl E. Mundy, Jr., the 30th Commandant of the Marine Corps, in the authoritative U.S. Naval Institute *Proceedings*:

> In the future, we will often be forced to operate in economy-of-force theaters, and we will also be operating in a political environment in which there is an "economy of national will." The American people will not tolerate high casualties in military operations they do not view as critical to our national security. . . . This is truly the heart of the matter: the naval expeditionary force must be able to project credible, sustainable combat power directly against a foe's center of gravity, without becoming tangled in prepared defenses. . . . We will be expected to get it right—with minimum casualties and material cost—the first time.[6]

Chapter One

Belief and Disbelief, 1945–1950

E ven before the atomic blasts that obliterated the Japanese cities of Hiroshima and Nagasaki inaugurated the nuclear age, planning had begun on the requirements for America's postwar armed forces. Defense strategists initiated thoughtful debate and extensive planning on the postwar defense strategy of the United States. General George C. Marshall, Chief of Staff of the Army (1939–45), and other senior officers sought to avoid the intense interservice rivalry that had characterized decisionmaking at the Joint Chiefs of Staff level during the war. Key planners within the Army and the Army Air Corps urged that a single Secretary of Defense at the cabinet level, supported by a unified general staff, replace single-service secretaries.

Initially, the fractious debates between senior officers and pundits on Capitol Hill focused on just which service appeared best suited as the deliverer of nuclear munitions. The Army Air Corps argued passionately for the efficacy of the manned bomber in support of a protracted land campaign, a line of reasoning endorsed wholeheartedly by the Army. The Navy presented an opposing view, reminding the generals that it required naval superiority to deliver these weapons of mass destruction effectively. The admirals cited the example of the Marianas campaign in 1944, which provided advance bases for B-29s and the aerial bombardment of the Japanese homeland. Moreover, manned bombers alone had failed to defeat either Japan or Germany, despite the impassioned prewar prophesies of Giulio Douhet or Billy Mitchell.

Clearly, public reaction to the nuclear age had alarmed the generals and admirals. Allegations that conventional forces were obsolete found currency. For navalists and their supporters, answers had to be provided in response to a nagging question: since the embrace of the theories of Alfred Thayer Mahan at the turn of the century, navies existed for defeating other navies; but in the 1945–50 time frame, whose Navy? Taking the offensive, the admirals presented the case for a postwar Navy centered on the flexibility of carrier task forces and argued that naval aviation no longer be limited to naval targets. Indeed, carrier-based aviation could strike both tactical and strategic targets within the great land masses of the world. The Navy's greatest fear, apparently, was that the proposed unification and structural changes within the defense structure would strip it of carrier aviation and the Marine Corps.[1]

Admiral Ernest J. King, Commander in Chief, U.S. Fleet and Chief of Naval Operations noted as early as February 1941 to his alarm and dismay that Marshall and the Army staff did not appreciate the experience and competence of the sea services in amphibious operations. Four years later, Secretary of the Navy James Forrestal took the issue to Capitol Hill. In his testimony, Forrestal emphasized the role of the amphibious Navy in a protracted conflict when he included among the purposes for a post–World War II Navy the "[maintenance of] auxiliary ships and landing craft adequate to support operations by ground forces."[2]

While Marines and their supporters tended to focus on the supposedly separate and distinct existence of the smaller of the naval services, in reality it was Leatherneck aviation and not ground elements that propelled interservice acrimony. Since the 1930s the admirals had argued passionately that carrier aviation was merely an arm of seapower in the modern age; by 1945, the carrier admirals especially could point to the war in the Pacific and argue convincingly that naval aviation had been a decisive factor in bringing the Empire of Japan to its knees. Senior Navy officers posited that the fleet air arm would surely dominate any future naval confrontation just as it had in the war in the Pacific. The admirals emphasized that naval aviation provided the bulwark upon which the Navy was configured for battle, including strategic bombing and the conduct of amphibious operations. They now championed a new flexibility involving carrier aviation, submarines, and amphibious operations.

Army and Army Air Corps critics postulated that carrier aviation, which included Marine Corps aircraft, duplicated the air arms of the other services. The token Marine Corps aviation assets in the debate only added fuel to the controversy, as detractors noted that Leatherneck aviation forces in the Pacific War had rarely operated as an integral element of amphibious task forces. From the Navy's perspective, the goal of the Army Air Corps and its Army supporters appeared clear to navalists: emasculation of the fleet air arm by transferring all fixed-wing assets to the emerging Air Force. Senior Marine Corps and Navy officers alike viewed such a proposal as anathema, the death knell of the aircraft carrier and the first step in the transfer of the amphibious arm of the Navy to the Army.[3]

An off-the-record speech by an Army Air Forces brigadier general in 1947, while intended to be humorous, underscored the heated controversy: "You gentlemen had better understand that the Army Air Force is tired of being a subordinate outfit. It was the predominant force during the war. It is going to be the predominant force during the peace. We do not care whether you like it or not." Then, warming to the subject and his bemused audience, the senior officer added: "The Army Air Force is going to run the show. You, the Navy, are not going to have anything but a couple of carriers which are ineffective anyway, and they will probably be sunk in the first battle."

Turning his attention to America's amphibious force, the speaker appeared to harken back to the Army–Marine Corps rivalry that had existed since the epic battle of Belleau Wood in 1918: "Now, as for the Marines, you know what the Marines are. They are a small, fouled-up Army talking Navy lingo. We are going to put these Marines in the regular Army and make efficient soldiers out of them. The Navy is going to end up by only supplying the requirements for the Army Air Corps and the Army forces, too." To the alarm of senior officers of the naval services, no one disavowed his brash sentiments. The remarks seemed to underscore an acrimony rapidly reaching a crescendo. Many senior Marines feared that, as minor players in the drama, the Marine Corps might become a postwar casualty.[4]

Much to the chagrin of most Marines, the future of America's amphibious arm appeared increasingly to be a minor irritant in the debate between the Army and Navy. By then, the Army Air Forces had achieved a distinct if not official existence, and spoke smugly and strongly for the subservience of all aviation assets under one administrative and operational umbrella. The hard lessons of joint and combined operations, learned so painfully during the years of World War II, seemed increasingly distant. Parochialism held sway in the highest councils of the separate armed services and in the offices of the service secretaries. Critics of amphibious warfare probably agreed with the pithy rejoinder of a Canadian observer, clearly wearied of the argument south of his border: "Let us have a bit of honest-to-God soldiering instead of messing about with this wet stuff."[5]

After years of rancorous debate and bitter infighting among the armed services, Congress enacted legislation that among other things protected the existence of the Marine Corps and preserved America's wartime amphibious capability. But it was not without cost. By 1950 Secretary of Defense Louis Johnson and Secretary of the Navy Francis P. Matthews had agreed on the prospective reduction of the Fleet Marine Force to six battalions of infantry and twelve squadrons of aircraft. In 1948, the enlisted strength of the Marine Corps totaled only 76,844. A year later that figure had fallen to 67,025 men. Supposedly, the urbane Johnson muttered to a confidant: "The Navy is on its way out. . . . Amphibious operations are a thing of the past . . . that does away with the Marine Corps. And the Air Force can do anything the Navy can do nowadays, so that does away with the Navy."[6]

The rhetoric became axiomatic, however, with the invasion of South Korea by communist forces from North Korea. On 25 June 1950 six divisions of the North Korean People's Army (NKPA), supported by Soviet-built T34 tanks, crossed the 38th Parallel and struck south. The U.N. Security Council, goaded by the United States, held that the naked aggression had to be halted in its tracks. From the perspective of Washington, the incursion across the demilitarized zone separating the two Koreas confirmed the widely held theory that the forces of international communism—inspired and directed by the Kremlin—intended to enslave the free world. A Security Council resolution condemning the invasion passed on 25 June; two days later, the members passed a second resolution recommending that forces provided by the U.N. membership assist the Republic of Korea in repelling the invasion. Between these two dates, President Harry S. Truman named General Douglas A. MacArthur (then serving in Japan as Supreme Command to the Allied Powers [SCAP]) as Commander-in-Chief, Far East (CinCFE).

Reeling under the onslaught, the forces of the Republic of Korea fell back in disarray while a division of U.S. troops sent hurriedly from occupation duties in Japan failed to deter the tank-led assaults. On 28 June, Seoul fell to the invaders and the next day the light cruiser *Juneau* (CL 119) began shelling communist positions on the east coast of South Korea. Initially, the Pentagon believed that air and naval assets from Japan could repel the invasion. When they failed, a naval blockade of the peninsula began on 28 June. MacArthur requested an additional five infantry divisions, but the Joint Chiefs of Staff (JCS) demurred fearing the potential for Soviet aggression in Europe or in Southwest Asia.

By the end of the month, a second American infantry division, also summoned from occupation duties in Japan, had taken up positions to repel the invasion. But both divisions on the line, the 24th and 25th, were manned with troops softened by occupation duties, and less than 20 percent of the men had any combat experience; the few antitank weapons proved ineffective against the Soviet-built armor. Subsequently, General MacArthur fed the U.S. 2d Infantry Division, U.S. 1st Cavalry Division, 5th Regimental Landing Team (RLT), a regimental landing team of Marines, and a brigade of British Commonwealth troops into the lines around the southern port city of Pusan as the situation grew increasingly worse. Meanwhile, CinCFE sought a strategy to break out of the perimeter and free his Eighth Army to strike against the mechanized columns converging on the southern half of the Korean peninsula.

MacArthur and his staff sought a bold strategy to alter the situation in the southern half of the Korean peninsula. On 2 July CinCFE notified the JCS of his plan: Operation Bluehearts called for the landing of the Army's 1st Cavalry Division, then based in Japan, spearheaded by a Marine Corps RLT, at Inchon on the northwest coast of South Korea. The site chosen contained the harbor facilities serving the capital, Seoul, and intelligence reports suggested few enemy troops garrisoned there. On 4 July, MacArthur met with Rear Admiral James H. Doyle, Commander, Amphibious Group One (ComPhibGrp 1), and Col. Edward H. Forney, the senior Marine on the PhibGrp staff. CinCFE told his visitors of a plan to land behind the NKPA lines, at either Inchon or Kunsan. MacArthur hoped to launch Operation Bluehearts on 22 July, but he needed a Marine brigade accompanied by an air group.[7]

The previous July, CinCFE had requested that the entire 1st Marine Division and 1st Marine Air Wing be in his theater by 10 September. MacArthur also asked that the Marine regimental landing team at Pusan be brought up to full strength. To meet manpower demands, Headquarters Marine Corps called up its entire reserve establishment (1,800 officersand 31,648 enlisted men) and transferred 6,800 regulars from the 2d Marine Division. In 1950, the table of organization (T/O) of a Marine division numbered 22,342 men. When the brigade left Camp Pendleton, it gutted the base of available manpower leaving only 3,386 Marines behind. On the east coast, the forces at Camp Lejeune fell to 3,928 men as drafts mounted out to fill the ranks in California. Air assets plummeted sharply as well; after

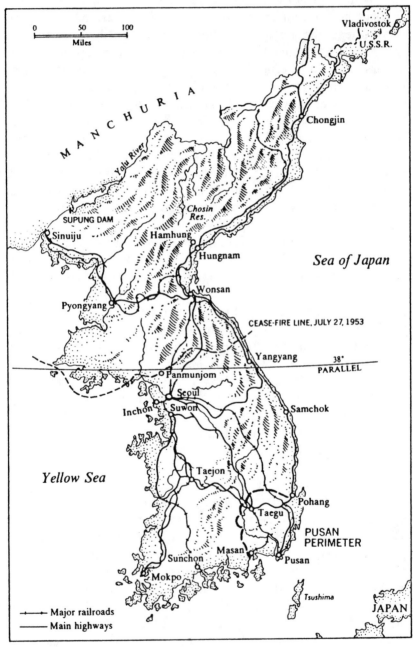

Korea, 1950. (From E. B. Potter, ed., *Sea Power*, 2nd ed. [Annapolis: Naval Institute Press, 1981]: 364.)

the first air group mounted out from El Toro, only 2,500 Marines remained. Clearly, the demands of the Korean War drew on almost the total assets of the Marine Corps, gutted by budgetary and manpower reductions.

Vice Admiral C. Turner Joy, Commander, Naval Forces Far East (COMNAVFORFE) concluded swiftly that his meager assets could not support the scheme, but a subsequent decision by the JCS made his opinion self-evident. The Chief of Naval Operations (CNO), Admiral Forrest P. Sherman, informed MacArthur through Vice Admiral Arthur D. Struble, Commander, Seventh Fleet (COMSEVENTHFLT) that the Marine regimental landing team would not arrive until August. MacArthur requested it anyway, along with an engineer brigade trained in amphibious warfare and an airborne regimental combat team. CinCFE already knew that the Army division designated for Bluehearts was slated to be fed into the rapidly deteriorating situation around the southern port city of Pusan. On 10 July, MacArthur proposed using the 2d Infantry Division, an under-strength division preparing to move from the west coast of the United States to Korea, for the amphibious assault. But as the situation around Pusan deteriorated, MacArthur ordered it into the lines of the Eighth Army instead. Subsequently, CinCFE suggested the 7th Infantry Division in Japan for a possible amphibious mission. But this division had already been drained to provide replacements for Walker's Eighth Army.

MacArthur's hopes for a "saltwater" end-run remained alive because of a visit by Marine Corps Lt. General Lemuel C. Shepherd, Jr., Commanding General, Fleet Marine Forces, Pacific, and his forceful and articulate Assistant Chief of Staff, G3, Col. Victor H. Krulak, on 10 July. At this meeting, Shepherd urged CinCFE to ask for an entire Marine division and assured him that the Marine Corps could meet the commitment. The information that initial elements of the 1st Marine Division could arrive in Korea by 25 July kept the notion of an amphibious envelopment 150 miles behind enemy lines alive, but not the bold concept. Operation Bluehearts died of necessity.[8]

U.S. Air Force aircraft flying from bases in Japan carried sharply reduced payloads of ordnance because of the distances involved, so CinCFE relied heavily on carrier-based air support. Initially, only the *Valley Forge* (CV 45) was available as a Seventh Fleet asset. On 3 July, the British provided HMS *Triumph*. As the situation worsened, Admiral Sherman ordered the *Philippine Sea* (CV 47) detached from the Pacific Fleet to bolster the naval air arm in Korean waters. Two escort carriers,

Badoeng Strait (CVE 116) and *Sicily* (CVE 118) began air operations in Korean waters in early August.

During the remainder of July, the forces of Lt. General Walton Walker's Eighth Army fell back toward the southern end of the peninsula. By then, four U.S. infantry divisions with British Commonwealth troops and a Marine Corps brigade had been fed into the lines in the south. Nine North Korean infantry divisions and an armored division pushed relentlessly against the beleaguered defenders. Taejon fell on 20 July and the NKPA forces pressed hard against the U.N. defensive perimeter around Pusan. To break the siege and the backbone of the communist offensive, MacArthur proposed an amphibious flanking movement by landing an entire Marine Corps division, followed in trace by an Army infantry division and nine thousand Korean troops, at Inchon in September. Operation Bluehearts thus became Operation Chromite (OpPlan 110-8).

By then the JCS had grown skittish and believed that MacArthur had overcommitted himself; the addition of a major amphibious operation might be more than even CinCFE could manage. Determined, MacArthur explained his strategy again: "I am firmly convinced that an early and strong effort behind his [NKPA] front will sever his main line of communication and enable us to deliver a decisive and crushing blow." Moving boldly, MacArthur then chided the JCS for hesitating: "Any material delay in such an operation may lose this opportunity," he intoned. CinCFE then reminded his superiors of the obvious: "The alternative [to an amphibious landing at Inchon] is a frontal attack which can only result in a protracted and expensive campaign to slowly drive the enemy north of the 38th Parallel."[9]

On 10 August, Admiral Sherman buoyed MacArthur's hopes with the news that another Marine Corps RLT was on its way to Korea and that the entire 1st Marine Division would be up to strength by the end of the month. MacArthur's message to the JCS, which simply stated: "operation planned mid-September is amphibious landing of a two-division corps in rear of enemy lines," caused even the Army and Air Force generals to wonder just how the indefatigable CinCFE could accomplish such a feat.

The CinCFE staff presented two options for a landing in September: withdraw the 2d Infantry Division and the Marines from Pusan to provide the troops for the amphibious assault; or use the 7th Infantry Division in Japan plus the Marines for the landing. But

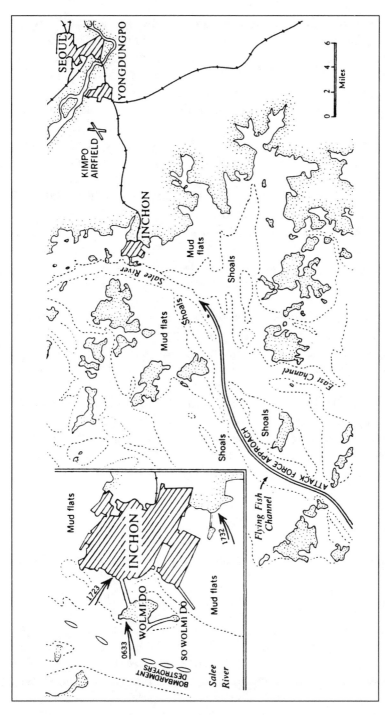

Inchon, 1950. (From Robert D. Heinl, Jr. "Inchon, 1950," in Merrill L. Bartlett, ed., *Assault from the Sea* [Annapolis: Naval Institute Press, 1983]: 340.)

extraction of a division from Pusan would clog the port's already jammed facilities, and the division in Japan would not be ready for amphibious operations for another year. Time was of the essence, however, and favored the attacker in the near term.

During 15–18 September, tidal surges at Inchon rose high enough to cover the mud flats and allow passage of landing craft. Tidal heights varied between twenty-three and thirty-three feet; the dock landing ships required twenty-five feet of freeboard while the LSTs needed twenty-nine feet. The high tides on the proposed D-day—15 September—crested at slightly more than thirty-one feet, barely enough to float the LSTs. A week later, the tides dropped to 27 feet and thus were too shallow. The morning high tide on 15 September crested at 0659 while the evening high tide peaked at 1919—only thirty-seven minutes after sunset. The next optimal tidal range occurred on 11 October, and MacArthur squelched any notion of delay by declaring that it would be too late to alleviate the increasing pressure on Walker's Eighth Army.

The CinCFE meteorologist reported a morning high tide at 0650 and an evening high tide at 1920 on D-day. Besides the unusual tides, other hydrographic and geographic features of Inchon harbor influenced the landing plan. Small islands dotted the channel and prevented swift passage through the harbor. The islet of Wolmi-do, thought heavily fortified, dominated the entrance to Inchon; thus, the assaulting amphibians must perforce seize this prominent land mass before assaulting the city. Seawalls ranging in height from twelve to fourteen feet fronted the waterfront along its entire length, requiring the landing force to scale them before moving ashore. No landing beaches in the traditional sense existed.[10]

Once it was ashore, commanders anticipated that the landing force would assault a sizable built-up area inhabited by perhaps 200,000 people. Estimates of the number of enemy troops garrisoned in the region varied, but the numbers did not appear to present a formidable problem. MacArthur's critics, both in East Asia and in Washington, remained nonplused and thought the idea fraught with unacceptable risks. Ominously, intelligence sources failed to report that the Soviet naval mine depot at Vladivostok had already shipped mines to Wonson and Chinnampo. Worse, the Soviets reportedly were prepared to load another shipment south to provide the North Koreans with the capability to mine the harbors at Inchon, Kunsan, Haeju, and Mokpo. On 4 September a U.S. destroyer reported mines off Chinnampo. Six days later, a South Korean patrol boat sank a North Korean minelaying sloop off Haeju. On 8 September, U.S. naval forces sank three North Korean minelayers in South Korean waters. The threat from enemy mines did not deter CinCFE.[11]

Meanwhile, the situation reports from the Eighth Army grew increasingly grim, and fueled the urgent planning for Operation Chromite. The pounding by the NKPA invasion force continued unabated; the beleaguered U.N. force barely held on. By then, a desperate General Walker at Pusan had excoriated his command: "there will be no further yielding under pressure of the enemy. From now on, let every man stand or die."[12]

On 22 August, Maj. Gen. Oliver P. Smith, the Commanding General of the First Marine Division, arrived in Tokyo. Admiral Doyle met him at the airport, and only then did Smith learn of the proposed landing and the date of D-day. The following day, Smith reported to MacArthur and his chief of staff, Maj. General Edward N. Almond. In a briefing Almond conducted, Smith learned that the First Marine Division would strike inland from Inchon, seize Kimpo Airfield, cross the Han River, and recapture Seoul. The veteran Marine wondered how his forces would cross the Han River without bridging equipment, but Almond dismissed his protestations by airily suggesting that they were matters of insignificant detail and that CinCFE must not be bothered.

MacArthur left no doubt that Almond had discussed the employment of the Marine division before Smith's arrival, and CinCFE's decisions appeared to be influenced heavily by Almond's opinions. The *New York Times* described the aristocratic Almond as "an insufferable martinet," an uncharitable observation shared by most senior naval officers involved in Operation Chromite. His Leatherneck critics would have been chagrined to learn that Almond had turned down a Marine Corps commission in favor of the gold bars of an Army second lieutenant in 1916. Almond had CinCFE's ear, and MacArthur continued to insist the boldness and daring of his plan overcame any obstacles. The patrician and patronizing Almond (age fifty-eight) annoyed Smith (age fifty-seven) by calling the veteran Leatherneck "son."[13]

Almond's arrogance did little to reassure the amphibians. The CinCFE chief of staff told Smith and Doyle that he and MacArthur had no interest in landing anywhere else; potentially less costly sites, such as Kunsan south of Inchon or Wonsan on the east coast, were not sufficiently close to the NKPA main line of communications. Inchon was secondary to the goals of Chromite; the primary objective was the recapture of Seoul. A closer alternate landing site at Posung-Myan did not have the road network to support a rapid breakout from the amphibious objective area in which to ease an advance on Kimpo Airfield and the South Korean capital. Obviously, MacArthur intended to emerge as the liberator of the South Korean capital.[14]

Senior officers converged on Tokyo in late August. Admiral Sherman summoned Admiral Arthur W. Radford, Commander-in-Chief, Pacific Fleet (CincPacFlt); Vice Admiral Joy, COMNAVFORFE; and Vice Admiral Struble, COMSEVENTHFLT, to join him in a full-dress meeting with MacArthur and his staff. In a conference on 23 August, heavily dominated by MacArthur's imposing personality, the CinCFE attempted to convince the reluctant navalists to support Chromite. When Admiral Sherman shifted the persuasive might of his position to MacArthur's side, it caused the lesser naval flag officers to acquiesce. The strategy settled, it was left to the amphibians, Admiral Doyle and General Smith, to accomplish MacArthur's bold stroke.[15]

Although the JCS subsequently approved the plan, it suggested that MacArthur also assault Kunsan as a diversion. Then, perhaps to remind MacArthur of the chain of command, the JCS rebuked him for not keeping the Pentagon informed and for requiring it to send two members of the JCS to Tokyo to learn his intentions. Moreover, the terse reprimand suggested that the JCS was distancing itself from Chromite in the event the operation failed. "We desire such information as becomes available with respect to conditions in the possible objective areas and finally information as to your intentions and plans for offensive operations," the JCS message stated flatly.[16]

Two days later, the naval officers who would direct Operation Chromite met to hammer out the details and sort out the problems. All the senior Navy and Marine Corps officers, especially Doyle and Smith, urged a reconsideration of the alternate landing site at Posung-Myan. Subsequently, CinCPacFlt sent General Shepherd to ask for MacArthur's reconsideration. Again, CinCFE and his stuff rebuffed the amphibians. MacArthur's earlier, prophetic declaration, "We shall land at Inchon and I shall crush them," hung heavy over future deliberations and stifled opposition.[17]

In a subsequent conference, Admiral Struble argued for tactical surprise by not bombarding Inchon prior to the landing, a notion Admiral Doyle and General Smith objected to vociferously and vehemently. Thus, on 13 September aircraft flying from four carriers struck targets in the amphibious objective area. Concurrently, a small Navy task force conducted a diversionary landing at Kunsan, southwest of Taejon. Two days later, the massive amphibious armada arrived in the Inchon area: 60,000 U.S. troops and 6,000 Koreans organized into two divisions (Smith's 1st Marine Division and Maj. General David G. Barr's 7th Infantry Division) assigned to X Corps. The force included Marine aviation assets in Brig. Gen. Thomas J. Cushman's Marine Air Group (MAG-33) and elements of the 1st Marine Air Wing's Headquarters and Headquarters and Service Squadron. MAG-12 supported Operation Chromite by flying from escort carriers. Admiral Doyle commanded the amphibious force from his flagship, *Mount McKinley*.

In a fit of interservice bias, at least as interpreted by Marines, MacArthur named Gen. Almond—his chief of staff and confidant— commander of the landing force instead of the more experienced and readily available Shepherd. Both the CinCFE Assistant Chief of Staff, Brig. Gen. Doyle G. Hickey, and Assistant Chief of Staff, G3 (Operations), Brig. Gen. Edwin K. Wright, urged the appointment of Shepherd and the designation of Headquarters, Fleet Marine force, Pacific to provide the tactical command of the landing force.

But MacArthur reasoned that he needed a staff for the invasion that was immediately available and, perhaps most important, subject to his direct supervision. Moreover, as Almond argued, the offensive operation after the initial landing and seizure of Inchon to recapture Kimpo Airport and Seoul was essentially a land campaign, and thus no further need for amphibians existed. MacArthur reasoned that Chromite would be completed successfully in a short period, and thus the invaluable and trusted Almond could return to CinCFE. Almond received the appointment during the third week in August, by which time an ad hoc planning staff had already been at work on Operation Chromite for over a week. CinCFE formally established X Corps on 26 August.[18]

Along with the baton of command, MacArthur presented Almond and X Corps with formidable objectives:

- seize the port of Inchon and capture a force beachhead line.
- advance rapidly and seize Kimpo Airfield.
- seize and occupy Seoul.
- occupy blocking positions north, northeast, and east of Seoul.
- using forces in the Inchon-Seoul area as an anvil, strike the communists with a stroke from the south by Eighth Army.[19]

COMNAVFE commanded the amphibious operation afloat, but Commanding General, X Corps, assumed command ashore. In both instances, Admiral Joy and General Almond reported directly to MacArthur. MacArthur directed Gen. George E. Stratemeyer's Far East Air Force to support the operation, to prepare for the lift of an airborne regimental landing team, and to back the offensive of the Eighth Army at Pusan. General Walker received orders to break out of the defensive perimeter on D+1 or 16 September.

As the impending date for the landing drew near, Washington grew increasingly nervous. On 5 September, the JCS rebuked CinCFE for failing to keep it more fully informed. Unperturbed, MacArthur calmly replied that "the general outline of the plan remains as described to you," and thus refused to allow Washington to micromanage the operation. For one last time, however, the JCS sought to remind the resolute MacArthur that America's defense assets had become increasingly spare. No more reserves remained, and those available had already been fed into the lines of the Eighth Army. The only major Army force left in the United States was the 82d Airborne Division. Senior Pentagon officials did not expect National Guard divisions recalled to the colors to be combat-ready for at least four months. D-day was only eight days away.[20]

Despite the urging of Shepherd, Joy, Doyle, and Sherman, the 7th Marines (one of the 1st Marine Division's infantry regiments) failed to arrive in Korea from CONUS until 21 September—six days after the landing. But even more disconcerting to the amphibians was the last-minute reluctance of the CinCFE staff to order the release of the Marine brigade from the Eighth Army at Pusan. Ultimately, MacArthur himself intervened to squelch the objections of Almond and Walker; at the last minute, Army planners even suggested replacing the veteran amphibians with a regimental landing team with no saltwater experience. But in fairness to Walker and the headquarters of the Eighth Army, the situation around Pusan had worsened.

The NKPA struck the beleaguered defenders on 2 September with thirteen divisions of tank-led infantry; the Marine brigade constituted the Eighth Army's strategic reserve, and Walker was loathe to lose it. Nonetheless, CinCFE's proposal to replace the 5th Marines in Operation Chromite with the 32d Infantry from the 7th Division made naval commanders increasingly fretful. In a showdown with Almond, Smith informed his arrogant commanding general that if the 5th Marines were withdrawn from the troop list for the amphibious operation, he would not bother to assault Red Beach into the environs of Inchon, but merely cross Blue Beach with his only Marine regiment. Fortunately, MacArthur interceded and the unwise notion disappeared. The 5th Marines withdrew from the Pusan perimeter on 5–6 September, only nine days before D-day at Inchon. Even then Almond and his staff suggested a three-day command-post exercise (CPX) to "war-game" the landing; the Marines blithely ignored the idea, and prepared their commands for an amphibious assault in the little precious time left before D-day.[21]

In the end, the Navy had to bring Operation Chromite to successful fruition. The narrow, twisting channel brought the amphibious ships within range of enemy shore batteries. Reduced speeds made the craft especially vulnerable. The 3d Battalion, 5th Marines, conducted the initial assault on the islet of Wolmi-do and clamored ashore on Green Beach with the morning tide. As the sun set, the remainder of the regiment stormed over the sea walls on Red Beach into the city, while the 1st Marines assaulted Blue Beach south of Inchon. At first light on D+1, the division advanced toward Seoul and took Kimpo Airfield on the same day. Also on D+1, the 7th Infantry Division landed at Inchon, swung southeast toward Suwon preparatory to linking up with leading elements of the Eighth Army.

On 20 September, X Corps began to cross the Han and by the end of the week had secured the city. Two days later a triumphant and emotional MacArthur returned the capital of South Korea to a beaming President Syngman Rhee. The landing resulted in only 22 Marines killed and another 174 wounded. Total casualties for all of X Corps during Operation Chromite numbered barely over 2,400, while the force took over six thousand NKPA prisoners and killed an estimated 13,666 enemy troops. But in its haste to participate, the Marine Corps had become a part of CinCFE's land forces—much to the discomfiture of tradition-minded navalists—and for the remainder of the war in Korea operated mainly as such. The subsequent attempt to repeat the amphibious triumph at Inchon by cutting off the retreating NKPA columns at Wonson failed. This time, the Soviet mines had been sown, a major deterrent to the proposed landing; ironically, the same Navy that proved successful at Inchon failed at Wonson because its mineclearing capability had grown far worse than its amphibious efficacy in the years since the end of World War II.

The 1945–50 time frame appears rife with ironies and strategic miscalculations. The era opened amid assumptions influenced heavily by the advent of the atomic bomb and in acrimonious interservice debate. While the armed services parried, even the most ardent of Navy and Marine Corps supporters wondered what if any role amphibious forces could play in the nuclear age. Yet despite the dire predictions of critics who grew increasingly alarmed at the Kremlin's threatening rhetoric, the first major clashes of arms in the era of the superpowers occurred not between the superpowers nor, apparently, at the unilateral behest of either global giant. The drama that unfolded on the Korean peninsula in the summer of 1950 saw neither nuclear explosions nor Soviet armed forces. Moreover, no evidence exists to suggest that Moscow directed Pyongyang to attack the south. Still, the theory of a communist monolith bent on enslaving a free world held sway throughout the clash of arms. The introduction of Chinese Communist troops in early 1951 appeared to support such a theory.[22]

For the landing at Inchon to succeed, the United States had to draw on its dwindling reserve of amphibious capability. By September 1950, the landing force could barely muster one Marine division—only by stripping the only other Marine division, thus leaving the United States woefully unprepared for a naval campaign in the Atlantic littoral. Worse, sizable numbers of the Navy's amphibious shipping had been scrapped, given or sold to Third World allies, or placed in mothballs. Of the 610 amphibious ships in commission in 1945, only 91 survived the naval reductions of the next five years. In 1948, 510 landing craft ended on the scrap heap, while the Navy received authorization to construct only one.[23]

Ultimately, however, MacArthur's decision to execute a major amphibious operation at Inchon enhanced the future of amphibious forces in the Cold War. When the admirals and generals met with MacArthur in Tokyo on 23 August 1950, the issue remained in doubt. Perhaps the Chief of Naval Operations, Admiral Sherman, understood the importance of Inchon more than any of the other conferees when he shifted his support against the operation to the argument in favor of MacArthur's bold stroke. If naval forces, especially amphibious forces, could not support Operation Chromite, one might conclude that the critics of the naval services—and Marines in particular—had been correct in their litany of limitations. Still, if Pyongyang had mined the harbor of Inchon effectively, or if reinforcements had been brought to bear between the landing sites and Seoul, the outcome for Operation Chromite might have been disastrous.

The JCS understood the grave risk MacArthur's amphibious gamble presented. On the eve of the landing, the Pentagon cabled CinCFE with a terse and demeaning message that caused MacArthur to bridle: "We have noted with considerable concern the trend of events in Korea. In light of the commitment of all the reserves available to the Eighth Army, we desire your estimate as to the feasibility and chance of success of [Operation Chromite]." MacArthur fired back a response that reflected more of his limitless store of optimism than any appreciation of the naval obstacles blocking the path of his forces in the recapture of Seoul: "There is no question in my mind as to the feasibility of the operation and I regard its chances of success as excellent." He added, "I go further and believe that it represents the only hope of wresting the initiative from the enemy and thereby presents the opportunity for a decisive blow."[24]

Although Admiral Sherman appeared to be reticent and ambivalent during the high-level conference on 23 August, in reality he had already decided that Operation Chromite must be supported wholeheartedly by whatever naval assets could be brought to bear. Sherman had already advised Struble that "you will recognize the importance of the Navy's doing everything possible for its success."[25]

For the near term, however, the faith of the amphibians had been bolstered on the west coast of Korea and not the least bit dimmed by the failure to duplicate the audacious landing with another at Wonson to the east. Pyongyang's failure to grasp the potential and lethality of an amphibious flanking movement in the south is inexplicable. On 14 September, just a day before the first Leatherneck waded ashore at Inchon, the New York Times reported that "an amphibious landing on the Korean coast well behind the enemy's front lines is an obvious and possible strategy."[26]

Chapter Two

The Amphibious Assault, 1952–1964

The confrontation on the Korean peninsula, especially with entry of the Chinese Communists into the fray, postponed earlier U.S. debate that questioned the efficacy of large-scale amphibious assaults in the nuclear age. For the Marine Corps, that debate had commenced when one of its most respected general officers, Roy S. Geiger, represented his armed service as an observer of the atomic tests at Bikini Atoll in July 1946. Alarmed by the implications of what he witnessed, Geiger wrote immediately to his Commandant, General Alexander A. Vandegrift, to call for a major review and analysis of the amphibious assault "[to find] a solution to develop the technique of conducting amphibious operations in the nuclear age."[1]

Vandegrift shared Geiger's concern. Less than two weeks after receiving the letter, the Commandant ordered the formation of a special board to assess the challenge posed to an amphibious operation by nuclear weapons. The gravity of Geiger's implication was reflected in the selection of the officers that Vandegrift chose for the ad hoc panel: Maj. Gen. Lemuel C. Shepherd, Jr., Assistant Commandant of the Marine Corps; Maj. Gen. Field Harris, Director of Aviation; and Brig. Gen. Oliver P. Smith, Commandant, Marine Corps Schools. A research secretariat, composed of Col. Merrill B. Twining, Col. Edward C. Dyer, and Lt. Col. Clair W. Sisler, collected data and provided documentation as the premier group formulated a plan for submission to the Commandant. Taking its cue from Geiger's prophetic warning, the analysis group focused on the vulnerabilities of the current ship-to-shore movement and the possibilities inherent in the employment of rotary-wing aircraft.

Shepherd and his cohorts prepared fairly detailed specifications for a helicopter suitable to the needs of the Marine Corps. The melancholy fact that nothing at all remotely existed to match the revolutionary design features failed to dissuade the optimism of the study group.

Planners envisioned an aircraft with a five thousand–pound payload, capable of flying at a speed of one hundred knots per hour at an altitude of four to fifteen hundred feet, and with a range of two to three hundred miles. But when the requirement passed to the Chief of Naval Operations for action and funding, Fleet Adm. Chester W. Nimitz refused to authorize spending for a separate Marine Corps aviation requirement. Instead, appropriations for the Marine Corps' rotary-wing aircraft became part of the Department of the Navy's budget for FY 1949. Meanwhile, the Marine Corps seized on the imperative of the moment, and used existing funding and aircraft to formulate doctrine to embrace the new technology.

In December 1947, Marine Helicopter Experimental Squadron (HMX-1) became operational at Quantico, ostensibly to test the HO3S and the HRP rotary-wing aircraft. Barely more than a month later, five HO3Ss embarked aboard the *Palau* (CVE 122) for Exercise Packard II on the coast of North Carolina. Although the tiny aircraft could only transport three combat-loaded troops per trip and required a total of thirty-five flights to transport sixty-six Marines plus communications equipment ashore, observers declared the employment of helicopters in the amphibious assault a resounding success. In a subsequent exercise in May 1949, Packard III, proponents of rotary-wing aircraft in the amphibious assault had their hopes buoyed when choppy seas swamped several landing craft. Even as one group pondered the operational initiatives and imperatives of the employment of helicopters in amphibious operations, another forthright body of Marines formulated doctrine.[2]

By late 1948, a study group headed by Maj. General Oliver P. Smith had assembled with a mandate not unlike that issued to their forebears by Maj. General Commandant Ben H. Fuller during the lean interwar years: "[Determine what] measures which the Marine Corps should take in order to fulfill its obligation in maintaining its position as the agency principally responsible for the development of landing force tactics, technology, and equipment." Smith's group concluded at the outset that the Marine Corps must obtain helicopters capable of carrying at least eight combat-loaded troops in one lift. Moreover, the aircraft had to be capable of being moved up and down flight decks and elevators, thus the requirement for folding rotor blades. Sensing the urgency of the moment, the group posited that HMX-1 be equipped with five HRP-1s by December 1948.[3]

By 1953, the group concluded, there should be one twelve-aircraft helicopter squadron on each coast with twice that number by 1954. Participants in these halcyon days shared an unbridled optimism. Lt. Col. Victor H. Krulak, while an ardent supporter, offered measured skepticism: "The best we could do was rationalize the operational principles, praying that they would turn out to be valid, since we had no real experience." Later, Col. Robert D. Heinl, Jr., captured the enthusiasm over the idea: "It was 1933 all over again. . . . This was not revolutionary; it was breathtaking."[4]

The new concept became interim doctrine with the publication of *Phib-31, Amphibious Operations—Employment of Helicopters (Tentative)*. Meanwhile, a joint Navy/Air Force program sought the acquisition and development of the XH-16 as a helicopter to meet the needs of both services. In March 1950, a board composed of Navy and Marine Corps representatives urged the development of a rotary-wing aircraft suited specifically for the requirements of the ship-to-shore movement. The group discarded the XH-16, which led to the development of the multi-engine Sikorsky XHR2S-1, capable of sustained operations from an escort carrier (CVE). By June 1952, each of the three Marine Corps air wings had a helicopter group with three helicopter squadrons in each group. General Shepherd's special study group recommended the acquisition of 180 HR2Ss by the late 1950s for a total of nine squadrons; however, Congress reduced funding for the optimistic acquisition so that only 140 aircraft were actually acquired in FY 1959. But by 1962 the helicopter had become a permanent fixture in Marine Corps aviation. Most ground elements trained in maneuvers involving the revolutionary idea. A total of 341 helicopters was counted in four groups, plus the reconfigured VIP squadron at Quantico (HMX-1). Six different models of helicopters flew in support of Marine Corps amphibious operations.[5]

Coincident with the revolutionary thought of a vertical platform in the amphibious assault was the requirement for new shipping. Initially, helicopter operations were conducted from the deck of the *Thetis Bay* (CVE 90; CVHA 1), but the Marine Corps scored the limitations of the escort carrier and asked instead for twelve carriers constructed, from the keel up, for amphibious operations. Faced with the parsimonious budgets of the Eisenhower years, the Navy elected to convert Essex-class carriers left over from World War II construction into the new Landing Platform Helicopter (LPH). Three such converted ships, *Boxer* (CV 21; LPH 4); *Valley Forge* (CV 45; LPH 8), and *Princeton* (CV 23; LPH 5) received the new designations and joined the active fleet between 1959 and 1961. Four keels were laid for LPHs: *Iwo Jima* (LPH 2); *Okinawa* (LPH 3); *Guadalcanal* (LPH 7); and *Guam* (LPH 9) in 1958. To increase speed of execution and provide additional troop lift, two commercial container ships, *Francis Marion* (APA 249) and *Paul Revere* (APA 248) underwent conversion into high-speed attack transports. Despite the initial enthusiasm for the new concept in amphibious warfare, only two LPHs were operational by 1960, but each could embark an infantry battalion and a composite helicopter squadron.

Helicopter operations in support of amphibious operations were not the only consideration on the minds of defense strategists during the 1950s. As the conflict on the Korean peninsula ground on indeterminably, forthright planners returned to the contentious issue faced when atomic bombs obliterated Hiroshima and Nagasaki. In February 1953, Headquarters Marine Corps published *Landing Force Bulletin 2: Interim Doctrine for the Conduct of Tactical Atomic Warfare.* Two planning documents followed in quick succession: number 17, *Concept of Future Amphibious Operations;* and number 24, *Helicopter Operations.*

Between 1951 and 1955, no less than six special study boards examined the future of amphibious operations in the emerging superpower rivalry with the increasingly bellicose Soviet Union. These efforts pointed toward a massive restructuring of the U.S. Marine Corps to face the challenges of the Cold War, rather than a refinement of the amphibious doctrine used in the naval campaigns in the central Pacific. As one respected luminary, Brig. Gen. Samuel B. Griffith, noted, "We are not prepared as we should be because both our amphibious doctrine and equipment are relevant to conditions that were entirely different from those that exist today or will exist tomorrow."[6]

On 4 June 1956, the Commandant of the Marine Corps—now General Shepherd—directed Maj. Gen. Robert E. Hogaboom to conduct a thorough study of the Fleet Marine Force and recommend necessary changes "in order to best perform its mission." Hogaboom directed a penetrating inquiry not only into the limitations imposed by nuclear weaponry, but in the employment of helicopters in amphibious operations. Appearing to propel the Hogaboom Board toward a preconceived conclusion was the earnest belief in some quarters that the arrival of rotary-wing aircraft meant all future amphibious operations would be conducted solely with helicopters for the ship-to-shore movement. At the outset, however, the Hogaboom Board disagreed with the self-styled prophets of "air-only assault." The parameters of the problem facing the study group showed clearly that the proposed changes would be effective for five to six years hence, and certainly no more than a decade. The anticipated numbers of helicopters available, or the existing or foreseen technology of improved models, did not support the concept of an all-helicopter transportable amphibious assault force.

The Hogaboom Board questioned whether amphibious forces would ever be employed in the European littoral in the face of the nuclear arsenal held by the nations of the Warsaw Pact. Instead, the study group focused on recommendations that rendered the Marine Corps a more flexible and utilitarian naval force in Third World conflicts. Rotary-wing aircraft appeared particularly adaptable to such confrontations: troops heli-lifted to the rear and flanks of the beach; beachheads seized from the rear, rather than from the water's edge, and prepared by heli-borne forces for follow-up landings by traditional water-borne conveyance; and helicopters used to provide tactical commanders with increased mobility and enhanced means of resupply. The traditional water-borne landing force, however, remained the linchpin of the amphibious assault.

The Hogaboom Board expected helicopters to aid the landing force commander to position his forces by maneuver, rather than squandering them—perhaps needlessly—in a frontal assault from the water's edge. By husbanding combat power, critical objectives would fall more quickly to the tactical commander. Although the study group eschewed the notion of total air mobility, it recommended the reorganization of the division into a much lighter force. The tank battalion, the division's heavier artillery, and motor transport and engineering units with heavy equipment moved to Force Troops. Meanwhile, the expansion of the reconnaissance company into a full battalion; the creation of an antitank battalion, armed with track-mounted recoilless rifles; and the addition of a fourth rifle company to each infantry battalion strengthened the sustaining power of the division.[7]

The revolutionary idea envisioned infantry battalions seizing widely separated key terrain, perhaps far from the landing beaches. Only then would traditional and perhaps heavier units come ashore. Clearly, heavy equipment within the division gave way to the requirement for increased mobility. Devotees of air-mobility appeared to have gained strength for their arguments for an entirely air-transportable Marine Corps division, but the Hogaboom Board continued to emphasize that only the assault elements in an amphibious operation were expected to be heli-transportable. In sharp contrast, the U.S. Army underwent a massive reorganization in anticipation of armed conflict in Europe, most likely against Soviet and Soviet-led mechanized columns crossing the Fulda Gap into West Germany, supported by tactical nuclear weapons.

The traditional infantry battalions and regiments within the Army divisions disappeared, replaced by five battle groups each containing four infantry companies and a heavy mortar battery. While the Marine Corps lightened its artillery regiment with the incorporation of 4.2-inch mortar batteries, the Army increased the number of its tubes in anticipation of combat with heavier, mechanized forces. Army critics of the Marine Corps' new organization argued that the potential existence of tactical nuclear weapons forced battlefield maneuvers most likely to the detriment of the landing force. Marine Corps planners gained solace from the fact that despite the prophesies of nuclear shrouds enveloping the battlefields of the post–World War II era, such had not occurred—or appeared even likely as the 1960s loomed on the horizon.[8]

U.S. defense strategists during the 1950s under the administration of President Dwight D. Eisenhower doubted the wisdom of preparing to fight smaller wars in the Third World. Defense planners of that era argued persuasively for a policy of "massive retaliation," using the specter of a nuclear holocaust to keep potential Kremlin expansionists at bay. Accordingly, most of the nation's defense budget skewed toward the development of manned bombers capable of dropping nuclear munitions and intercontinental ballistic missiles capable of delivering nuclear payload strikes against the Soviet Union. Navalists grew increasingly chary over the imbalances in the strategy and argued for retention of an adequate naval force. Despite these objections, the number of naval ships in service dropped from 860 in 1959 to 812 when Eisenhower left office two years later.[9]

Whatever major appropriations that were allocated to the Department of the Navy went mostly toward the goal of laying the keel for one *Forrestal*-class aircraft carrier each year, and the modernization of the submarine fleet with nuclear-powered ships. Thus, the fleet and the Fleet Marine Force that in 1953 stood at its peak since World War II declined drastically. Even as Secretary of the Navy Charles S. Thomas argued in 1953 for fast amphibious ships to incorporate the new idea of vertical assault, the Navy dropped in numbers from 800,000 men to 682,000, while the Marine Corps slipped from

250,000 to 215,000. By 1956, those figures had fallen even further to 657,000 bluejackets and 193,000 Leathernecks.

Despite modernization programs and new construction, most of the fleet retained ships of World War II vintage, and appeared better equipped for a landing at Saipan or Iwo Jima than at Novorossisk or Vladivostok. The only indication that defense planners had learned anything from the conflict in Korea was the decision announced on 20 August 1951 that four prototype minesweepers would be constructed. But President Harry S. Truman's defense budget allocated funds for the conversion of two heavy cruisers, Boston (CA 69) and Canberra (CA 70), into guided-missile cruisers that further reduced the fleet's ability to provide adequate naval gunfire support for an amphibious operation. In the conversion, both cruisers lost an 8-inch/55 turret, replaced with Terrier surface-to-air missile launchers. Officers in the Marine Corps and the Navy amphibious forces grew increasingly concerned, as it appeared that Pentagon strategists had relegated amphibious operations to a file of anachronistic scenarios not likely or envisioned.[10]

Given the imperatives of the Cold War, strategists in the West focused their attentions on the amphibious potential of the Soviet Union. By the end of World War II, that capability appeared formidable; the Soviet Naval Infantry had grown to more than 125,000 men. Then, inexplicably, this arm of the Soviet Navy disappeared from public scrutiny. Western defense analysts concluded that Soviet preoccupation with nuclear weaponry had resulted in the conviction that amphibious warfare offered little capacity for development as a significant military or naval option. But the manpower and material remaining from the war years still existed. In 1952 landing craft captured from the German and Italian fleets could be found in the Soviet Naval arsenal. Moreover, many LCMs, LCIs, LCVPs, and LCSs, remained from loans made by the United States during the war.

Near the end of the decade of the 1950s, however, indications came to the attention of Western defense analysts that suggested a renewed interest in amphibious warfare in the Soviet littoral. In 1959 the Ministry of Defense included a portion on "amphibious analysis" in its essay "Fundamentals of Naval Science," which appeared in Navy. The feature included photographs of Soviet Marines in a practice landing, circa 1953; and of amphibious vehicles in a parade in Red Square in November 1959. In that same year, a semi-official dictionary provided a contemporary definition of the Soviet Naval Infantry: "A special branch of troops in foreign armed forces. In our armed forces, the

Morskaia pekhota is a special branch of the Navy intended for use in naval amphibious landings." But in 1963, an essay appeared in the Soviet naval journal *Morskoi sbornik,* offering the argument that nuclear weapons had not ruled out amphibious landings; the same journal continued the dialogue in 1966.[11]

The British Royal Marines escaped outright disbanding following World War II, but with personnel reductions managed to subsequently field only a three-commando brigade. As in its prewar establishment, it lacked a combined-arms capability and relied on other UK forces to provide such support as artillery and engineers. Increasingly, the focus of training emphasized special operations rather than amphibious art. This lack of capability became apparent as Great Britain faced a major crisis in 1956.

On 26 July of that year, Egypt seized the British and French-owned Suez Canal. In response, the Admiralty offered to field a Royal Marine force to spearhead an invasion force. Beginning in early August 1956, amphibious planners participated in preparations for Operation Musketeer, the largest British amphibious operation undertaken since the United Kingdom's participation in the invasion of Normandy in 1944. Initially, planners envisioned the capture of Alexandria, an advance on Cairo, and then outright seizure of the canal. But the paucity of forces readily available, and the distances from suitable landing beaches and airstrips, resulted in planning for the invasion force to come ashore from the Mediterranean at Port Said. Both 40 and 42 Commandos would cross the beach from assault landing craft, the latter together with a squadron of Centurion tanks. The contingent from the Royal Tank Corps, other support elements, and the two commandos—more than 2,000 men and 550 vehicles—embarked in LSTs. Meanwhile, 45 Commando embarked in the carriers *Ocean* and *Theseus* in anticipation of landing by helicopter. But when commanders realized that an insufficient number of aircraft existed to heli-lift the entire brigade in one serial, 45 Commando became a floating reserve for the operation.

Eventually, twenty ships comprised the amphibious squadron for Operation Musketeer. The frigate *Meon* vectored the LVTs and LCAs four miles to a control point, from where the craft proceeded on a three-mile run toward the landing beaches. Each commando embarked two troops in LVTs in the leading wave, with a second wave in LCAs. The Egyptians failed to mine the landing beaches, but subsequently forces ashore discovered that the beaches of the alternate landing site had been heavily sown with mines. Facing stiff resistance ashore from Arab defenders, the landing force commander ordered 45 Commando ashore. The first aircraft touched down at 0815 in the beachhead—H-hour was at 0645—and in the next twenty-three hours 415 men and tons of supplies were landed from Whirlwind Mark 2s and Sycamore Mark 14s. Although three helicopters suffered damage in the aerial assault, the entire lift took less than 25 percent of the time required to transport a commando ashore in LCAs.

By D+8, brigade headquarters and two of the commandos had been withdrawn to Malta. Two weeks later, the last of the amphibians departed. The brigade counted only nine fatal casualties, and credited helicopter medical evacuation for saving the lives of the remaining sixty wounded men. Operation Musketeer resulted in significant reevaluation within the admiralty, and within the Ministry of Defense. More helicopters and an efficient platform to launch them was necessary; subsequently, the converted light-carriers, *Albion* and *Bulwark*, appeared in the inventory as LPHs. The lack of amphibious assault shipping underscored a long-dormant request for new construction that finally reached fruition with plans and appropriations to construct two ships, *Fearless* and *Intrepid*, as LPDs. Engineering specifications for these 12,120-ton ships specified that they be capable of transporting four LCUs, four LVCPs, and five helicopters and to embark four hundred troops for an extended period or eight hundred men for short deployments.[12]

Other Western nations maintained small units of amphibious forces in the post-World War II era. Typically, the size of such "marine" organizations varied from a battalion to a regiment. While the focus of training and mission remained "amphibious," local security requirements and political imperatives relegated these forces, in many instances, to a role as either a special-operations elite or "palace guard." Typically, some nations attempted to duplicate the training and operational skills—albeit on a small scale—of the U.S. Marine Corps. In Latin America, marine-type organizations appeared in the defense establishments of Argentina, Brazil, Peru, Venezuela, Columbia, Haiti, and Mexico. In Asia, the Republic of China (Taiwan), the People's Republic of China, and the Republic of Korea (South Korea) maintained divisional units of marines or troops with an amphibious capability. Elsewhere in the Pacific Rim, small amphibious units appeared in Thailand, the Philippines, Republic of Vietnam (South Vietnam), and Indonesia. Two decades later, defense analysts reported similar organizations in Singapore, Vietnam, and North Korea. In Western Europe, only the Netherlands maintained a sizable force of marines, at first to bolster a waning colonial empire and then in support of NATO. Elsewhere, Spain hosted a unit of marines, while France, Italy, and Denmark maintained a token force of soldiers or sailors with a special operations-amphibious capability.[13]

The first major U.S. amphibious landing in a potentially hostile environment after the Korean War occurred neither in the face of Soviet nor Warsaw Pact defenders, armed with nuclear weapons, nor on shores defended by lightly armed Third World forces. On 14 July 1958 the fragile political balance of the Arab world, still smoldering because of the creation of the state of Israel in 1947 and the Western-Israeli military intervention in the Suez Canal crisis of 1956, went further askew with a coup d'état in Iraq and the murder of its pro-Western monarch, a cousin of Jordan's King Hussein. Lebanon, teetering precariously with a polyglot population composed of Christians and an assortment of Moslem sects, faced open rebellion. Ominously, Syrian troops, armed and trained by the Soviet Union, massed on Lebanon's borders. Lebanese President Camille Chamoun appealed for assistance, and President Eisenhower responded with Operation Bluebat.

An old contingency plan, Bluebat called for the landing of two Marine battalion landing teams (BLTs) north and south of Beirut, while the British flew in an airborne brigade from Cyprus. The changing geopolitical situation eliminated the British—or any Western military coalition, for that matter, as Western leaders feared an escalating confrontation pitting a Western alliance against the Arab world—with Soviet intervention always a possibility. American naval planners had BLT 1/8 near Malta, nearing the completion of its normal Mediterranean deployment; its nominal relief, BLT 3/6, had just arrived in the Mediterranean. Another BLT, 2/2, stood off Cyprus along with the headquarters of the Second Provisional Marine Force, a deployment in anticipation of a combined amphibious exercise with the British Royal Marines and the Italian Navy. As Navy and Marine Corps planners prepared to carry out President Eisenhower's order, diplomats on the scene attempted to delay the intervention, fearing that it might ignite a major confrontation in the Arab world and draw the superpowers to further estrangement and perhaps an outright clash of arms.[14]

Despite the dire predictions of the diplomats, and the long-held fears of strategists pondering the possible intervention of the Soviet

Union and the employment of tactical nuclear weaponry, nothing untoward occurred. At 1500 on 15 July 1958, BLT 2/2 landed over Red Beach just four miles south of Beirut. Smiling Lebanese sunbathers and soft-drink peddlers, not Soviet-armed surrogates, met the combat-laden Marines. By the following evening, the BLT had moved into Beirut, secured the dock area, and established security around critical buildings and the U.S. embassy. On 16 July, BLT 1/8 landed over Yellow Beach four miles north of Beirut just as BLT 2/8 began arriving from Camp Lejeune at the city's international airport. BLT 3/6 remained in the eastern Mediterranean in reserve.

As tensions mounted, the British airborne brigade in Cyprus deployed to Jordan to bolster the confidence of King Hussein. The Joint Chiefs of Staff ordered in the 24th Airborne Brigade from Germany to replace the British force in Operation Bluebat, and directed it into position between BLT 1/8 and BLT 2/2. But on 31 July national elections resulted in a defeat for President Chamoun (discredited politically because of his request for military support from the West), and the installation of General Fuad Chehab, commander of the Lebanese army, as Lebanon's new president. Between the initial landings in July 1958 and the elections that fall, the three Marine BLTs departed for CONUS. The last U.S. amphibious forces departed Lebanon by 18 October.

Although containing some refinements in amphibious doctrine that had emerged since the days of the Central Pacific drive in World War II, the landings in Lebanon reflected more of Saipan and Inchon than any rebirth of revolutionary amphibious lore. Rotary-wing aircraft played no part in Operation Bluebat; the landing force came ashore in assault craft differing little from those carrying Marines to the beaches of Iwo Jima. The names borne by much of the amphibious shipping standing off Lebanon would not have been unfamiliar to the amphibians of an earlier generation. Perhaps most prophetically, the clash of arms with the Red Army or Soviet-armed surrogates failed to take place. Thus, Operation Bluebat neither validated newer doctrines of amphibious warfare nor tested its efficacy in a superpower confrontation involving nuclear weaponry. The U.S. ambassador to Lebanon, Robert McClintock, argued ruefully that the incursion confused the local political situation. In his view, the amphibious force should have remained offshore as a "show-of-force."[15]

The potential for the deployment of amphibious forces waxed and waned during the late 1950s. Continued saber-rattling by both the Republic of China in Taiwan and the Peking-based People's Republic of China, a wide assortment of communist-inspired insurgencies in Southeast Asia, and no lessening of bellicose posturing on the Korean peninsula, resulted in the establishment of a battalion landing team embarked aboard a squadron of amphibious ships as a semi-permanent fixture with the U.S. Seventh Fleet known as the Special Landing Force. A Marine Corps division began a long-term deployment to the U.S. administered island of Okinawa in the Ryukyu chain just south of Japan. The Seventh Fleet retained its home port in Yokosuka, while Marine Corps aircraft units deployed separately from ground units (MAG-11 deployed to Taiwan in 1958 and a helicopter squadron was sent to Thailand in 1958).[16]

Continuing estrangement between the royalist government of the Kingdom of Laos and the Pathet Lao, a North Vietnamese-controlled insurgent group that was equipped and financed by the Soviet Union, resulted in the deployment of Marine forces to Thailand in 1962. But all of the deployments after the crisis in Lebanon, which used amphibious forces in various ways, were amphibious only in the sense that amphibious shipping provided at best some transportation; the traditional concepts of amphibious warfare, delineated in 1933 and refined in the early 1950s, had yet to be tested fully or operationally in the era of the superpowers. Perhaps most disconcerting to naval strategists was the growing uneasiness and uncertainty of applying President Eisenhower's policy of massive retaliation in Third World confrontations in which the Soviet Union and Warsaw Pact nations were not overtly involved.[17]

The potential for the deployment of amphibious forces in a full-blown scenario involving the Soviet Union came during the Cuban missile crisis in the fall of 1962. On 22 October, President John F. Kennedy announced to a stunned nation that aerial reconnaissance had provided undeniable proof that the Soviet Union was in the process of installing nuclear-armed missiles in Cuba, clearly aimed at the United States and within easy striking distance. In the anxious days that followed, American armed forces prepared urgently for war. A sizable amphibious armada—the largest assembled since the invasion of Inchon—put to sea in anticipation of a seaborne invasion. Fixed-wing aviation assets moved to airfields within striking distance of the communist-controlled island nation, and U.S. Army armored and infantry units converged on ports of embarkation.

Initially, President Kennedy's advisors recommended implementation of OPlan 312-62, which designated mostly naval aviation assets to strike selected targets. Like previous administrations, this one hoped to avoid the political fallout from ground combat casualties in a lengthy confrontation ashore. But when analysts reminded senior defense strategists and those closest to the President that the Soviet leader, Nikita Khrushchev, had purposely emasculated his conventional forces in favor of nuclear-capable delivery systems, President Kennedy and his advisors decided to implement OPlan 316-62, which specified a joint military operation and the invasion of Cuba. This particular strategy rested its potential success on the fact that Khrushchev had allowed the Soviet Navy—and the Soviet Naval Infantry—to atrophy.

OPlan 316-62 envisioned the deployment of an entire Marine Expeditionary Force, composed of the Second Marine Division, the Second Marine Air Wing, and the XVIII Airborne Corps, the last built around two airborne divisions. In addition, two additional Army divisions, one armor and one infantry, staged for the invasion. Planners added the Fifth Marine Expeditionary Brigade from the West Coast-based First Marine Division to provide the expeditionary force commander with additional combat power or as a floating reserve. Critical shortages of amphibious shipping, which both Navy and Marine Corps spokesmen had scored since the guns fell silent in the Korean conflict, plagued planning staffs. Ultimately, the Navy chartered commercial LSTs, activated additional LSTs from the reserve fleet, and contracted for twenty commercial cargo ships to move the massive invasion force to the waters off Cuba.

As each side tensed, fearing a nuclear exchange, President Kennedy ordered a naval quarantine into effect. Strategists envisioned an airborne drop of two divisions behind Havana. Meanwhile, the Second Marine Expeditionary Force would establish a beachhead at Tarara, followed in trace by the 2d Infantry Division. The heavier 1st Armored Division would land at the port of Mariel. When the assaulting force had secured Havana, strategists expected the armored division to roll up the flanks of the invasion and isolate the Cuban capital.

Initially, aviation assets from the Second Marine Air Wing deployed to Key West, Florida; Roosevelt Roads, Puerto Rico; and aboard the carriers *Independence* (CVA 62) and *Enterprise* (CVAN 65). To forestall any Cuban threat to the U.S. naval base at Guantanamo Bay, a battalion landing team plus two Marine infantry battalions arrived to bolster local defensive positions. Ultimately, approximately

25,000 Marines deployed in anticipation of an invasion of Cuba with a logistical tail sufficient to support the expeditionary force for fifteen days. The brigade from Camp Pendleton, built around Regimental Landing Team-1, arrived in the Caribbean reinforced with two additional infantry battalions.

Between 5 and 11 November, nine Soviet ships departed Cuba. By then, U.S. Navy warships had effected the regional naval quarantine of the region, but the Soviets never attempted to reinforce its garrison or to bolster the Cuban armed forces. On 26 November, Khrushchev accepted the fact that he had grossly underestimated the determination of America's young president, and the will of the citizenry to support the removal of foreign nuclear weapons from the Western Hemisphere. The missiles departed Cuba on that date, and the Soviets agreed further to withdraw the IL-28 aircraft from the island within thirty days.

The amphibians gleaned numerous lessons from the planning and deployment. Guantanamo Bay as a landing and staging site would have been too far from Havana and involve a confrontation too costly in terms of the limited objectives in subjugating the Castro regime. The defense of the isolated facility, even with massive reinforcements, caused planners to question its worth. The reliance on commercial shipping underscored shortfalls apparent for over a decade. Finally, a Navy ship configured for command and control of an amphibious operation of this size simply did not exist. Ultimately, an estimated quarter of a million men marshaled for the largest potential D-day since the invasion of Normandy.[18]

Continued unrest in the Caribbean resulted in further amphibious deployment to the region. Just as Leathernecks in a "floating battalion" deployed to the waters off America's southernmost neighbors between the Spanish-American War and World War One, a battalion landing team in the Caribbean became a permanent fixture in the 1960s. In addition, a battalion of infantry rotated through Guantanamo Bay to provide additional security for the U.S. naval base. Marine Corps units routinely used the Puerto Rican islands of Culebra and Vieques to hone amphibious skills.

The next challenge to law and order in the region occurred in the fall of 1965. Four years of normality and civilian leadership with a popularly elected presidency did nothing to stabilize the political fortunes of the Dominican Republic. As the political situation deteriorated, with both the Pentagon and the White House fearing the emergence of another Castro in the power vacuum should the Santo Domingo government slip into anarchy, a new president, Lyndon B. Johnson, displayed a relentless willingness to involve America in foreign imbroglios.

On 28 April 1965, the 6th Marine Expeditionary Unit, composed of Battalion Landing Team 3/6 and composite helicopter squadron HMM–264, stood off Santo Domingo. Helicopters delivered Marines from the *Boxer* (LPH 4) to secure the capital, and then a brigade of the 82d Airborne Division arrived by air transport. Quickly securing Santo Domingo, the invasion force evacuated U.S. and foreign nationals. Ultimately, over six thousand Marines deployed to the Dominican Republic. All of the amphibians departed by 6 June 1965.

While the deployment served to enhance the confidence of defense, congressional, and presidential decisionmakers in the usefulness of amphibious forces, the general implication of the minor incursion caused concern among critics of American foreign policy. The new president appeared far too willing to interject America's military and naval might into foreign situations in which the nation had questionable long-term interests, and that offered the potential for either escalating confrontations or a lengthy involvement. Writing from retirement, General David M. Shoup, former Commandant of the Marine Corps, observed, "Only a fraction of the force was needed or justified. A small, 1935-model Marine force could probably have handled the situation."[19]

Despite the hubris and military-politico posturing that punctuated the years after the successful amphibious operation at Inchon and the incursion into the Dominican Republic, the most important water-borne scenarios involving sizable numbers of amphibians occurred in two peacetime training exercises conducted early in the 1960s. In Operation Steel Pike and Operation Silver Lance, many of the prophetic analyses and conclusions that visionaries cut of the same cloth as William F. Fullam, Eli K. Cole, Robert H. Dunlap, and John A. Lejeune had posited almost half a century before surfaced anew.[20]

The first of these major exercises, Operation Steel Pike, tested the capability of the Atlantic fleet to deploy an entire Marine Expeditionary Force from the United States across the Atlantic to land near Huelva, Spain, with a small force of Spanish Marines. The imaginative exercise involved a complete transit to the amphibious objective area under combat conditions during October–November 1964, and even involved an anti-submarine warfare exercise. Operation Steel Pike afforded commanders and their staffs a unique opportunity to hone skills in planning and executing a large-scale amphibious operation.

The initial task organization reflected the imperatives in any amphibious operation: mission, threat, force structure, command and control, and concurrent planning. The tactical situation differed little from amphibious scenarios that had evolved in fleet maneuvers throughout this century. The terrain enveloping the amphibious operating area, characterized by limited beach exits and poor cross-country trafficability, required the addition of specialized engineering support in the assault echelon of the amphibious task force.

While ideally the entire Second Marine Expeditionary Force had been assigned to the exercise, realistically, units already committed to afloat contingencies in the Caribbean or the Mediterranean could not be included. Likewise, the infantry battalion detached as a security force for the base at Guantanamo could not be involved in the troop list. Despite these drawdowns, insufficient numbers of amphibious ships existed and the task force employed Military Sea Transport Service (MSTS) merchant ships, many of which could not be configured to transport amphibian vehicles, tanks, and heavy engineering equipment. Even then, niggardly appropriations resulted in insufficient contracts for MSTS shipping. Eventually, Marines of II MEF assembled over four thousand vehicles and almost a million square feet of cargo for Operation Steel Pike. A total of 21,642 troops embarked in forty-three assault ships and seventeen MSTS hulls for the transit from North Carolina to Spain. This was a huge amphibious task force by postwar standards. Even then, planners estimated that the assault echelon lacked ten AKAs, four LSDs, and eleven LSTs necessary for the amphibious lift. The amphibious force flagships (AGCs) proved wholly inadequate in providing working spaces and communications equipment necessary to support the many staff layers of both the amphibious task force and the landing force.[21]

Even more ominous to Marine Corps observers were inadequate air and naval gunfire support. To many critics it appeared as if the hard lessons of the Central Pacific Campaign in World War II had been lost to a new generation of amphibians. The pre-assault fires, at H-hour and L-hour, appeared insufficient. Many heavy bunkers in the landing area were not destroyed by the time the first wave touched down. Although these targets had been struck with five-inch ordnance fires from direct-support destroyers, their size mandated larger caliber ordnance of eight inches or more. To the dismay of naval gunfire specialists, the two heavy cruisers normally assigned an assault division—one for each assault regiment—consisted only of the *Newport News* (CA 148) and *Boston* (CAG 1).

No one needed to be reminded that in the later days of World War II a battleship normally supported each division in the amphibious assault. Worse, in the opinion of amphibians observing the operation, was the wholly inadequate close air support. Just one carrier, a CVS, had been assigned, obviously for the anti-submarine play of the exercise. Only by dismissing any threat of enemy air in the scenario could planners ignore the shortages of fixed-wing naval assets in support of Steel Pike. Umpires noted that a counterattack on the night of D-day or a concerted effort to overcome the initial landing waves could not have been repulsed given the paucity of air and naval gunfire support. John A. Lejeune and his senior officers echoed precisely the same concerns in a similar scenario in the fleet exercises held in Hawaii in 1925.[22]

Operation Steel Pike was the first time that amphibians attempted to land the assault elements of an entire regimental combat team by helicopter. Critics noted that the operating spaces provided by three LPHs and two LPDs did not provide the requisite platforms for such an undertaking. By the time the cargo lift began, the sequence had slipped into disarray. By the afternoon of D+2, the serials designated for heli-lift had slipped an alarmingly twenty-three hours behind schedule. Meanwhile, surface off-loading proceeded apace and on schedule. Even then, the shortage of LCMs required the employment of LSTs in a ferry mode in order to land heavy equipment.

Despite its many problems Operation Steel Pike educated a new generation of Navy and Marine Corps officers in the enormously difficult business of amphibious warfare. As such, it was worth the great expense and frequent stress. The observation of a chief observer reflected the judgment of the senior Navy and Marine officers who participated: "Unquestionably, it was one of the smoothest operations ever executed, including the heavy reliance on MSTS shipping. . . . Many of the real problems encountered, both Navy and Marine Corps, were in areas that the exercise was designed to check or judge, and in this Steel Pike served its greatest purpose."[23]

Like their counterparts in Steel Pike, planners for Operation

Silver Lance hoped to test the embarkation and deployment of an entire Marine Expeditionary Force by ships of the Pacific Fleet. For Silver Lance, planners wrestled with fewer problems involving port facilities because of a lesser number of ships available and a greater number of ports of embarkation spread along 250 miles of Southern California coastline. Almost fifteen thousand personnel participated, embarked on twenty-five assault ships and three MSTS vessels; and 3,300 vehicles and more than a half million cubic feet of cargo accompanied the deployment.

In contrast to Steel Pike, which concentrated on the embarkation and landing, Silver Lance focused on differing criteria and objectives. Planners envisioned an extremely complex scenario, including sizable civil affairs and counterinsurgency play in the exercise. Held at Camp Pendleton, California, Silver Lance provided participants at least a modicum of what faced them in Southeast Asia. Even as Marines from the 1st Marine Division waded ashore or disembarked from helicopters, their comrades-in-arms from Okinawa and Japan landed in the northernmost provinces of South Vietnam or stood by on station in the South China Sea as communist insurgents menaced the government of Vietnam. In Operation Silver Lance, a Marine Corps brigade landed at the behest of a friendly government, assailed by a larger neighbor. When the aggressive neighbor attacked the government forces and the brigade, a much larger amphibious force landed to protect the host government and the initial landing force.

While Steel Pike came to fruition with significant shortfalls in shipping and thus necessary heavy equipment and weapons never entered the play of the exercise, Silver Lance evolved to its successful conclusion because commanders had the luxury of turnabouts in amphibious shipping, MSTS augmentation, and beach-to-beach lifts from the Del Mar Boat Basin to the amphibious objective area farther up the coast line. Although Steel Pike witnessed significant deficiencies in close-air support aircraft and aircraft carriers assigned, three carriers (two CVAs and one CVS) participated in Silver Lance. Still, only one heavy cruiser and only thirteen assorted destroyers (one DLG, eight DDs, two DEs) provided naval gunfire support.

Both Operation Steel Pike and Operation Silver Lance should have provided a wake-up call for both the Pentagon and the Oval Office. Heavy reliance on merchant shipping, inadequate close-air and naval gunfire support, and embarkation difficulties that clogged East Coast ports suggested serious problems in moving a Marine

Expeditionary Force, perhaps followed in trace by a field army, to the European or Mediterranean littoral. While Operation Silver Lance realized fewer such difficulties, its over-adaptability to problem areas by using local resources foreshadowed an unrealistic reliance on Marine and Navy ingenuity and resolve. In any event, the counterinsurgency focus in Silver Lance remained heavy over the debate on the future efficacy of amphibious warfare as U.S. forces prepared increasingly to fight in the anti-guerrilla environment and against native insurgents bent on communist-inspired wars of national liberation.[24]

Chapter Three

Amphibious Warfare and the Vietnam War

Beginning in the 1960s, serious interest by American militarists and strategists in amphibious warfare waned sharply. For most of a decade, the focus of attention for senior U.S. Marine and Navy amphibians shifted from the honing of skills germane to the time-honored projection of sea power ashore to support of a protracted land campaign in Southeast Asia. Except for a token commitment of advisors; members of the staff, Commander, U.S. Military Assistance Command, Vietnam (COMUSMACV); and highly specialized small units, involvement by the U.S. naval services did not begin in earnest until the spring of 1965. A decade later, the same services collaborated in an epic withdrawal of residual Americans, and indigenous personnel fleeing impending victories in South Vietnam and Cambodia. Even then, the persistent problems of the region continued to plague Washington. Less than a year after the humiliating and disquieting withdrawal, U.S. amphibious forces became embroiled in a costly and controversial attempt to recover the crew of a merchant ship after forces of the new communist rulers of Cambodia seized it on the high seas.

The origins of U.S. intervention in Southeast Asia may be traced to the anticommunist tensions of the early Cold War era. Especially after the frustrating end of the Korean conflict, strategists both in and out of uniform were influenced increasingly by the initiatives and imperatives emanating from the Kremlin. On 6 January 1961, shortly before the inauguration of President-elect John F. Kennedy, Soviet Premier Nikita Khrushchev startled the West by declaring global support for unconventional "wars of national liberation." When Kennedy countered with his promise "to go anywhere, bear any burden" in support of liberty, the stage was set for a new and deadly chapter of the Cold War. While nuclear war would remain a standing threat, the rivalry between the superpowers for the next dozen years focused on nationalism and counterinsurgency in the Third World.

By 1960, disquieting native insurgencies smoldered in various degrees of intensity in every nation in Southeast Asia. But in the government of the Republic of Vietnam (RVN or South Vietnam [SVN] in the vernacular), which had eschewed political ties or reunification with the communist-dominated Republic of Vietnam (DRV or North Vietnam [NVN] in the vernacular), the flames of insurgency burned increasingly brighter and threatened the pro-Western regime. In 1961, the government of NVN, led by the venerable Ho Chi Minh, began full-scale support of an insurgency in the southern half of the Vietnamese peninsula. Communist insurgencies in nearby Cambodia and Laos supported the machinations of the Vietnamese Workers Party, the political arm of the NVN government.[1]

Earlier, when the Geneva Accords of 1954 failed to achieve reunification of the two Vietnams, President Dwight D. Eisenhower had directed material aid to the fledgling RVN. Subsequently, President Kennedy increased U.S. involvement with the introduction of advisors to ground combat units and assignment of special warfare units "in-country." By 1964, the Viet Cong insurgents (Vietnamese Communists, or VC in the vernacular) in the south and their mentors in Hanoi appeared increasingly to threaten the Saigon government. A seemingly minor incident occurred at this point that caused the conflict on the Vietnamese peninsula to escalate sharply.

Among many widely ranging and imaginative plans formulated by national security planners in Washington during the early 1960s was OpPlan 34A. This special warfare plan entailed covert sabotage and amphibious raids by SVN forces along the coast of North Vietnam, and the employment of Thai pilots in old T39 propeller-driven aircraft in support of royalist forces in Laos. On 2 August 1964, the U.S. destroyer *Maddox* (DD 731) reported a torpedo attack by NVN patrol boats while steaming in international waters. Two days later the *Turner Joy* (DD 951) reported a second and similar attack. The North Vietnamese apparently believed the ships to be participants in infrequent SVN raids along the coast. President Johnson responded swiftly and in kind by ordering retaliatory air strikes by carrier-based aircraft on military facilities along one hundred miles of the North Vietnam coastline. Two days later Congress passed the so-called Tonkin Gulf Resolution with wide, bipartisan support and thus appeared to give President Johnson a free hand in the escalating conflict in Southeast Asia.[2]

U.S. amphibious forces reacted immediately in response to the Tonkin Gulf incident. Battalion Landing Team (BLT) 2/3, the currently deployed ground component of Commander Seventh Fleet's (COM-SEVENTHFLT) Special Landing Force (SLF) had barely disembarked at Subic Bay in anticipation of training ashore. News of the NVN attack followed quickly with orders to reembark aboard amphibious shipping. Throughout August and into the fall, the SLF—which grew at times into an entire Marine Expeditionary Brigade (MEB)—steamed up and down the coast of the two Vietnams, awaiting orders and planning various amphibious contingencies. For the most part, the president and the Pentagon concluded that Hanoi had learned the folly of its reckless actions the previous summer, and the SLF off-loaded at White Beach, Okinawa, in November. However, tensions remained high throughout the Western Pacific for the remainder of 1964 and into early 1965.

The political-military situation in South Vietnam deteriorated sharply in February 1965. Viet Cong attacks on U.S. facilities at Pleiku and Qui Nhon killed 31 Americans and wounded 147. When retaliatory strikes by carrier aircraft against NVN military targets failed to deter Viet Cong activities, the United States on 2 March initiated Operation Rolling Thunder, the sustained bombardment of NVN by U.S. Navy and Air Force planes. This strategy produced mixed results; the Americans and South Vietnamese were running out of options. As the military situation in SVN grew increasingly precarious in early 1965, Pentagon planners urged President Johnson to commit ground forces, if only to bolster the defense of vital coastal enclaves and the resolve of the RVN government.

From Saigon, both General William C. Westmoreland, COMUS-MACV; and General Maxwell D. Taylor, the U.S. ambassador to Saigon, urged the introduction of a modest and low-key contingent of troops. Specifically, Westmoreland wanted heavily armed Marines because of their amphibious capabilities and organic logistical support. Decisionmakers in Washington and Saigon agreed that the Leathernecks would cross the beaches at Da Nang in the northern province of Quang Nam that spring. At the last minute, Assistant Secretary of Defense John M. McNaughton attempted to replace the Marines with the Okinawa-based 173d Airborne Brigade, arguing unconvincingly that the lightly armed and equipped paratroopers could be introduced "in the most inconspicuous way feasible." Navalists responded quickly by suggesting that, once again, interservice rivalry had skewed rational decisionmaking. Westmoreland remained obdurate, however, insisting that he wanted the Marines because of their staying power.[3]

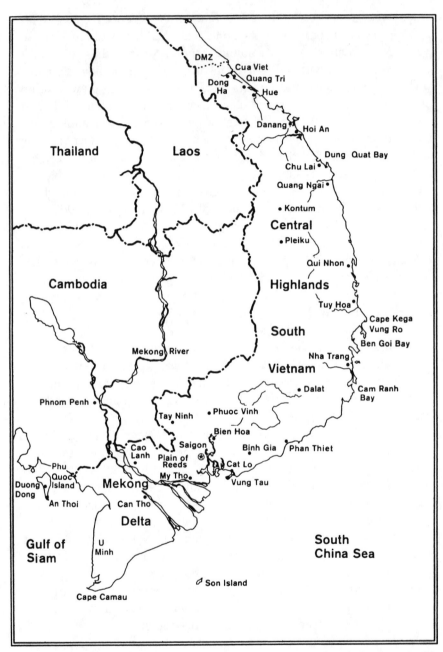

South Vietnam. (From Edward J. Marolda and Oscar P. Fitzgerald, *The United States Navy and the Vietnam Conflict*, vol. II, *From Military Assistance to Combat, 1959–1965* [Washington: GPO, 1986], p. iii.)

Even before the first infantry battalions crossed the beaches or exited aircraft onto Vietnamese soil, Marine support and service support elements had taken up positions in-country. A medium-lift helicopter squadron, HMM-163, relieved HMM-365 at the end of the unit's deployment on 17 February. Coincidentally, on the same day, Company C, 7th Engineers, arrived at Da Nang. Just a week before, Battery A, 1st Light Anti-Aircraft Missile Battalion (LAAM) had assumed a firing position in defense of the airfield at Da Nang; the remainder of the battalion arrived in-country on 17 February. Thus, even before the decision to land elements of the SLF and fly in additional Marines from Okinawa, Leatherneck strength in Vietnam numbered 1,248—including those assigned advisory duties or to the COMUSMACV staff.

Once the long-awaited order to deploy to SVN reached Navy and Marine Corps units, two battalions of infantry—with full combat support and combat service support—and squadrons of aircraft descended on the northern provinces of SVN. On 8 March, the 9th Marine Expeditionary Brigade (MEB) took up positions at Da Nang. BLT 3/9 landed across Red Beach near the city, while BLT 1/3 disembarked from transport aircraft at the combined military and commercial airport just outside the huge commercial hub of Da Nang. A day later, the arrival of HMM-162 doubled the helicopter assets available. On 10 April Navy Task Group 76.6 landed assault troops of BLT 2/3 across Red Beach, then off-loaded heavy equipment and supplies on the Tiensha Peninsula across the Da Nang River. The arrival of BLT 2/3, fresh from Operation Jungle Drum III on Thailand's Kra Isthmus, brought the 9th MEB to full strength. On the same day, VMFA-531— the first squadron of F4B Phantoms—landed at Da Nang to begin air operations in support of 9th MEB. Meanwhile, a detachment from BLT 2/3 deployed to Phu Bai to provide security for a vital signal intelligence facility located just outside the ancient capital of Hue. On 14 April Navy Task Group 76.7 assembled off the mouth of the Song Huong (or Perfume River), debarked troops of BLT 3/4 into landing craft, and guided them eleven miles upstream to Hue. The Marines, expecting the worst, were greeted by throngs of Vietnamese who lined the river banks to cheer the arriving Americans. The buildup continued at a rapid pace.

On 6 May, Headquarters, III Marine Expeditionary Force—later changed to Marine Amphibious Force (MAF) so as not to remind the Vietnamese of the hated French Corps d'Expéditionnaire—assumed tactical command of all Marine Corps units in the five northernmost provinces of SVN (also known as I Corps or I Combat Tactical Zone). The day after III MAF established its headquarters ashore, 3d MAB (Marine Amphibious Brigade) landed at Chu Lai in southern I Corps, fifty-seven miles south of Da Nang. The Chu Lai operation was then the largest amphibious landing under combat conditions conducted by American naval forces since Inchon. Rear Admiral Donald W. Wulzen, commanding Task Force 76, landed five thousand troops to establish a third enclave of sea soldiers ashore in the RVN. III MAF assigned the landing force the mission of constructing a "Short Airfield for Tactical Support (SATS)" in Chu Lai's soft sand. The expeditionary strip, complete with catapults and arresting cables, was ready to receive the first aircraft on 1 June, just twenty-five days after the landing.[4]

Despite the hubris surrounding the deployment of Marines to SVN, the amphibious landings themselves revealed many flaws in the planning and execution. Although normal security precautions prevailed, details of the forthcoming deployment appeared in Okinawan newspapers, greatly embarrassing senior officers. Commanders and staffs learned to their collective dismay that despite years of schooling and practice, loading appeared flawed. Congested beaches and landing craft floating offshore for hours frustrated shore party and beachmaster personnel. Planners learned that the cube of amphibious cargo, not the weight, was the determining factor in efficient embarkation. Supposedly, a modern attack transport probably could haul five hundred tons of cargo; to the surprise of planners, the *Lenawee* (APA 195) carried 850 tons to Chu Lai and 2,000 tons on a subsequent resupply mission.[5]

Doctrinal and strategic considerations surfaced almost immediately. The landing of the 9th MAB had seriously depleted the Fleet Marine Force (FMF) in the Seventh Fleet. Both Lt. Gen. Victor H. Krulak, Commanding General, FMFPac; and Vice Adm. Paul P. Blackburn, Commander in Chief, Pacific Fleet (CinCPacFlt) agreed that the SLF should be reconstituted as quickly as possible. Besides the usual contingencies requiring amphibious forces, both senior officers anticipated future amphibious operations in support of the burgeoning war in Vietnam.

Subsequently, COMUSMACV and CinCPacFlt agreed upon a coastal surveillance campaign, Operation Market Time, in hopes of interdicting North Vietnamese resupply to Viet Cong units in the south. As part of the effort, Vietnamese Marines and Marine Corps battalions would collaborate, and conduct amphibious raids. Four of the planned amphibious raids did take place, but none produced significant results. Planners at Headquarters, III MAF anticipated employment of the SLF as part of future operations ashore. To the dismay of senior Navy and Marine officers, however, COMUSMACV viewed the SLFs as a readily available source of manpower, the employment of which was not constricted by troop ceilings mandated by the Pentagon.[6]

Thus, for the remainder of the Second Indochina War (1965–1973), amphibious elements operated as part of Commander Seventh Fleet's (COMSEVENFLT) support of COMUSMACV and usually with III MAF operations in the northern provinces. The initial, and the most successful foray, occurred during the late summer of the Marines' first summer in Vietnam. Intelligence sources revealed the presence of the 1st VC Regiment south of Chu Lai in the Van Tuong Village complex, with an estimated strength of two thousand men. Operation Starlight took place during 18–24 August 1965, and began initially with the 4th Marines (1/7, 2/4, 3/3). When the assaulting force encountered unusually strong resistance from the well dug-in enemy, BLT 3/7 from the SLF joined the fray. After the two-day operation ended, commanders reported 623 VC killed at a cost of fifty-four Marine lives. Subsequent agent reports revealed that the 1st VC Regiment had suffered 1,430 dead and was no longer an effective combat unit.[7]

During the remainder of the year, amphibious forces from Seventh Fleet shipping deployed ashore in a half dozen occasions: Operation Piranha (7–10 September), in the Van Tuong Village complex again; Operation Blue Marlin (Phase II, 16–18 November), just south of Hoi An; BLT 3/7 landed to reinforce an Army of Vietnam (ARVN) ranger battalion south of Quang Ngai; and BLT 2/1 and HMM-261 conducted an amphibious raid seventy miles east of Saigon. The year ended with the second of the Marines' most successful operations, Harvest Moon, conducted twenty-five miles south of Chu Lai to deny the rice harvest to the VC. BLT 2/1 from the SLF joined Task Force Delta ashore, netting 407 VC killed. For the remainder of U.S. involvement ashore, III MAF grew increasingly to draw upon the SLFs as readily available reinforcements.[8]

By the beginning of 1966 the SLF constituted CinCPacFlt's only amphibious force and only strategic reserve, because all of III MAF (minus the SLF) operated solely in-country. Operation Double Eagle, the largest amphibious operation to date, took place when Task Force Delta—including the SLF—landed in Quang Ngai Province, and moved into the Que Son Valley (28 January–7 March). Despite the crush of friendly forces, none failed to engage sizeable enemy units. The lack of significant results fueled existing questions concerning future amphibious operations in Vietnam.

Observers already ashore concluded that the amphibious phase of the operations lingered longer than necessary. Command and control needed to be passed ashore far more quickly from the landing force to the local force conducting the larger operation. But both Lt. General Krulak and Lt. General Lewis W. Walt (Commanding General, III MAF) balked. Neither Krulak nor Walt wanted SLF assets considered as merely another of COMUSMACV's sources of in-country manpower. Both commanders insisted upon the maintenance of the SLF's integrity and independence. The command relationships were distinctive: III MAF belonged to COMUSMACV; the SLF belonged to COMSEVENTHFLT, a component of CINCPAC; and thereby independent of COMUSMACV.

These recurring questions led to a full-blown conference on Okinawa, 25 February–1 March 1966, at the instigation of Admiral Roy L. Johnson, CinCPacFlt. Conferees were tasked to review SLF command and control procedures, amphibious operations in the Vietnamese littoral in general, and amphibious operations with other COMUSMACV or in-country forces. The attendees envisioned four types of SLF employment:

- SLF is supporting a larger operation;
- SLF is an integral part of an in-country operation;
- SLF & in-country forces are usually III MAF forces;
- landing force is composed entirely of III MAF forces.

The participants ended the conference by encouraging the speedy end of the amphibious phase and the passing of operational control ashore. In addition, they concurred in the encouragement of more utilization of helicopters to allow amphibious forces to strike further inland.[9]

Later in the spring, the SLF participated in an unusual operation far removed from I Corps and III MAF's Area of Operations (AOA). During Operation Jackstay, 26 March–6 April 1966, the SLF entered the Rung Sat Special Zone to disrupt enemy operations along the waterways south of Saigon. Although only partially successful, the SLF uncovered arms and supply caches. Again, COMUSMACV voiced concerns over command and control issues. Although COMUSMACV reported to CinCPac, the SLF reported not to III MAF (who reported to COMUSMACV), but to ComSeventhFlt (who reported to CinCPacFlt), who in turn reported to CincPac. These concerns and queries led to yet another conference to address issues of command and control.[10]

Again held on Okinawa, the conference (25–28 May 1966) reached three important conclusions: early concurrent and parallel planning based on decisions reached mutually by COMUSMACV and CinCPacFlt; the need for acquisition of timely intelligence; and an improvement of amphibious reaction by streamlining procedures to improve the responsiveness of the SLF to COMUSMACV. General Westmoreland simply wanted more flexibility when requesting deployment of the SLF. The recommendations in turn assured CinCPacFlt that the command relationships delineated in NWP-22(A) would pertain to all amphibious operations in Vietnam as much as possible.

Renewed enthusiasm for amphibious landings following the Okinawa Conference, 1966, led to SLF participation in the Deckhouse series of operations. From 18–30 June 1966, the SLF participated in a nine-battalion force with elements of the 1st Air Cavalry Division in Operation Nathan Hale, conducted in II Corps. In midsummer, BLT 3/5 from the SLF joined III MAF forces on Operation Hastings, fifty-five miles southwest of Hue, to disrupt movement of the NVA 324B Division south across the Demilitarized Zone (DMZ). Deckhouse III, conducted with the 173d Airborne Brigade sixty miles southwest of Saigon, reaped little in the way of tangible victories. Finally, the SLF operated with III MAF forces ashore in Operation Prairie eight miles northeast of Dong Ha, hard against the DMZ.[11]

By the beginning of 1967, opinions varied widely over the deployment of the SLF. CinCPacFlt considered the amphibious force as just that, a naval contribution to the war effort in SVN also available for any naval mission in the Pacific. COMUSMACV viewed the SLF as a ready source of manpower, not counted as part of in-country ceilings imposed by the Pentagon or the White House. Marine wing and division commanders wanted to control their own assets and resented the siphoning off of infantry battalions and helicopter squadrons to man the SLF. Commanding General, III MAF, in turn, wanted troops in-country and in contact with a resolute enemy that appeared not only capable of replacing combat losses but reinforcing its units in I Corps. Furthermore, in the background of any discussion at COMUS-MACV concerning the SLF, the thorny issue of control of fixed-wing air assets was likely to surface.

Existing amphibious doctrine authorized the task force commander to establish an Amphibious Objective Area (AOA) throughout the airspace surrounding the operation for the duration of the landing. With the AOA, the amphibious task force commander maintained control of all aircraft, military or civilian. This single aspect of amphibious doctrine kept the U.S. Air Force at loggerheads with the Navy and Marines for thirty years. It was especially controversial during the Vietnam War. Seventh Air Force remained defiant on the issue. Some senior officers argued that existing doctrine granting such control to the amphibious task force commander was nullified because Free World Military Armed Forces (FWMAF) operated in-country at the behest of the RVN. Because Seventh Air Force command-and-control vehicles and procedures were already in place, supplanting them with a Navy and Marine Corps system made little sense. For the time being, however, General Westmoreland bowed to the naval side in the dispute—perhaps because FMFPac had CinCPac's ear on the subject.

Whatever doubts senior officers in Saigon or in the northern provinces harbored concerning the efficacy of amphibious forces in a war of counterinsurgency, Honolulu and Washington apparently believed the deployment of an SLF in Southeast Asia strengthened U.S. resolve in the region and reinforced the efforts of FWMAFs in Vietnam. In January 1967, CinCPacFlt directed the addition of an LST (landing ship, tank) to the SLF. This augmentation increased the shipping assigned to an amphibious ready group (ARG) to a total of five: one amphibious assault ship (LPH), one landing ship, dock (LSD), one attack transport (APA), one amphibious transport, dock (LPD), and the LST. Then, in the same month, the Joint Chiefs of Staff authorized creation of a second SLF, either for extended operations in Vietnam or in support of Seventh Fleet contingencies.

Operation Deckhouse V, a combined operation with the SLF and Vietnamese Marines, began on 6 January 1967 in Kien Hoa Province, IV Corps. Poor communications, rough seas, and harried planning contributed to unspectacular results. Ominously, Philippine news reported the departure of the SLF from Subic Bay with the information that the force intended to land somewhere in the Mekong Delta. Most significantly for the future of amphibious operations in SVN, Seventh Air Force again raised the contentious issue of fixed-wing air control in SVN airspace. Because an Air Force air control system was already in place, senior Air Force officers loathed supplementing the existing program or to supplant it with one provided by the amphibious task force. In this imbroglio, General Westmoreland still sided with the amphibians, but the nagging controversy foreshadowed a decision to confine future SLF operations in I Corps.

In the next twelve months, both SLF Alpha and SLF Bravo participated in a total of twenty-three amphibious operations in I Corps. Most of the landings were conducted in support of existing operations ashore, with the SLFs used in a reinforcing role. None produced spectacular results or sizeable counts of enemy dead, which unfortunately had become the chief measure of effectiveness in the war by that time. Increasingly, U.S. amphibious operations in Vietnam, while validating overall doctrine and special ships and equipment within the Department of the Navy, did little to enlist new converts from other armed services or national security experts.[12]

The parochial views regarding employment of the SLFs continued into 1968; the enemy's Tet Offensive of that year only deflected further debate on the subject. Despite the efforts of COMUSMACV, III MAF, FMFPac, and CinCPacFlt to resolve the differences, the procedures agreed upon in 1966 still precipitated occasional controversy. From General Krulak's perspective, the maintenance of the SLFs as components of the 9th MAB's commitment to COMSEVENTHFLT's operational requirements maintained the amphibious character of the organizations. COMUSMACV, however, continued to view the SLFs as merely squadrons and battalions, and not Marine Air-Ground Task Forces (MAGTFs) or combined-arms units. But even FMFPac could recognize that exigencies might occur which required the deployment of either or both SLFs in-country for extended periods; the Tet Offensive provided just such a scenario. In an attempt to balance the competing views, Lt. General Robert E. Cushman, Jr., Commanding General, III MAF, suggested that SLFs refit at Subic Bay in the Philippines, rather than through Okinawa and thus be more responsive to the needs of COMUSMACV.

By 1968, many Marine commanders expressed reservations about employment and overall worth of the SLFs. Was the cherished amphibious objective area still worth fighting for when American control of air space and all landing sites already existed? Did all the provision of NWP-22(A) apply to the enormous air-ground war in Vietnam? Navy and Marine amphibious commanders continued to argue that the SLFs constituted COMSEVENTHFLT's reserve force; moreover, other potential crises existed elsewhere in the theater. Still, when emergencies such as the Tet Offensive occurred, COMUSMACV could well wonder why two fully armed and equipped infantry battalions floated offshore when reinforcements were sorely needed. But the SLFs gave COMUSMACV a flexibility that it apparently did not appreciate fully, and General Cushman continued to demand adherence to doctrine. Cushman informed his division commanders that he wanted "the SLFs used in an amphibious role according to current doctrine for amphibious operations."[13]

Ironically, even while the debate over the military usefulness of amphibious operations with South Vietnam continued, the COMUS-MACV staff was preparing plans for a proposed U.S. landing north of the DMZ. This planning initiative, code-named Durango City, was not widely known. The objective of Operation Durango City was the surprise disruption of an estimated thirty thousand NVA troops assembling in their presumed "sanctuary" prior to infiltrating across the DMZ into Quang Tri Province. Planning was hampered by interservice squabbles—the Seventh Air Force objected to the establishment of an AOA even outside RVN—but most military officers yearned to see even a temporary opening of "a second front" along the NVN coastline. Here, it seemed, was a legitimate opportunity to employ America's amphibious expertise. But the war in Vietnam was fast becoming a political liability in Washington, especially after the domestic repercussions following the Tet Offensive. There was little top-level support for military initiatives north of the DMZ. To the great disappointment of many serving officers in-country and afloat, Operation Durango City died stillborn. Unlike Korea, the Vietnam War would have no Inchon.[14]

As infiltrating enemy units massed in the northern provinces, both SLFs remained ashore. From January through June, both of their infantry battalions operated as such with units of the 3d Marine Division. Thus, the exigencies of the tactical situation resulted in a realization of what both COMUSMACV and III MAF wanted, and apparently without opposition from 9th MAB, COMSEVENTHFLT, or CinCPacFlt. Beginning in the summer and for the remainder of the year, the SLFs participated in operations ashore just as in 1967. Still, however, many issues over employment of the SLF remained unresolved. 9th MAB believed that III MAF or its subordinate units actually concocted operational scenarios ashore to force deployment of the SLFs in a reinforcing role—in effect, providing additional troop strength despite the MAGTF character of the SLFs. Only thirteen amphibious operations, deploying either or both of the SLFs, occurred in 1968.[15]

The two landing forces, Alpha and Bravo (designated by the Navy as Task Groups 79.4 and 79.5) continued under the command of 9th MAB in Okinawa. At sea, the SLFs came under Commander, Amphibious Task Force, Seventh Fleet; ashore, under the operational control of III MAF. Until 1969 any infantry regiment assigned to III MAF could be required to provide a battalion to an SLF. But near the end of 1968, with the reconstitution of Regimental Landing Team (RLT) Twenty-Six, both SLFs drew their ground elements from that RLT. In like fashion, two medium helicopter squadrons (HMMs) were tasked to deploy with the SLFs on a permanent basis.

The year 1969 witnessed fourteen SLF operations, as compared to thirteen the year before and twenty-five in 1967. Of these, Operation Bold Mariner constituted the largest amphibious operation since the Korean War. A brigade-size landing force, including both of the SLFs, joined with elements of the American Division eighteen kilometers south of Chu Lai to root out the enemy stronghold on the Batangan Peninsula. Sizable Viet Cong units had estimated well-entrenched positions in the flatlands and rolling hills of the region. The operation began on 12 January and achieved substantial results, including the capture of an entire enemy unit virtually intact. Meanwhile, U.S. Navy task forces continued to execute amphibious landings by the Korean Marine Corps on Barrier Island, south of Da Nang. These assaults were well executed; unfortunately, they were also well-advertised. Viet Cong forces usually had enough advance warning to evacuate the objective area.

Upon redeployment of the 3d Marine Division to Okinawa near the end of 1969, the assets of III MAF—now on Okinawa—were used to provide the manning of the SLFs. As such, the SLFs could no longer deploy to Vietnam without specific authorization from the JCS. In CinCPac's view, only a major enemy offensive could result in either of the SLFs deploying in-country. Nonetheless, such a contingency remained as a possibility. CinCPac directed the SLFs to maintain a 120-hour reaction time.[16]

The cycle of SLF operations in support of COMUSMACV and III MAF operations in South Vietnam ended coincidently with an American withdrawal and "Vietnamization" in full swing. The 31st Marine Amphibious Unit (MAU) participated in a final SVN operation, Lam Son 719, by providing helicopter support on the eastern side of the border with Laos. The operation, conducted in February–March 1971, ended with an amphibious demonstration by the MAU near the NVA airfield at Vinh in the southern part of North Vietnam. As the 3d MAB, which had assumed control of III MAF's forces after the latter redeployed to Okinawa, prepared to stand down and redeploy itself, the normal 120-hour response time of the SLFs was decreased to 72 hours as senior commanders voiced concern over the possibility of renewed enemy hostilities. Despite the feared collapse of the Saigon government in the face of the communist Easter Offensive in 1972, and a heightened alert status, amphibious forces never received authorization to deploy ashore in SVN.[17]

Nonetheless, CinCPac and COMSEVENTHFLT ordered III MAF units into the waters off Vietnam, with 9th MAB providing security for COMUSMACV and emergency evacuation if needed. Ultimately, four amphibious groups in sixteen ships responded. With the imminent collapse of the government in the south in 1975, amphibious elements of the Seventh Fleet participated in a herculean effort to evacuate the remnants of the U.S. population from Cambodia and South Vietnam, along with scores of the indigenous population fearful of life under a Marxist-Leninist regime. On 12 April 1975, SLF elements extracted remaining U.S. personnel from Pnom Penh as Cambodia collapsed under the communist onslaught. Amphibious forces executed Operation Eagle Pull without serious incident. In nearby South Vietnam, SLF units transported the residual U.S. presence and any Vietnamese that could wrangle passage out of Saigon on Operation Frequent Wind on 29 April. This operation, exceedingly difficult to plan and execute, made full use of forward deployed amphibious forces. The South Vietnamese government collapsed immediately; America's longest war shuddered to its unhappy ending.

The final employment of American amphibious forces in combat in Southeast Asia occurred through an unlikely scenario. On 12 May 1975, an overzealous local Khmer Rouge commander ordered a gunboat to capture an unarmed U.S. merchantman, the SS Mayaguez, in the Gulf of Thailand. As the Cambodians ferried the luckless crew of the vessel to the mainland, planning for an amphibious assault on Koh

Tang Island commenced. Finding the *Mayaguez* deserted, Marines of BLT 2/9—arriving in Air Force helicopters from an air base in Thailand on 14 May—fought a determined opponent on the island. In an operation fraught with command-and-control difficulties, punctuated by far too many conflicting chains of command, and unbalanced by political intrusions at the highest level, the episode ended with the embarrassing disclosure that the Cambodians had already released the crew following what had clearly been a mistake. The sorry episode claimed the lives of fifteen U.S. servicemen (plus three men reported missing and later declared dead), forty-nine wounded, and another twenty-three dead servicemen in a related helicopter crash. The entire affair served to underscore the need to reestablish amphibious capabilities and improve joint-service planning after so many years' preoccupation with counterinsurgency.[18]

During the Second Indochina War and after, critics faulted the Marine Corps for failing to embrace the concept of riverine warfare and its obvious adaptation to the waterways of the Mekong Delta. But the difference between "brown water" and "blue water" operations is more than color variance. Amphibious warfare by definition is an assault launched from the sea against a hostile shore. By such terms, the landing up the Perfume River by Task Group 76.7 in 1965 was technically an amphibious assault—the surprise appearance of cheering natives not withstanding. To employ these same assets—amphibious troops and helicopters, naval landing craft, and beachmasters—in protracted patrolling operations along inland river networks would waste a unique military capability. CinCPacFlt and CG, FMFPac strove to protect this capability (reduced to the SLF) throughout the war. Both commanders kept their focus on future naval requirements as well as the very real threat of additional communist influences in other "wars of national liberation" which may well have erupted elsewhere in the Pacific. And it is doubtful if CinCPacFlt and CG, FMFPac would have allowed such a drastic alteration in the traditional employment of Fleet Marine Forces; redeployment to IV Corps in a riverine warfare role would have required transfer of III MAF assets to the operational control of the corps commander—most likely, an Army officer.[19]

While U.S. Marines performed yeoman service ashore in the northern provinces, they were operationally divorced in most respects from the Navy, and the experience spawned a generation of Leathernecks woefully ignorant about the special demands of amphibious warfare. Beginning even before the landings in 1965, the primary interest—if not the unspoken emphasis—at Marine Corps schools focused on counterinsurgency. So many adaptations and field expedients to modify NWP-22B and LFM-01 made many amphibians question current doctrine altogether. Perhaps the most debatable navy issue to emerge from the decade of U.S. involvement was the controversial authority of the amphibious task force commander to control air traffic within the AOA, even during the protracted land campaign. The acrimonious debate over control of fixed-wing assets and air space exacerbated interservice issues. Amphibious doctrine, undersubscribed and misunderstood for several years, seemed out of vogue with military thinkers.[20]

By the end of III MAF's deployment ashore, even junior officers spoke openly of SLF operations with derision. Some eschewed assignment to the 26th Marines, opting instead to join a unit operating full-time ashore. Even senior officers suspected that the many SLF operations had the taint of concoction about them. One distinguished Marine, Col. (later Lt. Gen.) John R. Chaisson, speaking from his experiences serving on the COMUSMACV staff, suggested that "the SLF operations were by and large sort of contrived. It was almost a concept looking for a home." Lt. General Victor H. Krulak, commanding FMFPAC throughout 1964-1968, saw the SLF from a broader perspective: the institutional need for the corps to retain its amphibious roots. "I stuck to it [the SLF] like a drunk hangs on to a lamp post," he recalled, insisting that "we had to have a mobile, amphibious element at all times." Col. Robert H. Barrow (later Gen. and 27th Commandant) served as Krulak's G-3 during 1964–1967, but viewed the SLF differently than his commander. In Barrow's judgment, the "malemployment of the SLF" was "one of the sad stories of the Vietnam War." He believed the Navy-Marine Corps team missed many opportunities for effective employment of the SLF by "not raising our sights high enough." Most SLF landings were limited to shallow coastal enclaves and hampered by the perceived requirement to offload everything—including heavy tracked vehicles of marginal utility inland. "We should have tailored and employed the SLF as a hard-hitting, almost exclusively helicopter-borne force," he concluded, preferably using a full regimental landing team capable of significant strikes twenty to forty miles from the coast.[21]

Maj. Gen. (later Lt. Gen.) Ormond R. Simpson commanded the 1st Marine Division in Quang Nam Province throughout 1969. He was not impressed by SLF incursions in his tactical area of responsibility.

"They were not very effective in the Quang Nam area," he recalled. "They invariably suffered greater casualties from mines and booby traps than a regularly assigned battalion." He added, "I know that in my area the enemy didn't worry about the SLF." On the other hand, Simpson admitted his appreciation for the SLF being retained offshore. "They did keep alive the idea of the threat of amphibious assault. . . . From the standpoint of overall Marine policy, it was a good idea."[22]

No less a luminary than noted historian Allan R. Millett has argued persuasively that the entire Vietnam experience, fought so assiduously and with such professionalism by the Marine Corps, provided few lasting benefits in the long term. Perhaps General Robert E. Cushman, Jr., perceived the problem when he declared, shortly after becoming Commandant of the Marine Corps in 1972, "we are pulling our heads out of the jungle and getting back into the amphibious business. . . . We are redirecting our partnership with the Navy and our shared concern in the maritime aspects of our national strategy."[23]

Chapter Four

Back to Basics

Each American war in the twentieth century has been followed by a period of critical examination of the roles and missions of its armed forces by the nation's political leadership. In particular, those U.S. Navy and Fleet Marine Force units comprising the amphibious force throughout the Vietnam War were singled out for an intense review. Indeed, the amphibious mission itself came under outspoken and critical scrutiny almost before American involvement in the Vietnam War ended.

These developments compared directly with the Korean War. Amphibious forces proved highly useful during the first year of that conflict. As the war lost much of its mobile character over time, the utility of such units began to decline. So it was in Vietnam. After 1965 the war became compartmentalized and less mobile; subsequently, amphibious forces played a more peripheral role.

Five years of counterinsurgency operations by American forces took a toll in the U.S. capacity to conduct more conventional forms of combat. Within the Fleet Marine Forces, the sustained preoccupation with inland "search and clear" operations caused a sharp atrophy in the skills needed to conduct amphibious operations. The ranks lacked junior officers and NCOs with experience in devising a sequential plan for fire support coordination, or the ability to prepare embarkation plans to support the scheme of maneuver ashore.

The Fleet Marine Forces that deployed from Vietnam to prewar operating bases in the early 1970s therefore accorded high priority to rebuilding amphibious expertise. The key first step in this process was to reestablish linkage with the fleet, an essential objective. Among the many institutional casualties of the long war in Vietnam was the forfeiture of the fragile operational consensus between Navy and Marines, so essential to any nation's ability to wage amphibious war.

The postwar distraction of both services due to problems of force reductions, budget constraints, and disciplinary matters complicated rebuilding of the Navy-Marine Corps amphibious team. The Navy's operations and programming focused understandably on the growing threat of the Soviet Navy's surface, submarine and long-range naval aviation assets. Service with the amphibious "Gator" navy had largely been discredited as a career choice. The Marine Corps, having worked rather closely with the Army and Air Force in the last years of the war, suddenly found itself cast adrift from, and already in unfavorable competition with, those services. For the Marines, the situation paralleled its experience in the years after World War I. It was past time to return to their naval roots.

The difficulties involved in rebuilding a mutual Navy-Marine Corps focus on amphibious warfare were experienced along all points of contact between the two sea services. The extent of the problems can be illustrated on a lower echelon level. The missions of certain Marine Corps units—air and naval gunfire liaison (ANGLICO) companies, shore party battalions, force reconnaissance companies, transport helicopter squadrons, amphibian tractor battalions, for example—mandate a more frequent interface with the fleet. Among these naval-oriented units, perhaps none has such an absolute requirement for recurring "coexistence" with the operational navy than amphibian tractor battalions. The "main armaments" of such battalions consist of several hundred LVTs (Landing Vehicle Tracked, later Assault Amphibian Vehicle or AAV), which typically comprise the initial assault waves of any surface landing. The battalions are therefore totally dependent on the amphibious navy for unit training, deployment to the objective area, and guidance to the target beach. Prolonged separation from the fleet, in peace or war, does both sides disservice. Marine Corps "amtrac" battalions deployed ashore in Vietnam in the later years of that conflict became "AmGrunts," dismounted infantry, their vehicles parked and out of action. Rebuilding amphibious expertise with these forces was particularly difficult.[1]

The LVT itself appeared as part of the problem in reestablishing ship-to-shore skills among the veteran amphibious tractor battalions after the war. The U.S. Marine Corps in Vietnam was equipped with the LVTP-5A1 family of vehicles. The Marine Corps developed the P-5 after the Korean War and designed it for a projected operational environment of 80 percent sea/20 percent land. Working within that envelope of primarily seaborne operations, the vehicle performed adequately. Marines lauded its spectacular performance in the high surf, built to withstand 15-foot plunging breakers. This was a wasted capability, however, because the remainder of the surface assault—the other assault waves, all on-call waves, the floating dumps and other critical landing force supplies—were typically embarked in open landing boats with surfing capabilities limited to six-eight feet at the most. In Vietnam, after the initial assault landings, battlefield commanders used the P-5 for tactical mobility ashore, to the extent it operated at all. The vehicle ashore was clearly out of its element. At thirty-five tons and a unit ground pressure of 9.3 pounds per square inch, the vehicle mired easily in paddies, swamps and estuaries, and it proved fatally vulnerable to shape-charge antitank mines.[2]

The Marines in the redeployed amphibian tractor battalions after the war thus had to learn again how to operate their vehicles in a maritime environment (rules of the road, signal flags, basic navigation, abandon-vehicle drills, and line handling, for example). Progress was slow and costly. A disastrous early deployment of an amphibian tractor unit from Okinawa for service with the Seventh Fleet amphibious force illustrated the range and depth of training deficiencies among these units. An outgoing P-5 drifted beyond the channel in Oura Wan Bay, struck a coral head and sank; the crew barely escaped with their lives. Once aboard ship, another vehicle—improperly dogged down on the well deck—broke loose in subsequent high seas, crushing a crewman to death as he attempted to reconnect the chains. The whole experience underscored an unwelcome but vivid reminder of the necessity of maintaining amphibious expertise at all levels.

The Navy and Marine Corps did not solve these problems quickly. Funding restraints made opportunities for shipboard training uncommon and over subscribed. Personnel turbulence in the ranks of both services required starting over often. A number of commanders and senior staff officers also lacked expertise, and critical mistakes continued to occur throughout the decade of the 1970s. The primary control officer for a surface landing during a well-attended NATO exercise in Saros Bay, Turkey, vectored the assault waves to the wrong beach on a one-mile run in broad daylight. A year later, someone launched an unprepared LVT at night in the Mediterranean; as it slowly sank, panic ensued among the crew and embarked troops because insufficient life jackets had been issued and no emergency evacuation procedures had been explained. Two Marines drowned, and two rescue craft collided in the dark, killing a third man. For an overly long period in the 1970s, it almost seemed as if all the amphibious experience developed by the Navy-Marine Corps team during the halcyon years of 1935–65 had evaporated. Many critics of maintaining an amphibious capability seized upon the situation. Had amphibious warfare in fact outlived its usefulness in the American defense establishment?

On 6 October 1973, barely five weeks after the last United States combat unit redeployed from the Southeast Asia mainland, a regional conflict of unprecedented ferocity erupted in the Middle East between Israel and several Arab states, principally Egypt and Syria. The Yom Kippur War (War of Ramadan to the Arabs) was sudden, violent and sophisticated, arguably the first fully "high tech" war in history. Both sides expended missiles and other munitions at astonishing rates, and the losses among primary weapons systems were appalling. Both superpowers made significant efforts to resupply their clients from national or alliance stocks. Within three weeks the war ended, leaving the major powers shaken and the terrain littered with fifteen hundred destroyed tanks and five hundred downed aircraft. The 1973 war shattered many premises harbored by defense planners in Washington and Moscow and demanded a sweeping reassessment of future fighting capabilities.[3]

The results of the Yom Kippur War caused a particularly sensitive jolt to the United States. For one thing, there was the obvious comparison between this conflict and the protracted, inconclusive and generally lower-technology war in Vietnam. For another, the fact that Egypt and Syria had attained strategic and tactical surprise against a nation with one of the best intelligence services in the world was unwelcome news. Existing scenarios dealing with a potential NATO war against the Soviet Union regularly assumed an extended period of "rising political troubles," a handy checklist of warnings and indicators that would allow NATO's North American allies time to mobilize and deploy their general-purpose forces well before hostilities began. The sudden ascendancy of Soviet anti-air missiles and artillery, particularly the mobile SAM-6, which called into question the viability of troop-carrying helicopters and close support aircraft in amphibious operations, added a third sobering realization. Much of the American defense establishment seemed bloated, unresponsive and ill-equipped for such conflict. Terms like "crisis management," "high-intensity conflict," and "strategic mobility" came in vogue among defense analysts and commentators.

This critical reassessment in the mid-1970s seemed to appear particularly applicable to U.S. Navy and Marine Corps amphibious forces. The atrophy of amphibious utility during the later years of the Vietnam War contributed to the dilemma. In Vietnam, as in World War I and Korea, the Marines appeared to have spent the bulk of their combat ashore operating as a duplicate land army. While few critics questioned the valor and ingenuity with which the Marines had fought throughout the I Corps sector of Vietnam, many questioned the size of the Corps and the value of the expensive amphibious hardware retained by the Department of the Navy. The aftermath of Vietnam also left a persistent public mood against foreign intervention, particularly by ground forces, no matter how noble the cause might be.

The Yom Kippur War caused additional criticism of amphibious warfare. The aggregate lift capacity of the nation's amphibious ships had dropped just when the Marine Corps began a force modernization program that increased the configuration, complexity and support requirements of its new weapons systems. Critics scored the amphibious force/lift disparity. A Corps of Marines sized at a mandated level of three amphibious forces (each comprising roughly one infantry division, an air wing and an equivalent combat support unit) seemed far too large for a fleet of sixty-some amphibious ships that could at best lift the assault elements of only 1.15 of these combined-arms forces— provided the Pacific ships had time to join the Atlantic ships, or vice versa. Time was the new crucial measure of effectiveness in force planning. After the Yom Kippur War, it was no longer considered acceptable to be able to muster the ships, embark the troops and effect a thirty-day "closure time" at some NATO or Middle East port or beachhead. Thirty days was a lifetime. The war could well be fought and lost by that time.

The Yom Kippur War further called into question the issue of vulnerability of the amphibious force, both in its transoceanic deployment and during its ship-to-shore assault. The Soviet Union had taken advantage of America's costly distraction with Southeast Asia to expand its naval forces and develop weapons systems with global reach. In the 1970s, this new capability seemed to pose a very real threat to amphibious task forces attempting to deploy overseas. Moreover, all surface ships revealed vulnerabilities to less expensive but equally deadly missile systems exported to smaller powers. In 1967, during an earlier Mid-East war, Egyptian *Komar*-class gunboats engaged the Israeli destroyer *Eilat* (formerly HMS *Zealous*) and sank her at a range of twelve miles with Soviet Styx missiles, the first loss of a combatant ship to guided missiles in naval history. Most potential adversaries now possessed similar surface-to-surface missiles and incorporated these systems into their counter-landing defenses. American amphibious ships, landing craft, and assault vehicles appeared readily targeted for destruction by such systems. Protecting the task force by launching assault troops by helicopter from extended ranges was not deemed by some observers to be much of an improvement. Critics pointed out that the United States lost 1,777 helicopters to ground fire in South Vietnam during the first five years of that war against relatively unsophisticated air defenses.[4]

The Marine Corps itself contributed to public confusion and doubt over the future utility of amphibious warfare by the sharply divided opinions of its own officer corps. Once before, in the early 1930s, the senior officers of the Corps became disunited over the question of whether to maintain an army-oriented mission and force structure or return to the fleet for development of a naval mission. The Corps of that era, under the leadership of commandants Ben Fuller, John Russell, and Thomas Holcomb, returned to its naval roots and, with the Navy, developed the modern amphibious mission. Forty years later, professional opinions varied widely again. Some Marines opted to continue the "small wars" approach, emphasizing light, readily deployed forces for low-intensity operations in Third World arenas. Contingencies in support of NATO's Central Front and the perceived need to embrace the Army, in the process fielding mechanized infantry units as well as acquiring heavier tanks and more self-propelled artillery, attracted others. A third group of officers envisioned the continued usefulness of a modernized Fleet Marine Force, a task-organized, force-in-readiness available for global commitment to protect the nation's enduring maritime interests.

Into the middle of this debate in 1975 stepped General Louis H. Wilson, newly appointed as the 26th Commandant of the Marine Corps. Wilson faced many pressing problems, but he could readily see that the Corps needed to reaffirm its amphibious mission in tandem with the Navy and convince Washington and the public that this was indeed an essential and efficient military capability. To help answer the nagging questions of utility, mobility, vulnerability and force structure, Wilson established an ad hoc study group under the leadership of Maj. General Fred E. Haynes, Jr. The Commandant challenged the "Haynes Board" to take an unblinking look at all the operational problems and limitations facing the Corps and suggest corrective action. The Board did good work; unfortunately, an ominous wave of public criticism had begun sweeping over the Corps.

Secretary of Defense James Schlesinger set the tone for this period of reappraisal by questioning in early 1974 (and again in mid-1975) whether the nation still needed "an amphibious assault force which has not seen anything more demanding than essentially unopposed landings for over twenty years." Former Marine Francis J. "Bing" West, Jr., then Professor of Management at the Naval War College, admitted that the Yom Kippur War had shown the lack of responsiveness of large-sized amphibious forces, units rendered impotent and subject to defeat in detail due to geography and lift limitations.[5]

Martin Binkin and Jeffrey Record, military analysts at the Brookings Institute, published a scathing monograph in early 1976 entitled *Where Does the Marine Corps Go From Here?* Citing cost, lift and threat factors, Binkin and Record criticized the Corps for clinging to the amphibious mission, that "peculiar type of combat." They argued that "the Corps must shift its principal focus from seaborne assault to a more appropriate mission. . . . The golden age of amphibious warfare is now the domain of historians, and the Marine Corps no longer needs a unique mission to justify its existence." The analysts also criticized Marine aviation as extravagant and redundant, and suggested a significant downsizing of the entire Corps with either a geographic (i.e., "mostly Asian") or operational ("Strike Force") mission. While many Marines and naval officers disputed some of the study's assumptions and conclusions, most realized that their amphibious mission was indeed in disarray.[6]

Another defense analyst, William S. Lind, surfaced at this time. Lind, defense advisor initially to Senator Robert Taft, Jr., then for Senator Gary Hart, became a prolific writer and lecturer who advocated a revised mission for the Marine Corps. Most Marines expressed ambivalence about Lind: they either strongly opposed his theories or they warmly embraced them. A student of European military history and advocate of Guderian and Von Seekt, Lind analyzed the Yom Kippur War, looked at the anachronisms in Marine Corps force structure, and proposed revolutionary changes in the way Marines thought about combat. He denounced the attrition warfare of much of World War I, Korea, and Vietnam, and persuasively advocated the principles of "maneuver warfare." Lind helped spark a reform movement among the officers of the Marine Corps.

He certainly caused Marines to begin "thinking about the unthinkable." In Lind's view, amphibious operations were not incompatible with the tenets of maneuver warfare. Indeed, the principles of surprise, initiative, mobility and mass involved in a well-planned and executed amphibious assault lent themselves favorably to maneuver war. The problem, as Lind saw it, was to train leaders to trust their subordinates with mission orders and to equip each unit with sufficient firepower and maximum tactical mobility. It was the lack of tactical mobility that attracted the most criticism from Lind. In an essay written with Jeffrey Record in a 1978 issue of *Naval Institute Proceedings,* Lind linked the perceived diminished utility of the Corps to its historical penchant for foot soldiers, eschewing mechanization in the interests of strategic mobility. Again using the Yom Kippur War as a yardstick, the writers concluded that the Marine Corps epitomized "an undergunned, slow-moving monument to a bygone era in warfare."[7]

The period also saw considerable unrest within the amphibious navy community. The *Proceedings* published consecutive feature stories in 1978 by two retired admirals, both former amphibious force commanders of considerable distinction. Vice Admiral Robert S. Salzer's essay expressed alarm at the proliferation of Soviet "anti-invasion" weaponry and concern over the vulnerability of a mass helicopter assault against the ubiquitous, shoulder-fired SA-7 surface-to-air missile. Salzer also deplored the Navy's diminishing lift capacity and the almost total disappearance of suitable naval gunfire to support an amphibious assault. He took the Marine Corps to task for "gold-plating" the requirements for new amphibious ships during a period of fiscal austerity. Saltzer concluded that the future of amphibious warfare lay in its contributions to wartime sea control.[8]

Vice Adm. Frank W. Vannoy's essay viewed the vulnerability of the amphibious task force to cruise missiles as the most severe future threat. He warned that the radiation emitted by any concentration of ships invited disaster. Vannoy lamented the decline of the U.S Merchant Marine and the diminishment of true lift capacities. He saw a continued need for amphibious capability, but not without some joint Navy-Marine Corps endeavors to reduce vulnerability and increase lift.[9]

Not all analysts expressed gloom in their assessments. Frank Uhlig, Jr., then a senior editor at the U.S. Naval Institute, urged the Corps to return to its naval roots, and apply its amphibious virtuosity to sea control missions, especially in the preemptive seizure of the critical choke-points in the prosecution of a naval campaign. He reminded readers of the historic value of an amphibious assault as a strategic offensive followed by an initial tactical defensive.[10]

Repeated public questioning of the need for amphibious forces began to take a toll. The Navy and Marine Corps continued to battle the Defense Department, especially under the administration of President James E. Carter, on priorities for amphibious ships and weapons in the annual "Consolidated Guidance" documents. As late as 1979, Secretary of Defense Harold Brown remained unconvinced for the need for amphibious capability, commenting to Congress that "in many cases, administrative . . . lift can do the job, instead of amphibious lift." This led a defense journalist to conclude that, when it came to the Marine Corps, "the Administration still has not decided what their mission is, how they will operate with the fleet or be configured for the 80's."[11]

General Wilson harbored no such doubts. Throughout his tenure as commandant, Wilson continued to advocate an upgraded amphibious mission for his Corps, always emphasizing readiness, combined arms, and the need to protect the multiple interests of the maritime nation. His testimony before the Senate Armed Forces Committee in early 1976 is illustrative: "Our first and paramount characteristic is readiness," he emphasized. "This mission is meant to provide the fleets with a ready capability to project combined arms combat power ashore." The following month, the Haynes Board reported to the same committee. General Haynes recommended that the Marine Corps remain a global strategic force-in-readiness, as opposed to being limited to a specific theater of operations. While admitting the need to improve firepower, increase mobility and generally modernize the force, Haynes declared the Corps ready for mid and high intensity wars. With regard to Marine aviation, General Haynes added: "We reject out of hand any reduction in the close support attack role."[12]

General Wilson used the forum of the *Naval Institute Proceedings* in late 1978 to express his views on the amphibious mission. He reminded readers of the effect of OPEC's oil embargo of 1973–74. Wilson addressed the national mood of opposition to future foreign entanglements by pointing out that amphibious forces offer swift reaction, long distance deployment, rapid prosecution and timely withdrawal. He stated that amphibious forces could make positive contributions to three key naval missions: presence, power projection, and sea control. Wilson forecast a prominent role for amphibious forces in support of NATO, not necessarily on the Central Front, but in the North Atlantic campaign to seize and control the islands along the Greenland-Iceland-United Kingdom littoral, and then as an "ace in the hole," poised on the flanks, tying down a substantial enemy reaction force indefinitely. His closing argument in effect restored the pre-1965 Navy-Marine Corps operational consensus:

> The Marine Corps stands unique . . . as a ready force of combined arms, linked solidly to the Navy through integrated doctrine, training and structure. It is truly a mobile force, prepared to respond to contingencies anywhere in the world, using any available and suitable means of strategic lift. At the same time, it retains its amphibious character, providing not only the institutional memory but also the expertise necessary to keep the state of the art of amphibious warfare in step with the times.[13]

Restoring and upgrading amphibious capability within the U.S. sea services did not occur overnight, but under General Wilson's leadership the Marine Corps clarified its own roles and missions, answered its critics, and joined actively with the Navy to further refine the art. Other factors came to bear. The expansion of Soviet military and political influence in Latin America, the Pacific, Africa and the Mideast displayed the need for mobile, flexible forces. The experiences of Vietnam notwithstanding, the world remained a dangerous place. The ability of the United States to forward deploy even token amphibious forces in contested waters began to attract renewed appreciation from defense planners. Further analysis of the Yom Kippur War caused a reassessment of airlift capabilities in a major emergency. Although incomparably faster than sealift, the limited capacity of airlifts to deliver major weapons systems or large quantities of critical munitions came under sharp criticism. Political problems with staging, overflights and landing rights also surfaced.

General Wilson demonstrated a willingness to leave the Central Front of NATO to the U.S. Army and other allied armored forces. "There are 8,000 miles of coastline between Europe's North Cape and Greece," he observed, "and we are the only ones who can project this power ashore." The Marines and Navy thus reestablished their commitment to amphibious warfare, at least within the art of the possible and affordable. The time appeared propitious to reexamine amphibious doctrine in view of increasing vulnerabilities and some evolving new capabilities.[14]

The prolonged institutional fight to reestablish amphibious credibility after the Vietnam War shifted perceptibly in the late 1970s from mission validation to one of cost justification for new ship construction and assault aircraft procurement. The dispute became localized between the Marines and the Navy over amphibious lift requirements for the foreseeable future. A series of secretaries of the Navy tried with varying degrees of success to mediate the intradepartmental feud. The issue of amphibious lift, as an integral subset of national strategic mobility, dominated naval planners and budget analysts for years.

Initially, it seemed that amphibious shipping posed no particular problem. In spite of the atrophy of amphibious capability in the later years of the Vietnam War, the Defense Department of Robert McNamara's administration (1961–1968) had previously made substantial funds available to support a major upgrade in amphibious ships to replace the aging World War II fleet. This initiative resulted from a rare concurrence between Navy and Marine leaders. Secretary of the Navy Fred Korth signed a document in the early 1960s which designated $3.16 billion in ship construction funds, praising the "one voice, one statement" consensus it represented.[15]

The first fruits of this amphibious ship modernization program appeared in the fleet in time for combat employment in the South China Sea in support of operations in Vietnam. Amphibious squadrons featured a scattering of the impressive new *Iwo Jima*-class LPHs (helicopter assault ships) and *Raleigh*-class LPDs (landing platform dock) along with 1944 vintage *Haskell*-class APAs (attack transports). A few years later, the new 1179 class LSTs (tank landing ships) joined the fleet, and McNamara's "20-knot amphibious force" became a reality.

A significant program decision in the late 1960s led to an agreement between the two sea services to delete ten *Newport*-class LSTs in exchange for construction of the new, multipurpose *Tarawa*-class LHAs (amphibious assault ships). The LHA experienced a decade of tortuous development and acquisition before five of the class (reduced from nine) eventually slid down the ways. The ship's ever-increasing production cost, which eventually exceeded $300 million, emerged as an issue. Bitterly, the Navy accused the Marines of "gold-plating" their requirements for the ship. Indeed, the LHA was to become all things to all amphibious planners: it contained a large well deck, extended flight deck, and berthing accommodations for a reinforced battalion landing team. At 40,000 tons and 840 feet in length, the *Tarawa* (LHA

1) and her sister ships loomed larger than many World War II aircraft carriers. In fact, the ship was too large and valuable a target to risk her close ashore for launch of conventional assault amphibians. Modifications would be needed to reconfigure the well deck for the forthcoming air-cushioned landing craft. And the ship required six fathoms of water under the hull to safely ballast down to launch causeway warping tugs. Nevertheless, the LHA was an impressive warship in its own right, well suited for presence, power projection and sea control missions.[16]

The *Blue Ridge*-class LCC (amphibious command ship) appeared as a response to the command and control deficiencies revealed during Exercise Steel Pike a decade earlier. Two such ships joined the fleet: *Blue Ridge* (LCC 19), assigned to the Pacific Fleet, and *Mount Whitney* (LCC 20), assigned to the Atlantic Fleet. The new ships provided the amphibious task force commander and his counterpart, the landing force commander, with sufficient control and communications facilities to conduct a full-scale amphibious operation. The ships, with their abundance of transmitters, receivers, satellite systems and remote operating modules, consolidated in one hull those features that in World War II were distributed among several ships of lesser capabilities. The LCCs provided facilities to coordinate all supporting arms, collect and disseminate intelligence and permit direct communications, as needed, with national command authorities. An expanded naval tactical data system provided the critically needed capability of positive control of all aircraft—military and civilian, fixed and rotary winged—operating within or traveling through the designated amphibious objective area.

The amphibious command ships filled an immediate need and both sea services received them well. Unforeseen by the original designers, however, was the burgeoning nature of all command and control staffs, plus the natural attraction of such a useful, mobile, communications suite to non-amphibious staffs. As an example, the *Mount Whitney* sailed for Exercise Northern Wedding/Bold Guard in 1978 with not only Commander, Amphibious Group Two and Commanding General, 4th Marine Amphibious Brigade embarked, but also Commander Second Fleet/Commander Striking Fleet Atlantic, plus a tactical air control group and a large tactical exercise coordinator staff. The ship was "top-heavy" with staff officers.[17]

By 1978 the amphibious ships authorized by the construction agreements in the 1960s had joined fleets. The Atlantic Fleet, for example, contained one LCC, one LHA (with another soon to arrive), four LPHs, one *Raleigh*-class LPD, six *Austin*-class LPDs, four *Thomaston*-class LSDs (dock landing ships), two *Anchorage*-class LSDs, ten *Newport*-class LSTs, two *Charleston*-class LKAs (amphibious cargo ships), and one *Paul Revere*-class LPA (assigned to the naval reserve). The amphibious ships of the Pacific Fleet roughly matched those in the Atlantic, and numbered thirty-one. Despite this modernized flotilla, the Marines remained discontented. Their complaints centered on the lingering force/lift mismatch, a looming block obsolescence of many older ships, and the rapid disappearance of naval gunfire support from naval combatants elsewhere in the fleet.[18]

As early as 1972, the Commandant of the Marine Corps, Gen. Robert E. Cushman, Jr., testified before Congress that "the amount of amphibious lift capability available in 1973 will be at its lowest point since 1950." Cushman also warned against the lack of naval gunfire support. General Wilson essentially repeated these concerns five years later in testimony before the Sub-Committee on Sea Power, House Armed Service Committee. The need to modernize other elements of the fleet, in response to the perceived Soviet threat, justifiably distracted senior Navy officers. Faced with escalating construction costs and declining manning levels, the Navy sought and obtained permission to abbreviate the LHA program, delay significantly new construction of the LSD-41 ships and prolong the usefulness of certain older ships by service life extension programs.[19]

To the Marines, the Navy appeared to provide amphibious ships as an after thought, and then only by fits and starts. In their view, the well had run dry after the abundant building program of the 1960s. By 1981, the Marines complained that of 203 shipbuilding starts over the past decade since the LHAs, only one had been an amphibian. The specter of block obsolescence, even when diffused somewhat by "service life extension programs," grew increasingly troublesome.[20]

The Navy viewed the problem differently. Whereas Marine Gen. Wallace M. Greene Jr. had persuaded the Secretary of the Navy with his "one voice, one statement" approach many years earlier, the Navy now perceived the Marines as clamoring with several strident voices. And always, in the Navy's view, the exact definition of lift requirements was a moving target—ever upward. Marines presented amphibious lift requirements in four categories: troops, square footage, cubic footage, and helicopter operating/storage spots (expressed in CH-46 medium helicopter equivalents). Any force modernization or restructuring would have an obvious ripple effect on these equations. So would recalculation of ammunition or fuel consumption rates, fundamental decisions on days of supply that had to be embarked with the landing force, the extent of landing force operational reserve material prepositioned on shipping, and any tinkering with a unit's table of organization and its supporting table of equipment. As an example, development of the new light armored vehicle (LAV), an eight-wheeled, helicopter-transportable system, caused a significant increase in helicopter deck spaces. No one questioned the need for LAVs for maneuver warfare missions; the Navy simply saw the new lift requirements and rolled its eyes again. This debate continued for years.

The Marines had a real reason for concern about the disappearance of naval gunfire support. Many senior officers could still recall the glory days of the Iwo Jima assault in 1945 when ten battleships, twelve cruisers and fifty-five destroyers expended more than 210,000 rounds of major-caliber ammunition (five-inch and above). By contrast, when the heavy cruiser *Newport News* (CA-148) went to the scrap heap in 1975, the sea services lost their last big guns; a steadily dwindling number of five-inch mounts followed as missile launchers replaced naval rifles. As these, too, began to disappear, the Marines took their concerns to Congress. Marines described a Navy proposal to build a "gunless destroyer," the DDGX, as "one of the more recent expressions of missile age thinking carried to an unfortunate extreme."[21]

The Navy had a greater concern for missile defense in surface-to-surface and surface-to-air warfare. The tight fiscal environment was not conducive to additional funding for guns just to support one narrow field of naval operations. Nevertheless, planners formulated certain prototype solutions. Temporary reactivation of the inshore fire support ship *Carronade* and three other rocket ships for the Vietnam War briefly encouraged Marines. But a modernized version, the proposed Landing Fire Support Ship, died stillborn in budget cuts of the postwar period. At the insistence of the Marines and their allies in Congress and the Office of the Secretary of Defense, the Navy experimented for years with such programs as the "major caliber lightweight gun" and the five-inch semi-active, laser-guided projectile, the SAL GP. Both showed promise, waxed and waned during various fiscal tides, and eventually flickered out. The most persistent suggestion concerned reactivation of the *Iowa*-class battleships, launched at the end of World War II and recalled periodically for shore bombardment roles (Korea, Vietnam, Beirut, the Gulf War).

As early as 1963, then-Rear Admiral John S. McCain proposed modification of the *Iowa* class to fill both amphibious lift *and* naval gunfire support missions. McCain's "commando ships" featured a large helicopter deck and lower hanger astern in lieu of number three turret, the addition of davits for LCM-6 landing craft on each side and berthing accommodations for a battalion of Marines—plus retention of two turrets of sixteen-inch naval rifles. The commando ship program failed to gain funding support, although the old battleships later won the admiration of yet another generation of troops. In the bleak period 1979–81, however, the Marines sensed a growing indifference to their stated needs for shore bombardment.[22]

The Marine Corps supported one expensive new weapons system with enthusiasm during this period: the AV-8 Harrier vertical-takeoff attack aircraft. The AV-8A entered the inventory in 1971, and while some disturbing malfunctions (with resultant fatalities) remained among the first four squadrons, the V/STOL aircraft evolved as the most revolutionary new aircraft fielded by the sea services since the helicopter. The Harrier's operational impact was felt immediately. Not only could the aircraft operate from paved roads and other improvised hardstands close to the front lines ashore, but its deployability aboard LPHs and LHAs also made it a superb enhancement to amphibious assaults.

The Marines had yearned for a seagoing platform for their own attack aircraft since the 1930s. For the first time, the landing force commander was assured of his own responsive close air support. The amphibious task force commander stood to benefit as well, not only from an upgraded assault support capability but from sea control assets immediately available in emergencies during the movement to the objective area. The improved AV-8B program sought to replace the original Harriers, but the tightened defense budgets and generally unresponsive support from the Carter administration delayed this program by several years.[23]

The Marine Corps also fielded the CH-53E "Sea Stallion" heavy helicopter during this period. The E model provided increased operating ranges up to five hundred nautical miles. More significantly, the new helicopter promised a payload of sixteen tons. This increased capacity caused General Wilson to proclaim in 1977 that fully 93 percent of organic division material could now be heli-lifted, including towed artillery, its prime movers, and heavy engineering equipment.[24]

Generally, the surface Navy community expressed appreciation for these aviation developments. Yet the decade-long dispute between the two services about amphibious ship construction programs versus lift requirements continued to undermine good relations. Some Navy officers pointed out that the Harriers simply complicated further the alleged shortage of helicopter operating spots, while the CH-53E occupied one and a half times the space of the CH-46. At best, the two services agreed to disagree while trying to address other pressing problems. There remained the persistent vulnerability to ships and landing craft during the waterborne assault, historically the Achilles Heel of amphibious warfare.

Amphibious planners since the 1930s had viewed the vulnerability of ships and craft during the waterborne assault as the potential fatal flaw in the doctrine. The arrival of the transport helicopter added a remarkable new dimension by providing the opportunity to launch an assault from underway ships far over the horizon. There were just so many helicopters and a finite number of seagoing platforms. The rapid buildup of combat power ashore continued as the historical imperative in amphibious warfare. Helicopters alone, even the new CH-53E, could not fully satisfy that requirement.

In 1951, Lt. Col. Lewis W. Walt, a hero of the Guadalcanal and Bougainville campaigns and future Assistant Commandant of the Marine Corps, looked askance at the state of amphibious warfare and concluded "the time is past when assault infantry can be placed as helpless victims aboard slow-moving landing craft, several miles from the shore, and expect that a sufficient number of them will reach a defended beach to initiate an attack." Walt proposed several alternatives, including paratroop insertions, gliders, submarines, futuristic helicopters or even transport seaplanes.[25]

Other alternatives emerged over the years. One naval officer proposed using LSTs in the assault waves. Other developers tinkered with exotic landing craft using hydrofoil, hydrokeel or the ancient Archimedes "marsh screw" technology. The Marine Corps considered each option in turn, but evaluated and eventually discarded them all.[26]

In 1972 the Marine Corps completed a seven-year development program that brought into operational use the LVTP-7 family of assault vehicles to replace the P-5 of Vietnam vintage. Although lacking the superior surfing capability of its predecessor, the P-7 proved, overall, a safer, more versatile assault vehicle, particularly for sustained tactical mobility ashore. The vehicle's waterjet propulsion system gave it more agility in the water, and the vehicle was adept at crossing rivers and negotiating marginal terrain—but the P-7 was still a displacement hull amphibian. Its top water speed of 8.6 knots hardly demonstrated an improvement over the original 1937 version, and users found its advertised fifty-mile waterborne range laughable. Usually, embarked troops endured the combination of claustrophobia and seasickness for at best a half hour, which translated to a typical launch distance of only four thousand meters offshore. This was nowhere near being "over the horizon (OTH)"; in fact, it was only slightly to the seaward of the surf zone and in full view and range of any conventional weapons an enemy might choose to employ. Clearly, the Marine Corps needed another assault craft that could combine the water speed, stand-off range, sea worthiness, and surfing capabilities inherent in a true OTH waterborne assault system, *and* serve as a suitable cross-country tactical vehicle during subsequent operations ashore.[27]

Efforts to produce a hybrid craft with such multidimensional capabilities began almost immediately after the introduction of the LVTP-7 to the Fleet Marine Force. Plans for a successor system made rapid progress: on 15 May 1975, the Commandant approved top priority R&D rating to the program. The Marine Corps development team had every reason to expect success. But affordable engineering technology that permitted the fusion of both a seagoing and cross-country armored vehicle proved elusive. Two major programs, the LVA in 1979 and the LVTX in 1983—both born with high hopes—suffered design, cost and operational setbacks and the Commandant abruptly canceled them. Meanwhile, the conventional LVTP-7, originally built with 1950s–60s technologies with an expected life-cycle of ten years, remained the principal means of waterborne assault for U.S. armed forces. Various initiatives in the past decades had enabled the vehicle to be up-gunned and upgraded, subjected to a service life-extension program and provided with an array of product improvements. It served well in peacetime exercises—for example, a ten-thousand-meter transit of North Sea waters in Sea State three to land at Oksboel, Denmark, within thirty seconds of H-hour, seasick troops notwithstanding—and in combat (Falklands, Grenada, the Gulf War). But the vehicle is still a dog in the water, and its earliest replacement is now not expected until 2006. In the lengthy meantime, the vulnerability of the initial phase of the surface assault has been reduced only around the margins.

Its collective inability to solve this problem throughout the Cold War chagrined the American defense establishment. Sea service leaders found it particularly vexing to be reminded of the capability long held by the Soviet Union and several Warsaw Pact nations to land their naval infantry well beyond the high-water mark by means of successive families of air cushioned assault craft. In the West, many planners considered air-cushion technology as the answer to all assault vulnerabilities from as early as the first years of the 1960s. After all, the technology was hardly new. Commercial air-cushioned ferries had operated in the English Channel for decades. American visitors to Montreal's Expo '67 could ride such a high-speed craft along the St. Lawrence River for two dollars Canadian. What about air-cushioned vehicles for amphibious warfare?

The seminal study on this topic, "A 60-Knot Landing Force," by M. J. Hanley, appeared in the March 1967 issue of *The U.S. Naval Institute Proceedings*. Captain Hanley had served as the CNO Project Officer for Surface Effects Ships Study at the Center for Naval Analysis. He described with professional detachment a 147-ton flexible-skirt craft designed by Bell Aerosystems, the SK-10. Designers claimed it capable of delivering a sixty-ton payload at speeds of sixty knots in Sea State three or eighty knots at Sea State one for assault stage lengths up to one hundred nautical miles.

The prototype craft included other military design features: the ability to embark and debark from several well-deck amphibious ships in the open sea, bow and stern ramps to allow "roll-on, roll-off" cargo handling, the capability of skimming unharmed over most conventional minefields, a revolutionary freedom from the usual dictates of hydrography, thus providing striking opportunities far beyond the conventional beachhead. Hanley's remarkable essay visualized only two operational disadvantages: "the concentration of loads in a single vehicle and the essential aircraft construction without armor of the SK-10." He accurately predicted many of the capabilities and limitations of the landing craft air cushioned (LCAC) of the next decade. Persuasively, Hanley proposed a reasonably available solution to the vulnerability problem. What he could not predict was the slow response of the Navy-Marine Corps team, or that it would take more than ten years before the first over-water mission of the JEFF(B), the eventual prototype of the Navy's LCAC.[28]

With Secretary of Defense Harold Brown's approval for lead production of the LCAC in December 1980, the United States finally entered the military air-cushioned vehicle age. The LCAC was indeed a godsend, a surface craft at long last with the speed, range, payload, and over-the-beach capability to materially enhance the amphibious assault. As with every revolutionary new system, however, the amphibious forces of both services underwent an educational process.

The first thing to learn was that the LCAC was a landing craft not an assault craft. The difference in armored protection offered by an assault amphibian was piddling: the LVT's aluminum armor could at best deflect small arms fire and shell fragments. But the LCAC offered no protection at all; moreover, the craft demonstrated difficulties to retrieve, proved costly to replace, and appeared few in number. In the next year, the Navy procured only six LCACs; and limited the total program to less than sixty. A typical amphibious task force experienced difficulty in transporting more than a handful: the modified LHA could carry one; an LPD, only two; and the *Thomaston*-class LSDs, three. Only the new *Whidby Island*-class LSDs (LSD-41), long deferred throughout the period, appeared able to carry as many as four. The Marines also had to be reminded that, unlike LVTs, the landing force did not "own" the LCACs; they were naval craft, skippered by Navy petty officers and fully "owned" by the amphibious task force commander. Where the Marines might desire operational control of the LCACs for post-landing sorties along the littoral or extended inland maneuvers, the naval commander might instead need his craft for minesweeping operations or general unloading of follow-on forces. Clearly, the many problems showed the need for an operational concept, and amphibious planners from both services worked out the details in the years preceding the LCAC's initial deployment.

The LCAC's tumultuous arrival marked a milestone in American amphibious history, an expensive, specialized program without consistent top-level sponsorship that nevertheless survived years of budgetary pulling and squeezing. The craft's value as a genuine force multiplier was immediately evident to anyone taking their first ride, especially after years of sluggish wallowing in a displacement hull LVT. A legitimate means to get the landing force's tanks, artillery, light assault vehicles, and critical ammunition stocks ashore early in the assault had arrived.

The LCAC also lent itself nicely to the concepts of maneuver warfare being espoused by analysts like William Lind and members of the Military Reform Caucus in Congress. An example often cited in

Congressional hearings to illustrate the tactical flexibility afforded by the LCAC was that of an amphibious task force approaching Norfolk, Virginia, at dusk; with LCACs, the commander could be landing anywhere from Montauk Point, Long Island, to Myrtle Beach, South Carolina, by the next morning. Because the LCAC truly did not require a flat, gentle beach to cross, it further reduced the vulnerability of the task force. Where hydrography heretofore had limited naval landing craft like the LCU and LCM to perhaps 17 percent of the world's beaches, the LCAC increased the assailable beaches by a factor of four. The speed and versatility of the LCAC enabled the commander to operate easily within the reaction cycle of his defending opponent, a goal of maneuver warfare. Similarly, the LCAC empowered the commander to terminate an unpromising or stalled landing effort and reinforce another one, or initiate a new landing at a widely separated stretch of coastline. "The LCAC offers an opportunity we as a maritime nation must seize," affirmed General Robert H. Barrow, successor in 1979 to General Wilson as Marine Corps Commandant. The advent of the LCAC supplied at least the hardware to help solve the vulnerability problem. The time appeared propitious to experiment with existing doctrine to further reduce the operational hazards.[29]

NATO Exercise Display Determination was conducted in Saros Bay, Turkey, in the fall of 1977. A combined task force entered the Aegean and prepared to land American, Turkish and Italian marines ashore before a grandstand full of high-ranking political and military officials representing NATO's fifteen nations. The amphibious task force anchored two miles offshore on a bright, cloudless day. The Navy painstakingly launched amphibious craft and they made the rounds of the troop ships, collecting their assault forces and forming interminable circles. A pair of *Newport* class LSTs steamed slowly parallel to the line of departure at five knots, launching LVTs at intervals. Eventually, the combined assault waves turned toward the beach. Helicopters streamed overhead, while attack aircraft "prepped" beach targets. After some confusion, the waterborne elements touched down on Turkish soil, dropped their ramps at the water's edge and disembarked several companies of infantry, casting off their bulky life preservers as they lurched toward the dunes and the grandstand. It was the ultimate dog and pony show.

The NATO observers no doubt appreciated the impressive amphibious hardware and America's willingness to deploy it so far from home waters. On the other hand, even the most militarily unschooled of the dignitaries could not help but notice the slowness, predictability, and vulnerability of the entire assault. Equally appreciative of the Soviet Union's counter-invasion weaponry, most NATO observers concluded that the United States was still mired in World War II doctrine.

Senior U.S. amphibious officers of the time would have been quick to point out that the exercise was indeed a dog and pony show, 80 percent political and perhaps 20 percent military in value. Yet it is doubtful if any observer came away with a sense of reassurance about the usefulness of American amphibious forces employed in such a fashion. Fortunately, the lag between new amphibious ships, transport helicopters and V/STOL aircraft and an upgraded doctrine for their integrated employment did not last very long. Within a year, bold new ideas were being exchanged between the Americans and their allies. Some realities remained: show demonstrations, the vulnerability of the surface assault, the inability to carry all the preferred assault elements of amphibious forces in amphibious ships. Accepting those restrictions, amphibious planners made progressive strides forward in the late 1970s and early 1980s.

To the Marines, the ultimate goal remained inviolable. General Greene may not have been the first to articulate the vision, but his dream was the most persistent. Introducing the Marine Corps Long Range Plan in mid-1965, he wrote:

> The primary amphibious assault capability of the landing force will consist of fully V/STOL-mobile Marine air-ground teams, launched and supported from mission designed amphibious shipping under all conditions of weather and visibility. This will be complemented by a surface assault capability using high speed surface craft, either water or air cushion-borne, able to project troops, equipment and supplies onto the beach beyond the high water line.[30]

An early approach to reducing the vulnerability of the surface assault was the exploration of means of launching LVTs from underway amphibious ships. Hazarding any ship to an approach within four thousand meters of a hostile beach was considered fatally prohibitive. Perhaps, with training, a well-deck ship could make a twenty-knot approach with stern gate leveled and launch multiple columns of loaded LVTs along the line of departure. The Navy had previous experience doing this with landing craft, although not at flank speed. During

1965–66, the Marine Corps Development Center at Quantico teamed with field units from Fleet Marine Force Atlantic and ships of Amphibious Force Atlantic to conduct feasibility tests. Amphibious ships launched LVTP-5s successfully at speeds in excess of twenty knots without unusual jeopardy. (Most Marines still believe that launching *any* LVT from a ship is an act of deep faith.)

Everyone seemed to benefit from the new technique. For troops embarked for the minimum time there was no need for endless circling, and the ships could enter and depart the launch area rapidly. The *Ogden* (LPD 5), conducting a combat assault in Vietnam during Operation Bear Chain in March 1968, successfully executed an underway launch of LVTP-5s while simultaneously launching helicopters and performing as the primary control ship. The Fleet Marine Forces and both Amphibious Forces signed a Joint Tactical Note in July 1968. After incorporating it in NWIP 1-4(B) (*Experimental Tactics*) the following year, the Navy eventually accepted it as standard doctrine in NWP 22-3 (*Ship-to-Shore Movement*).[31]

Most amphibious practitioners expressed pleasure with these developments. Using underway launch techniques, the new LVTP-7 assault amphibians were tested as prototypes and did quite well. Sixty of the production vehicles were launched at high speed during Exercise Solid Shield 75 without incident. But then the technique seemed to fall from grace. One of the last operational LVTP-5s, launched from the underway *Nashville* (LPD-13) in April 1972 off Vieques, Puerto Rico, collided with another vehicle and sank. Investigations revealed that the ship's stern ramp had been depressed several degrees instead of dead level, thereby creating a cavitation bubble astern that trapped the launched vehicles and thus led to the collision. Although easily correctable, the news of the sinking, plus subsequent publication of photographs showing the eventual salvage of the hulk, caused a dampening effect on the enthusiasm among the captains of amphibious ships.

In practice, too, the Navy rarely provided well-deck ships for transporting LVTs, especially on prolonged deployments. LCUs and LCMs pre-loaded with tanks, artillery, or beachmaster gear required the wells. Commanders of well-deck ships expressed concerned about certain seamanship aspects of the high-speed launch. Steaming at high speed with stern gate open, a slight ballast aft and sloshing free water in the well caused increased pitching, varying draft, vibration resonance, and a phenomenon known as the "squat effect." The Navy voiced troubles with bottom-laid pressure mines. Since LVTs commonly embarked aboard LSTs, the Marines then tried to perfect the technique with these landing ships. Unfortunately, the *Newport*-class LSTs developed structural problems with their stern gate, and the underway launch, when conducted at all, limited them for years to a maximum speed of five knots. Engineering modifications eventually reached the fleet, beginning with the *Saginaw* (LST 1188) in the late 1970s. The procedure is thus still accepted practice, but it has failed of itself significantly to reduce surface vulnerability.[32]

Other options existed to reduce the age-old vulnerability. The obvious first choice was to make the surface assault subsequent and incidental to the heli-borne assault. Under ideal conditions, the amphibious task force commander could land two-thirds of the assault troops inland by helicopter under a scenario in which L-hour, the designated touchdown of the first heli-borne units, significantly preceded H-hour, the traditional touchdown for surface assault units. Troops landed by successive waves of helicopters and, fully supported by attack aircraft and naval gunfire, then seized initial landing force objectives, drawing defenders away from the beachhead. Judging it to be a good scheme, amphibians increasingly practiced this plan in spite of some questionable assumptions, including: acceptable conditions of weather and visibility; a favorable envelope of at least temporary air superiority and the ability to suppress anti-aircraft missiles; the ability of heli-borne troops to develop sufficient mobility and firepower ashore to attain tactical objectives; and the ability of both heli-borne and surface-borne elements to link up in time to avoid defeat in detail.

To help reduce ship-to-shore vulnerability, planners considered conducting the entire assault at night. Low visibility assault landings inconvenienced those who stage-managed dog and pony shows, but the operating forces clearly recognized the imperative necessity for mastering this technique under realistic conditions. The silent landing technique emerged as yet another development. Amphibious operations had previously been notorious for the volume of radio traffic and number of nets activated just prior to the assault—both dead giveaways in the emerging age of electronic warfare. Enforcing strict radio silence until the assault waves arrived on the objective might frustrate commanders and staff officers, but it represented a quantum improvement in operational security.

The Navy and Marine Corps developed, refined, and codified these techniques during the increasing number of combined amphibious operations that began during the late 1970s. Once the Marines had flirted with and ultimately rejected a mission role as reinforcing units in the Fulda Gap, they were able to work more closely with the Navy and several maritime allies in amphibious scenarios on both flanks of NATO. Landing exercises continued in the Mediterranean, but increasingly the Navy-Marine Corps team saw a principal role on the northern flank.

The first Marine amphibious unit to participate in NATO exercises occurred in Germany and Norway during 1975. The effort underwhelmed NATO allies, initially. The Marines' armored assets—a platoon of five overaged medium tanks and a dozen thin-skinned LVTs—were immediately suspect. Nor were the northern allies impressed with the U.S. landing force's antiquated cold weather clothing and equipment. The lingering effects of America's preoccupation with a counterinsurgency war in the jungles and rice paddies of Vietnam seemed evident. But the allies liked the Marines' aggressive spirit and their willingness to learn. NATO partners appeared impressed, although initially confused, by the integrated air-ground doctrine the Marines displayed, particularly at their ability to coordinate organic close air support with obvious precision. It was a start. Subsequent US amphibious units returned to the northern flank in greater numbers and at increasing frequency. Brigade-size joint amphibious exercises featured realistic landings in the Shetlands and Jutland in 1978 and in the Surnadalsora region of central Norway in 1980.

Exercises in Norway took on a special meaning as that country emerged as a likely site for contingency deployment of U.S. Marine amphibious forces in event of war with the Soviet Union and the Warsaw Pact. The number of combined command and control exercises and small unit arctic training deployments increased. A major policy decision committed a naval amphibious group and a counterpart amphibious brigade to Exercise Teamwork 84, conducted in northern Norway during the late winter of 1984—the largest arctic amphibious exercise ever conducted by U.S. forces.

Conducting combined amphibious exercises within the leads and fjords of Norway added a new dimension to the problems of task force vulnerability. Of necessity, amphibious rehearsals reverted from political demonstrations to full-scale tests of landing plans and communications capabilities. American staff officers found the coastline of western Scotland offered similar hydrography and topography to Norway.

Amphibians conducted useful rehearsals in the Sound of Sleat and Cape Wrath regions. Extensive "pre-assault operations" were conceived in which landing force elements were heli-lifted in force to seize the military crests of the mountains overlooking the fjords to protect the task force, coordinate air support and provide radio relay teams. These techniques and tactics worked. The combined exercises produced fertile grounds for further innovations and refinements.[33]

American amphibious forces had thus come full cycle within the first decade after the Vietnam War. The painful period of reestablishing credibility, as cited in Okinawa in 1970 and in the Mediterranean in 1977, evolved into a new era of validation and political usefulness. Significant problems remained: the force/lift mismatch, future ship construction, susceptibility to enemy mines and missiles, the lingering vulnerability of the surface assault forces, decreasing merchant shipping to handle increasing follow-on lift requirements, competing program priorities, and the expanding Soviet threat. But at least the Navy and Marines had established relative harmony with each other, and the value of amphibious capabilities seemed justified. The three years between Exercise Display Determination 77 and Exercise Teamwork 80 seemed more like three decades in terms of growth and improvements.

When President-elect Ronald Reagan's advance party arrived in Washington at the very start of 1981, it invited each armed service to explain its role, mission, and funding priorities. The Marines made a case for amphibious utility within the wide spectrum between brushfire conflicts and limited nuclear war. By 1981, they prepared to justify their "peculiar form of combat" with increasing confidence.

Chapter Five

Amphibious Force Deployment at the Height of the Cold War, 1973–1981

The prolonged Cold War between the United States and the Soviet Union witnessed several "heights"—periods of increased tension with an enhanced risk of open hostilities. Among these, the Berlin Wall crisis and the Cuban missile crisis come immediately to mind. The period 1973–81, however, was one of sustained political-military tension between the superpowers. The Soviet Union, emboldened by political disarray in the United States following the Vietnam War and the Watergate scandal, and flexing its own military muscles resulting from years of unrelenting force modernization, sought to challenge America for influence throughout the world.

The era included a variety of threats and alarms, direct and indirect confrontations, and interminable propaganda in the world's media and the halls of the United Nations. Both military powers readily used military forces as instruments of state policy. In almost all cases, the superpowers employed naval forces to deal with recurring crises. Amphibious elements of these forces played a significant supporting role throughout the epoch. The period began and ended with critical confrontations between the United States and the Soviet Union in the Middle East, starting with the Arab-Israeli War of 1973 and ending with the sustained naval standoff in the Indian Ocean following the Iranian revolution and the Soviet invasion of Afghanistan.

Leonid Brezhnev continued to lead the USSR throughout this period, although evidence of his declining health caused American analysts to worry about those who might succeed him. The vicissitudes of American politics likewise baffled the Soviets: Richard Nixon resigned in disgrace and was replaced by his vice president, Gerald Ford, who in turn lost to a Democratic Party candidate, Jimmy Carter.

The American public began to view Soviet military expansion and increased overseas commitments with alarm. Most Americans could readily see Soviet gains around the world as a net disadvantage to U.S. interests. Complete parity in nuclear and conventional arms no doubt gave the Soviets confidence to extend their political reach. A corollary of this expansion policy was the modernization of the Soviet Navy. While the Soviet submarine force had long presented strategic and conventional threats, the surface fleet had previously represented little more than a defensive force along the littorals of the motherland and the Warsaw Pact. Then, under the inspired leadership of Admiral Sergei G. Gorshkov, the Soviet Navy's longtime Commander-in-Chief, the Russian surface fleet and long-range naval aviation components grew exponentially during the 1970s. A bold willingness by Soviet political leaders to deploy these forces as instruments of state policy soon matched this enhanced naval capability.

Soviet naval units began to appear regularly in waters far from home. Port visits were conducted in exotic places with high visibility. More important, the Soviets also acquired naval bases at critical sites on the Arabian peninsula, both coasts of Africa, and even southern Vietnam (the former U.S. port at Cam Ranh Bay). While the Soviets did not attempt to duplicate the long-range, continuous steaming capabilities of the American task forces, they still managed to marshal all forces for spectacular global exercises like the *Okean* series in 1975 and 1980.

The increasing Soviet use of naval forces (and merchant marine units) in contested waters made the Americans even more uncomfortable. During the delivery of Cuban troops to Angola in 1975–76 and Ethiopia in 1978, observers noted the evidence of Soviet shipping. The USSR's Pacific Fleet also constituted a countervailing force in the South China Sea during Vietnam's invasion of Cambodia in 1978. And Soviet merchant ships delivered an increasing amount of sophisticated military hardware to Nicaraguan ports throughout the late 1970s and early 1980s.

The boldest Soviet gambit of the period, however, did not directly involve naval forces. The abrupt invasion of Afghanistan by Soviet airborne, KGB and *spetsnaz* units in December 1979 shocked the world. Not only was the invasion the first direct armed excursion by Soviet forces outside the Warsaw Pact since World War II, but it closely followed the revolution and subsequent power vacuum in neighboring Iran. Another energy crisis stalked the industrial nations, along with a great fear that the Soviets were reverting to naked aggression. The rapid buildup of more than 100,000 first-rate Soviet troops had a galvanic effect on the tenuous balance of power in the Middle East and East Asia. In one stroke, the Soviets had coopted a local civil war, outflanked the critical oil fields in Iran, threatened troubled Pakistan, and taken a giant step toward its ancient goal of acquiring a warm-water port.

The fleets of both superpowers drifted into confrontation in the remote emptiness of the Indian Ocean because of this situation in early 1980. For the Americans, already committed to the other oceans of the world, it was a long and expensive reach. And more unwelcome news punctuated the estrangement. Two new Soviet ships, the first of their class, entered the Indian Ocean then, a deployment that portended a significant shift in the power projection of USSR politics. The amphibious dock landing ship *Ivan Rogov,* with a battalion of Soviet Naval Infantry embarked, accompanied by the long-range replenishment ship *Berezina,* entered the Indian Ocean. The deployments raised the stakes of the Cold War again.

The American public, long distracted with local political issues and generally disenchanted with overseas commitments in the aftermath of the Vietnam War, could well question how all this occurred. American naval dominance had been the rule for more than thirty years. The unchallenged seapower embodied in the U.S. Sixth Fleet contained earlier crises in the region (Suez, 1956; Lebanon, 1958; the Arab-Israeli War, 1967). By October 1973, however, the Soviet Navy could deploy nearly a hundred warships, including amphibious forces, with its *Fifth Eskadra* in the Mediterranean, effectively countervailing against the Sixth Fleet. A brief but deadly serious threat of nuclear escalation resulted.

The two superpowers responded to the outbreak of the Yom Kippur War in 1973 by concentrating naval forces in the Mediterranean and using airlift and sealift assets to replace the unprecedented expenditure of planes, tanks and missiles by their respective clients in the conflict. The United States reinforced the Sixth Fleet to the point that it numbered more than fifty warships, including three carrier battle groups. The Soviet *Fifth Eskadra* matched the total number of ships soon after the conflict erupted, grew to eighty-five at the crisis point, and then increased further to ninety-six ships (including twenty-three submarines) by the end of October.

After two weeks of intense combat, the war slowly turned in favor of the Israelis. They soon recaptured ground lost in the initial invasion, crossed the Nile, and encircled the Third Egyptian Army. The Soviets, alarmed at the reversal of their client's fortunes and fearful of a major change to their favorable status quo in North Africa, called for a cease-fire. The United States expressed general agreement, but Israel—wounded and enraged—appeared to be in no mood to listen. As Israeli forces continued efforts to cut off and capture the Third Egyptian Army, Soviet policy makers began preparations for direct intervention; their signals were unmistakable.

The real crisis occurred during the two days beginning on 24 October 1973. The Washington Special Action Group (WSAG), led by Secretary of State Henry A. Kissinger, reviewed the warnings and indicators of Soviet intervention with grave concern. The Kremlin placed all seven active Soviet airborne divisions (some forty thousand combat troops) on special alert, along with certain Soviet Air Force units. One airborne division deployed to Belgrade, along with a tactical airlift squadron of thirty Antonov aircraft. An airborne command post had been established in southern Russia. As the crisis deepened, analysts could not locate a large number of the Soviet airlift fleet. In the Mediterranean, a force of seven Soviet amphibious ships, believed transporting naval infantry units, was reportedly underway for Egypt. And U.S. intelligence services speculated that a Russian ship, reportedly "leaking radiation," made preparations to dock at Port Said, possibly with nuclear warheads for a Soviet SCUD missile unit previously deployed near Cairo.

Faced with these reports to the WSAG, Kissinger paused in his intermittent dialogue with the Soviet Ambassador and the Israeli government to direct Secretary of Defense James R. Schlesinger to set Defense Condition III for U.S. forces worldwide. Setting DEFCON III (DEFCON I=war) sent an unmistakable signal in its own right. It was the highest readiness level directed for worldwide U.S. forces since the Cuban Missile Crisis of 1962. For added credibility, the Joint Chiefs of Staff directed the deployment of more than fifty B-52 bombers from Guam to the United States, placed the 82d Airborne Division on special alert, directed the *John F. Kennedy* (CV 67) carrier battle group to return to the eastern Mediterranean, and airlifted an additional U.S. Marine Corps infantry unit from Cherry Point, North Carolina to Sigonella, Sicily. The combined effect of these measures worked. The Israelis agreed to an immediate cease-fire, and the Soviet Union halted its intervention in time. But it had been a near thing.

The confrontation represented classic Cold War brinkmanship: with both sides deploying major forces with the perceived intent to engage in direct combat to salvage or protect their competing interests. While the naval forces of the original combatants contributed only marginally to the outcome of the war, the naval strength of the two superpowers—readily reinforced by their other power-projection forces—caused a regional conflict to escalate to a global crisis.

Amphibious forces of both powers played an integral role in the confrontation. Shortly before the war began, Soviet LSTs delivered a Moroccan armored brigade to Syria. That unit saw action against the Israelis on the Golan Heights, but an Algerian armored brigade that had to deploy overland took ten days to arrive and could not contribute. Soviet LSTs also evacuated Soviet advisors and "sensitive material" from Alexandria, Tartus and Port Said early in the war. Presumably, these were the same "Soviet ships with helicopters and landing craft [reported to be] sailing near the Egyptian coast" on 24 October.

The forward deployed Mediterranean Amphibious Ready Group, a five-ship squadron, contained an embarked Marine Amphibious Unit (MAU). Advance elements of a second MAU deployed aboard the helicopter assault ship *Iwo Jima* (LPH 2) from Morehead City, North Carolina, on 16 October, entered the Mediterranean on the critical day of the 24th, and reinforced other amphibious forces on station near Soudha Bay, Crete. Four additional amphibious ships deployed in mid-November. At the peak of the crisis, the ships of the Sixth Fleet had some 4,400 U.S. Marines embarked aboard, including the headquarters of the 4th Marine Amphibious Brigade.[1]

In the zero-sum mathematics of late Cold War confrontations, the United States was probably a "winner" in the October War crisis. Its favored client, Israel, had prevailed against Soviet-backed Arab states. Accompanied by an unexpectedly firm resolve to "play tough," its aggregate military muscle had enabled America to dissuade Soviet intervention. But, as noted in the previous chapter, the conflict also revealed critical shortcomings in U.S. military doctrine, equipment and deployability. The Yom Kippur War also disclosed the chilling expansion of Soviet naval projection forces, forecasting some grim crises. U.S. national security planners were further concerned by a subsequent doctrinal observation by Admiral Gorshkov in the Soviet naval journal *Morskoy sbornik* in 1974. Gorshkov proudly extolled the "special importance" of naval forces in pursuit of political objectives. The admiral's conclusion reinforced the enhanced role of the Soviet Fleet as the Cold War continued:

> The mobility of a navy, and its flexibility when limited military conflicts are imminent, enable it to exert an influence on littoral countries, and to apply and advertise a military threat at any level, beginning with a demonstration of military force and ending with an amphibious landing.[2]

Many interactions between the superpowers in the Cold War were based on perceptions. While the rivals spared no effort to gain advantage in their confrontations, they displayed an unspoken reluctance to resort to actual, direct force. This did not always apply to the indirect competition between their allies and clients. Here, the psychological and political use of force short of war was highly refined. And here an opponent's perceptions of one's capabilities *and* intent were vital.

As perhaps a coincidence, the appearance of Gorshkov's essay in *Morskoy sbornik* paralleled the publication in America of a small book, *The Political Uses of Seapower,* by naval theorist Edward N. Luttwak. In Luttwak's analysis, oceangoing navies possess a "peculiar usefulness" as instruments of foreign policy, even in situations without hostilities. He coined the term "armed suasion," defined as "all reactions, political or tactical, elicited by all parties—allies, adversaries or neutrals—to the existence, display, manipulation or symbolic use of any instrument of military power." "Naval suasion" meant those effects evoked by naval units. Further, naval suasion could be latent (deter or support by routine deployment) or active (support or coerce by deliberate action). Any armed suasion, according to Luttwak, was manifested only in others' reactions. Here, again, was the perception of capability plus intent. "The ultimate readiness to resort to force," wrote Luttwak, "is, of course, indispensable."[3]

Gorshkov and Luttwak, and the many other analysts from both countries, could readily illustrate their points by naval incidents throughout the Cold War. The American public, however, appeared reticent and uncomfortable about using military power to further state policies. Thomas C. Schelling's book, *Arms and Influence,* accurately described the use of military power in the Cold War, but his blunt declarations hardly made the public feel better about foreign affairs.

Schelling argued persuasively that military power in the Cold War was not so much exercised as threatened. "It is *bargaining power*," he observed, "and the exercise of this power, for good or evil, to preserve peace or threaten war, is diplomacy—the diplomacy of violence." Schelling considered latent violence, the threat of damage to come, more influential than actual damage in many cases. "To be coercive, violence has to be anticipated. . . . The power to hurt is bargaining power. To exploit it is diplomacy." And while many Americans considered "deterrence" to refer to nuclear retaliatory capability, Schelling applied the term to conventional naval forces as well. "Deterrence involves setting the stage—by announcement, by rigging the trip-wire, by incurring the obligation—and *waiting*. The overt act is up to the opponent."[4]

Setting the deterrent stage and waiting for the opponent's next move characterized the role of amphibious forces of both superpowers during the critical 1973–81 period. Both opposing navies organized to perform the usual spectrum of post–World War II missions in support of national strategy, ranging from presence to sea control to power projection to nuclear strikes. "Presence" represented the most common application of naval power by both sides in this period of the Cold War.

The superpowers used naval presence in the Cold War to "show the flag," creating desired perceptions among allies, clients and adversaries of national interest and resolve. Amphibious forces included in the task force represented a visible capability to intervene, as necessary. The appearance of Soviet amphibious ships and naval infantry in distant waters during the 1970s added instant credibility to the USSR's presence. The forces were smaller than those of the United States, but for the first time the Russians had in place visible evidence of a direct intervention capability. An additional American LSD and replenishment ship entering the Indian Ocean during the prolonged naval crisis of 1979–80 would hardly have raised an eyebrow. But the appearance of the *Ivan Rogov* and the *Berezina* in that critical region had a "catalytic" effect far beyond the limited power projection capabilities they actually represented.

"No navy builds ships primarily for the presence mission," wrote Admiral Stansfield Turner, President Carter's roommate from the Naval Academy Class of 1947, in an essay in *Foreign Affairs* in 1977: "Ship design reflects almost exclusively those qualities needed in battle. Moreover, a ship's fighting capability determines how other governments and navies perceive the weight of that ship's presence." Turner described seapower in the later stages of the Cold War as "a direct arm of foreign policy without a shot necessarily being fired." And he observed that the U.S. Sixth Fleet and its Soviet counterpart currently engaged in "presence" competition along the entire Mediterranean littoral.[5]

Presence, perception, latent and direct naval suasion, the power to hurt, bargaining power, the diplomacy of violence—these phrases capture the essence of the Soviet-American naval competition in the eight years following the face-off during the Yom Kippur War of 1973. The amphibious forces of both superpowers often "sailed in harm's way" during the era.

By 1977, Admiral Turner readily admitted that the Soviet Navy had become a formidable opponent in all three dimensions: surface, subsurface, and aviation. The advent of the Tupolev TU-26 Backfire long-range naval bomber, the *Oscar*-class submarine, and the *Kirov*-class cruiser provided the Soviet Union with impressive new platforms from which to launch cruise missiles and otherwise interdict U.S. Navy missions around much of the world. Admiral Gorshkov's predictions about the usefulness of advanced naval forces rapidly became operational realities. The opportunity to include amphibious forces among the Soviet Union's power projection forces was promptly seized. And the Soviets made some intelligent program decisions in the process, building capability before increasing forces. The force/lift mismatch in Soviet amphibious units would be insignificant compared to that being experienced by American forces.

The United States, however, maintained a clear advantage in amphibious forces throughout the period. In all categories of comparison—save surface ship-to-shore capabilities—the American ships, landing forces and command and control features appeared superior to those of the Soviet Union. But the shrinking size of the United States Navy overall continued as a vexing problem for Pentagon strategists. In May 1977, the Navy announced a reduction during the next fiscal year to a low of 462 active vessels, down from 926 only eight years earlier. The Chief of Naval Operations complained about having to face a "three-ocean requirement with a one-and-a-half ocean Navy."[6] Meanwhile, the Soviet Navy during the same period increased from 1,670 ships to 1,762. In 1979 the United States counted sixty-three amphibious ships, the Soviet Union ninety-one (although only twenty-six were considered transoceanic). The Soviet transition from "brown-water" to "blue-water" naval presence and projection forces was clearly well underway.[7]

During the period 1967–82, the Soviet Union made order-of-magnitude improvements in naval, airborne and airlift capabilities, programs that analyst Dennis M. Gormley described as "the classic indexes of direct military power projection." By the early 1980s, the Soviet amphibious force comprised ninety-six open-ocean ships and twelve thousand naval infantry divided into five regiments, augmented by amphibious units of certain Warsaw Pact allies and by Russia's own merchant fleet.[8]

This resurgence in Soviet amphibious capabilities did not establish precedent, however. In the mammoth Russian land campaigns against the Nazi armies in World War II, a series of 114 amphibious landings along the maritime flanks of the fighting occurred. Most of these assaults were small—3,000 troops from twenty warships, supported by ninety tactical aircraft. But at least nine major-sized amphibious assaults took place, including Kirkenes, Norway, and Pechenga in the northwestern Soviet Union, both during late 1944—difficult operations in low light and extreme cold. Following the war the Soviet Naval Infantry dwindled from its wartime strength of five hundred thousand men. Apparently absorbed by the Coastal Defense Forces, the organization then went out of existence in the mid-1950s.[9]

Western analysts conclude that the U.S. landing in Lebanon in 1958 influenced the Soviet leadership to revive its dormant amphibious force. In that crisis Nikita Khrushchev threatened to counter American and British interests in Lebanon by deploying Soviet "volunteers" to support the pro-Nasser rebels. It was then a hollow threat. The U.S. Sixth Fleet had already assembled a powerful armada in the eastern Mediterranean with three Marine Corps battalion landing teams embarked. Khrushchev's "volunteers" had no amphibious experience or capability. Shortly after this humbling experience, Khrushchev's Minister of Defense, Marshal Rodion Malinovski, ordered the reactivation of naval infantry units. The West's first unclassified glimpse of the Soviet "Marines" occurred with a photographic essay in *Kracnaja Zwezda* in July 1964. The pictures showed resurrected naval infantrymen in characteristic black uniforms with striped shirts; in addition, they wore black berets. The news article heralded them as a new elite force, but the euphoria appeared premature. Pentagon analysts during the Arab-Israeli War were unimpressed with the Soviet amphibious forces in the Mediterranean (one landing ship, two landing craft). The crisis, however, motivated Admiral Gorshkov to push for a long-range naval expansion program—involving larger ships, longer reach, and a greatly enhanced power-projection capability. Soviet naval forces then began deploying to the Mediterranean on a full-time basis.[10]

An astute politician, Gorshkov realized he could never gain Kremlin approval of an expensive ship construction program on the basis of the requirements of amphibious warfare alone. The Central Committee and the Politburo focused historically on general nuclear war, and considered conventional warfare only in terms of large land campaigns in western Europe or along the Chinese frontier. Gorshkov patiently integrated his visions of naval expansion with themes of nuclear deterrence against American carrier battle groups and submarines and theater support for land forces. He similarly integrated his plans for amphibious forcible entry with those evolving capabilities of Soviet airborne and airlift interests. As a result, Gorshkov presented realistically modest proposals.

Gorshkov never intended for the reactivated naval infantry or his impressive new amphibious ships and landing craft to mirror their large American counterparts. Soviet naval infantry was rather seen as a highly trained amphibious force in readiness, capable of working well with airborne and *spetsnaz* forces for early seizure of critical facilities and chokepoints in support of theater warfare. In larger amphibious assaults, where warranted, Gorshkov expected the naval infantry to function principally as the spearhead, an initial assault force that would pave the way for larger army combat units arriving in trace aboard merchant ships. Meanwhile, during the noncombatant rivalries of the Cold War, such forces served the state in presence missions, especially among the many Third World nations with seacoasts and harbors.[11]

Western analysts frequently misinterpreted the Soviet decision during this period not to try to match American naval projection forces. Intelligence reports appearing in the open press in the 1970s and early 1980s often predicted the appearance of a Soviet large-deck aircraft carrier. To American perceptions, there was no other purpose to modernize a fleet. But the Soviets built small V/STOL cruisers instead. The *Moskva* and *Leningrad,* each displacing fifteen thousand tons, deployed with eighteen Ka-25 or Mi-8 helicopters, principally used for antisubmarine warfare. Commendably versatile, the larger (forty thousand tons) *Kiev*-class "carrier" appeared later in the 1970s with the capacity of embarking a mix of thirty-five helicopters and fixed-wing aircraft, such as the YAK-36 Forger. The *Leningrad* used Mi-8 helicopters in a minesweeping role in the Suez Canal in 1974. Observers readily saw that embarked troop-carrying and assault helicopters could project forces ashore.

Admiral Gorshkov's naval construction program began to bear fruit in terms of amphibians and auxiliaries in the mid-1970s. Large air-cushioned landing craft, the *Aist* and *Gus* models, entered the Soviet navy in 1974–75. The first of thirteen *Ropucha* landing ships, built in Gdansk, Poland, received a commissioning pendant in 1975. A forty-thousand ton fleet replenishment ship, *Berezina,* appeared in 1977. Intelligence agencies reported an oceangoing hospital ship on the ways in a Polish shipyard the next year, when the Soviets also launched the first *Ivan Rogov*-class dock landing ship at their Kaliningrad shipyard. While the *Ivan Rogov* hardly compared with the new U.S.-built *Tarawa*-class amphibious ships in terms of lift, range, and mix of V/STOL, helicopters, and surface-craft launching capacity, the new Soviet amphibian still attracted a great deal of international attention. The thirteen thousand-ton ship loomed three times larger than any previous Soviet amphibian, the first to contain a heli-pad. The well-deck accommodated Soviet air-cushion craft, and the ship possessed the capability to embark a battalion of naval infantry. The *Ivan Rogov* represented a visible manifestation of increased Soviet projection capabilities.[12]

The appearance of a solitary, new Soviet amphibious ship, despite its capabilities, did not seduce some American observers. Those with an appreciation for the need for rapid reinforcement and sustainability in amphibious warfare looked instead at the quiet growth of the Soviet merchant fleet. What they saw was alarming. On a parallel but unheralded track with the selective growth of the Soviet Navy, the Russian merchant fleet had grown exponentially. By 1978 the Soviet Union boasted a merchant fleet numbering 1,700 oceangoing ships, the largest in the world. In comparison, the United States, with slightly more than five hundred ships, ranked tenth. Soviet merchant ships, heavily subsidized by the government, also possessed attractive military characteristics. The fleet included forty-five modern Ro-Ro (Roll-On, Roll-off) ships, extremely valuable in delivering military vehicles following an amphibious assault. In addition, by 1981 the Soviets had ordered two "Seabee" barge transports from Finland. Cargo from these ships is loaded onto barges from stern elevators, permitting rapid offload of military cargo even in damaged or primitive ports, a utility immediately evident in amphibious operations.[13]

Soviet power projection enhancements of the 1970s were therefore much more substantial than the launching of the *Ivan Rogov*. The Soviet policy decision to integrate *all* aspects of power projection— amphibious ships and craft, fleet auxiliaries, the merchant fleet, military-transport aviation, and the world's largest airborne force— produced a significant political boost to Soviet presence and credibility in most corners of the world during this period.

America in the 1970s retained a definitive edge in amphibious warfare, sea control assets, and strategic airlift, but the gap between the superpower rivals had narrowed considerably. As discussed in the previous chapter, the U.S. Navy-Marine team had shaken off the doldrums of the Vietnam War to reaffirm the amphibious warfare mission. The Soviet Navy may have commenced a full-time deployment in the Mediterranean, including occasional amphibious forces, but the United States had been providing full-time Marine Corps landing forces with the Sixth Fleet since 1948. The capability and credibility were there; what was uncertain was the political consensus to use force. Gradually, the political use of force became more acceptable, particularly in view of the appearance of Soviet naval forces seemingly in every troubled site in the world.[14]

Soviet willingness to sail their own naval forces in harm's way was readily quantified. "Between 1964 and 1976," observed James H. Hansen, "the scale of Soviet out-of-area forward naval operations expanded by a factor of almost fourteen, from less than four thousand ship-days annually, to nearly forty-eight thousand. The latter figure equates to over 130 Soviet naval ships operating outside of Soviet homeland waters each day."[15] Soviet combatants began making port visits in Cienfuegos, Cuba; Conakry, Guinea; and Berbera, Somalia. The ubiquitous Soviet AGI intelligence trawlers tracked every U.S. task force, observing each fleet maneuver and landing exercise. Soviet military writer V. M. Kulish set the tone for the epoch in an anthology he edited in 1972:

> In some situations, the very knowledge of a Soviet military presence in an area in which a conflict situation is developing may serve to restrain the imperialists and local reaction. . . . It is precisely this type of role that ships of the Soviet Navy are playing [in] the Mediterranean Sea.[16]

The superpowers did not have a monopoly in the use of amphibious warfare for political objectives during this period. Although renowned for its armored and air force prowess, Israel used amphibious techniques several times during repeated wars against neighboring Arab states. Indeed, Israeli use of amphibious deception in the 1967 War—repeatedly transporting the same tank landing craft across the Negev Desert toward the Red Sea—convinced the Egyptians of an imminent amphibious assault on Sharm el-Sheik, thereby causing Egypt to divert 30 percent of its naval forces to that region. In the October War of 1973, Egyptian naval commandos staged amphibious raids on Israeli facilities on two occasions, while Israeli forces assaulted Gharghada Harbor on the Red Sea. Nine years later Israeli amphibious forces supported the incursion into Lebanon by conducting successive assaults north of the Zahrani River, and then at Tyre, Sidon, and Damur. In 1974, Turkey used combined seaborne, heli-borne and airborne forces to invade Cyprus, landing six thousand troops and forty tanks in the first few hours. Still, the world's attention focused mainly on the "naval suasions" of the superpowers during the 1970s, as neither rival displayed much hesitation to use naval presence in pursuit of political objectives.[17]

In terms of U.S. forces, a study in 1978 by Barry M. Blechman and Stephen S. Kaplan for the Brookings Institution reported America had used armed forces for political objectives some 215 times during the extended period 1946–75 (less the Korean and Vietnam wars). Eighty per cent of these incidents (90 percent since 1955) involved naval units, including amphibious forces in at least a third of the events. Fleet commanders used battalion-sized amphibious forces on forty-four occasions. Such occasions did not always achieve successful political results and, eventually, mostly served only to buy time for a more appropriate diplomatic resolution. Regardless of long-term political results, ready amphibious forces on the scene proved invariably available and useful for political decisionmakers as instruments of foreign policy.[18]

In 1981 Kaplan produced another study for the Brookings Institution in which he appraised the Soviet Union's use of armed forces as political instruments. In the thirty-four-year period between August 1945 and August 1979, Kaplan documented 178 instances of such political muscle-flexing. Narrowing the scope somewhat, Kaplan reported that of forty-one incidents occurring between 1957 and 1979, two-thirds involved the use of naval forces. In a parallel study, analyst Abram N. Shulsky listed twenty incidents between 1967 and 1976 in which the Soviet Union employed naval forces as an instrument of coercive diplomacy. The figures serve to illustrate the growing political utility of the Soviet Navy as its force modernization program matured.[19]

The superpowers used amphibious units commonly as part and parcel of naval diplomacy during this period. A Soviet LST deployed South Yemen troops from Aden to Dhofar on the Omani border to support the Marxist insurgency in that region. Soviet amphibious ships took up almost-permanent station in the western Indian Ocean and in the eastern Atlantic off the coast of Guinea. U.S. and British amphibious forces evacuated their citizens from embattled Cyprus in 1974. A single Soviet LST with naval infantry embarked took a position off the coast of Angola during the prolonged airlift and sealift of Cuban troops into that country during the height of the civil war in 1975–76. Significantly, the United States declined to intervene. During the Lebanese civil war of 1976, the U.S. government sent a single, unarmed landing craft into Beirut harbor to evacuate American citizens, a situation particularly galling to those who recalled the forceful amphibious landing eighteen years earlier. The United States again used a restrained show of force in the 1979 evacuation of American citizens from Iranian ports during the revolution in that country. Meanwhile, Soviet amphibious ships and naval infantry played a support role in the deployment of Cuban forces into Ethiopia in 1978–79.

Direct naval confrontations between the superpowers after the 1973 Mediterranean crisis were uncommon. A *Moskva*-class helicopter carrier and its escorts closely shadowed the American evacuation of noncombatants from Beirut in 1976, further aggravating U.S. conservatives. The buildup of opposing naval forces in the Indian Ocean throughout 1980 taxed both rivals. The *Eisenhower* (CVN 69) and her carrier battle group returned to the United States just before Christmas of that year after 251 days, the Navy's longest deployment since World War II. At one point, the carrier spent 152 consecutive days at sea, largely in the Persian Gulf/Indian Ocean area. Earlier that year, a two-thousand-man MAU deployed in the Indian Ocean for seventy-five straight days under very crowded conditions. Such lengthy deployments strained the nerves of participants, Leathernecks and bluejackets alike.[20]

The conduct of large-scale naval exercises, including amphibious landings, by the two superpowers emerged as a common means of naval competition. These events progressed from small, bilateral exercises—the Soviets with the Egyptians, or the Syrians, and the United States with small amphibious forces of South American navies, for example—to theater-wide or even global naval maneuvers. As discussed earlier, American participation in NATO naval exercises in the Mediterranean and especially the northern flank region increased in scope and sophistication throughout the period. In the Pacific, Americans landed with allies and friends in South Korea, Thailand, the Philippines and Australia. Increasingly, the United States tended to test amphibious doctrine, equipment, and expertise under grim conditions of weather and terrain, such as in northern Norway or the Aleutians during wintertime. The open press reported Soviet Naval Infantry landing exercises in the Kurile Islands, much to the discomfiture of Japan. Meanwhile, both superpowers made good use of coalition partners in amphibious training. The Soviets drew professional admiration for their series of *Okean* exercises, particularly those involving amphibious landings in the Baltic with East German and Polish naval forces. In time, it became obvious that both the Kremlin and the Pentagon viewed these exercises themselves as instruments of naval diplomacy.[21]

Warsaw Pact operations in the Baltic provided observers a glimpse of the likely wartime employment of Pact amphibious forces worldwide: early seizure of the "narrow waters," the strategic straits of the world, to facilitate passage of the fleet or to protect the flanks of the ground war. Both sides began to discuss openly the relative value of such exotic straits or strategic islands as Malacca, Good Hope, Iceland, the Shetlands, the Faeroes, Shimonoseki, and the Azores. The Baltic Approaches seemed a likely flash point early in any NATO/Warsaw Pact war. The imperative to seize or reinforce Bornholm Island, or the race to mine and close the Belts and Skagerrak, took on special significance. NATO landings on Zealand and Jutland followed Soviet amphibious landings in the Baltic during *Okean* 80. Subsequently, Soviet exercises in the Kola Peninsula followed NATO training exercises in the leads and fjords of northern Norway.

Amphibious forces of both powers played an increasingly significant role in these Cold War demonstrations and confrontations, but they always reflected a means to a political end, never the end unto themselves. On the scale of coercive diplomacy, an amphibious squadron off the coast represented one value; the same force, integrated with carrier air, other surface and subsurface combatants, and coordinated with long-range deployment of land-based aircraft and airborne units, represented quite another quality. "Amphibs" represented an important part of the equation. Often, because of their potential for measured crisis escalation, they represented a highly visible capability; always, however, they delineated part of a much larger, more lethal cast.

The implications for direct intervention represented by forward deployed, fully supported amphibious forces usually gained the attention of the target government. Bradford Dismukes and James M. McConnell called this "coercive naval diplomacy." By their definition, such diplomacy is a "bloodless" negotiating instrument. "Its principal asset is the economy of blood and treasure involved for both parties to the negotiations. The objective is to keep 'events' within the realm of the mind, avoiding physical action," they noted.[22]

Thus, during the Yom Kippur War of 1973, the traditional amphibious capability of the United States, the emerging capability of Soviet amphibious forces, and the perceived amphibious capability of Israel all fulfilled useful tactical or political objectives. The Syrian perception that Israel planned and prepared for an amphibious assault on their coast caused them to redeploy two armored brigades from the Golan front. The sustained presence of both Soviet and American amphibious forces helped contain the conflict and prevent either superpower from gaining any significant advantage from the chaos of that short, violent war. Strategists took note of the diversionary potential of a ready amphibious force poised off the coast of a contested area. Subsequent events in the Persian Gulf eighteen years later convincingly demonstrated this "force multiplier" effect.[23]

The realization by a number of national security analysts that airlift posed serious limitations for the superpowers gave a backhanded boost to the use of amphibious forces as a ready political instrument in the late 1970s. Overflight rights and landing/refueling access emerged as critical political restraints. During the 1973 war such erstwhile allies as Greece, Turkey, Italy, and Spain refused landing and refueling rights by the United States, while Turkey even granted overflight rights to the Soviet Union for resupply of Arab states. American use of the leased facilities in the Azores, without prior permission by the Portuguese government, required some ticklish political fence-mending as a result. The Azores were critical. American C-141s would not have been able to participate in the emergency airlift resupply to Israel without that refueling site, the last one available in the theater.

During the opening weeks of the Angolan airlift of 1975, Soviet VTA aircraft flew over Egypt and the Sudan. Deteriorating political relations with those nations eventually caused the withdrawal of over-flight rights and the subsequent rerouting over West Africa, adding a third again the distance covered and reducing cargo lift accordingly. Similarly, an attempt by the Carter administration to show the flag in Saudi Arabia by deploying unarmed F-15 aircraft incurred both logis-tical and political problems. Only twelve of the eighteen fighters arrived; the move required thirty support aircraft; and Spain refused the use of its bases leased to the United States as stopover points for the deployment.[24]

The perceived erosion of national political and military clout had aroused the American public by the time of the 1980 presidential elec-tion. Many recent events overseas bothered potential voters: the "toothless" evacuation operations from Beirut and Iran; the unarmed F-15 deployment; the 1977 establishment of a rapid deployment force which appeared unlikely to live up to its name; the 444 days of frus-tration during the Iranian hostage episode, and the excruciating failure of the Desert One rescue operation in 1980. All of these flawed and untoward scenarios compared unfavorably with Israel's Operation Babylon in 1981 which destroyed Iraq's nuclear facilities at Towaitha in a masterstroke of planning and execution.

Naval War College professor of strategy Thomas H. Etzold spoke the mind of many despairing citizens when he asserted: "Events in Iran and Afghanistan in 1979 and 1980 have taught us painful but necessary lessons about the limits of military power. In both instances, it has become clear that despite 2.6 trillion dollars spent on American defense since World War II, the United States does not have global military reach."[25] The Republican Party platform called for military expansion, including the establishment of a U.S. Fifth Fleet in the Indian Ocean.

For a combination of political reasons, Republican Ronald Reagan defeated the incumbent Jimmy Carter. Moments after Reagan's inaugu-ration in January 1981, the Iranians released the American hostages, a decision received with great joy throughout America and most of the world. But Reagan's new Cabinet then turned to the same nagging problems that had beset the previous administration: how to deploy significant combat-equipped forces to the remote reaches of the earth in time to control a crisis situation and yet be heavy enough to stay and fight decisively if necessary. Meanwhile, in a previously quiet corner of the globe south of the Tropic of Capricorn, events already underway would test another nation's capability to conduct and support amphibious war very far removed from home waters. Both superpowers observed the development with professional interest.

Soviet Naval Infantry mounted in BTR-60PA amphibious armored personnel carriers approach a beach in a 1964 training exercise. This older version of the standard assault vehicle mounted a 12.7–mm machine gun on a forward pintle, carried twelve to fourteen troops, and could switch from waterjets to eight-wheel drive upon reaching the shore. [Marine Corps Association]

PT-76 light amphibious tanks of the Soviet Naval Infantry lead the ship-to-shore movement in this 1966 exercise. The thirteen-ton tanks mounted a 76-mm gun and featured twin hydrojets and a forward trim board in the amphibious mode. By Soviet doctrine, PT-76s comprised the initial waves of the assault landing. [Marine Corps Association]

Soviet Naval Infantry disembark from their amphibious vehicles during a 1972 landing exercise. Dismounting into the water like this was actually counter to Soviet tactical doctrine. Troops normally remained embarked in the BTR-60s until inland resistance developed, thus maintaining the momentum of the assault. [U.S. Navy]

Amphibious training at Camp Lejeune in April 1950, just before the onset of the Korean War. [U.S. Naval Institute]

Amassing combat power ashore at Inchon, Korea, after the D-day assault landings. [U.S. Naval Institute]

Combat-equipped Marines clamber down cargo nets into LCVP "Peter Boats" for amphibious training in the 1950s. [Official U.S. Navy Photo]

The dock landing ship USS *Thomaston* (LSD 28) launches medium landing craft for an amphibious assault along the coast of South Vietnam. [U.S. Naval Institute]

A Marine Corps "ONTOS" tank-killer, mounting six 106-mm recoilless rifles, splashes ashore in South Vietnam. [U.S. Navy]

Relearning old lessons: an LVTP-5 broached in the surf at Kin Blue Beach, Okinawa, 1969. [Official Marine Corps Photograph]

Marines of the Landing Force Sixth Fleet run ashore on a Mediterranean beach in the late 1960s. [U.S. Naval Institute]

Underway launch of AAV-7 assault amphibians from the well deck of the amphibious transport dock USS *Coronado* (LPD 11) off the coast of North Carolina. [Milt Putnam]

The *Haskell*-class attack transport USS *Lenawee* (APA 195), a veteran of the Iwo Jima, Korea, Da Nang, and Chu Lai landings. [U.S. Naval Institute]

The *Blue Ridge*–class amphibious force flagship USS *Mount Whitney* (LCC 20), the flagship in the late 1970s for Commander Amphibious Group Two and Commanding General, 4th Marine Amphibious Brigade. [U.S. Naval Institute]

The general purpose amphibious assault ship USS *Tarawa* (LHA 1). At the time she was the largest amphibious ship in the world. [U.S. Naval Institute]

The first operational air cushion landing craft (LCAC 001) enters the well deck of the underway dock landing ship USS *Pensacola* (LSD 38) in the Gulf of Mexico. [Official U.S. Navy Photo]

The USS *Whidbey Island* (LSD 41), the first of a new class of dock landing ships. [U.S. Naval Institute]

The *Wasp*-class multi-mission amphibious assault ship USS *Essex* (LHD 2), designed to be the centerpiece of an amphibious assault group. [Ingalls Shipbuilding Photo]

The British amphibious task force launching helicopters and landing craft in the assault on San Carlos, Falkland Islands. [U.S. Naval Institute]

Royal Navy medium landing craft in San Carlos Waters, Falkland Islands. [HMS Excellent, Plymouth]

A Soviet *Alligator*-class tank landing ship. [U.S. Naval Institute]

A Soviet *Repucha*-class tank landing craft. [U.S. Naval Institute]

The Soviet *Pomornik* air cushion assault craft, at the time the largest military version of this advanced technology in the world. [U.S. Naval Institute]

A Soviet *Ivan Rogov*–class dock transport ship. The Soviet Navy built three of these ships, each capable of launching naval infantry by both helicopters and air cushion landing craft. [U.S. Naval Institute]

Marine Corps landing forces embark aboard USS *Portland* (LSD 37) by both AAV-7 assault amphibians and CH-46 transport helicopters. [U.S. Naval Institute]

The Marine Corps triple-turbine-powered CH-53E heavy transport helicopter delivers a fourteen-ton bulldozer to an inland landing zone in amphibious training exercises. [Sikorsky Aircraft]

Marine Corps AAV-7 assault amphibians churn toward their landing point past the amphibious dock transport USS *Austin* (LPD 4) during a NATO training exercise in northern Norway. [U.S. Naval Institute, by Danny Layne]

A reconnaissance patrol of the Republic of Korea Marine Corps in action.

Countdown to Operation Desert Storm: an LCAC boards the dock landing ship USS *Mount Vernon* (LSD 39) for advanced amphibious training exercises. [U.S. Naval Institute, by Timothy L. Hanks]

"The Grunts Are Running" illustrates some of the constraints faced by today's amphibious forces. The best landing beaches are also prime recreational facilities or real estate development sites. [U.S. Naval Institute, by John Haley Scott]

Chapter Six

British Recapture of the Falklands, 1982

The largest opposed amphibious operation since U.S. forces seized Inchon in 1950 surprised most strategists and diplomats. With the world preoccupied with the Cold War rivalry between the superpowers, no one could have predicted the Falklands War of 1982. To imagine that Great Britain—clearly in the fading twilight of imperial glory, its armed forces reduced—would launch an invasion to recapture a group of forlorn islands possessing doubtful value to the Crown appeared remote. But such was the case, as first Argentina, attempting to regain a modicum of national pride after a decade of political oppression and economic frustration, seized the lightly defended islands on 2 April. Then, to the amazement of the world—and especially the military junta in Buenos Aires—the United Kingdom launched a massive naval campaign that culminated in the surrender of the Argentine occupation forces in the islands on 14 June 1982. Together, both sides counted over a thousand dead, thirty ships sunk or damaged, and 138 aircraft lost.

The disputed territories—East and West Falkland, South Georgia Islands, and South Sandwich Islands—had originally been claimed by Spain. Great Britain took undisputed possession in 1833. Argentina assumed that, having once been a colony of Spain, any Spanish territorial possessions in the region now belonged to it. With much solemnity and a dash of comic-opera buffoonery, the Argentine government named a governor *in absentia* each year. In 1965, the United Nations invited both parties to negotiate but in the next few years little evolved that altered the status quo.

The Union Jack still flew over the Falklands, and the local population—approximately two thousand hardy souls—endured the harsh winters of the South Atlantic with characteristic English resolve and stoicism, even while Britain's naval and military capabilities continued to decline. The disputed land seemed unappealing to outside observers: low hills, rocky outcrops, bog lands, and roads passable only in the best of weather dominated the desolate and barren landscape. The Falklands boasted only eight miles of paved, all-weather road in a land mass estimated to be 4,250 square miles. Still, the seemingly unimportant islands remained an irritating political problem for Argentina's national pride. In addition to and in spite of any substantive scientific data to support the claim, Buenos Aires believed the Falklands lay astride a large oil field.

In 1981 a new political regime came to power in Argentina, the latest in a series of juntas that had ruled the nation for over a decade, earning an unsavory international reputation for iron-fisted repression and maladroit economic management. Seizure of the Islas Malvinas (as the Argentines called the Falklands) appeared increasingly attractive to the ruling junta; in one action, the pesky diplomatic problem concerning sovereignty of the territories could be resolved in favor of Buenos Aires while the affair would detract from the dismal economic situation at home. A gross miscalculation followed, however, as Buenos Aires expected London to accept the seizure of the islands as an irreversible event not worthy of further confrontation—especially because the disputed territories lay 8,928 nautical miles from the United Kingdom.[1]

By early 1982 the Argentine junta concluded that an outright seizure of the Falklands could succeed. In what must remain as the major miscalculation of the epoch—perhaps comparable to Sadaam Hussein's belief a decade later that his Arab brothers would join him against the U.S.-led United Nations alliance that recaptured Kuwait—Buenos Aires expected the Crown to accept the loss of the Falklands with the good graces that it had displayed on losing other parts of the empire. That the island inhabitants were staunchly British in citizenship and disposition was a fact seemingly lost to Argentina's military government. Announcement of Britain's naval retrenchment, including the planned sale of several warships, fueled the junta's belief that in this instance the British lion would not roar but only sputter. Long-running border disputes with neighboring Chile added to the conviction that Argentina act before the onslaught of the bitter Antarctic winter.

Argentina also assumed, incorrectly as well, that world opinion would shift to its side of the dispute, given the tide of anticolonial feeling in the United Nations. The Argentine junta believed that the U.N. Security Council would not intervene. Given the colonial legacy of the

Falklands, the Argentines expected that the dispute would quickly become mired in a conflict between a sagging superpower and the passions of the Third World. To the shock and chagrin of Argentina's leaders, however, the Security Council came down on the side of the United Kingdom and demanded the immediate withdrawal of Argentina's military and naval forces from the islands. In another untoward assessment, Argentina's junta believed that the antiwar and liberal segment of the American electorate would keep the United States ostensibly neutral. Instead, when Washington's attempts to mediate the conflict failed, the administration of President Ronald Reagan supported the United Kingdom both overtly and covertly. Opinion polls revealed the American public favoring the UK in the dispute by 60 percent while only 19 percent of the survey expressed support for Argentina. Meanwhile, Argentina's long record of civil rights abuses and memories of its sympathies with Nazi Germany during World War Two prevented the development of any significant international support for Buenos Aires in the dispute.[2]

It took the Conservative government of Prime Minister Margaret Thatcher less than two days to decide to respond to the Argentine incursion by force of arms. Although Secretary of State for Defense Sir John Nott objected, the First Sea Lord, Adm. Sir Henry Leach, argued firmly and convincingly that he could form a naval task force and retake the Falklands. Thatcher moved quickly, approving Operation Corporate—the British recapture of the Falklands. In the opinion of at least one observer, the forthright and heady decision left Nott "turning white." It was, after all, 1982 and not 1882. While many observers might have shared Secretary Nott's incredulity, even a cursory glance at British history suggested that England would respond forcibly.[3]

On 5 April the first units—a nuclear submarine and special warfare contingents—departed from the United Kingdom. During the next two weeks, U.S. Secretary of State Alexander Haig's shuttle diplomacy accomplished little, except to underscore Argentina's obdurate wish to retain control and sovereignty over the island and British insistence that no diplomatic discussions could begin until the invaders had left the Falklands. Neither side displayed any willingness to negotiate further. Six days after Haig's mission ended in frustration, a contingent of Royal Marines landed on South Georgia to subdue the Argentine defenders and regain control of the island for the Crown. On 30 April the United States announced that it would support the British despite muttering from pundits fearful of damaging Washington's diplomatic and economic ties with South America.

Notwithstanding the United Kingdom's resolve to act decisively, the Crown's military retrenchment worried defense strategists. The old *Hermes* and smaller *Invincible* could together provide the carrier platforms for only a fraction of the fixed-wing aircraft needed for the invasion, causing planners to wonder if the requisite air parity for a successful amphibious assault could be provided. In its naval arsenal, Great Britain had only three modern ships capable of air defense: the destroyers *Coventry, Glasgow,* and *Sheffield,* all armed with Sea Dart missiles. For close-in air defense, it relied on type-22 frigates, and only three such ships were available to support the invasion.

Great Britain's amphibious capability had atrophied considerably. Naval planners found it prudent to siphon funds destined for maintaining amphibious ships and the commando brigade to weapons systems and other types of ships. The Admiralty's two amphibious assault ships, *Fearless* and *Intrepid,* faced sale to Third World nations even as the conflict in the South Atlantic erupted.

After disbanding the Sixteenth Parachute Brigade in 1974, England's only amphibious force consisted of 3 Commando Brigade, Royal Marines. To respond to the crisis in the South Atlantic, 3 Commando Brigade (40, 42, and 45 Commando, Royal Marines) was reinforced with the Second and Third Battalions Parachute Regiment. These additions, along with normal support and service support elements gave the brigade, commanded by Brigadier Julian Thompson, RM, an approximate strength of three thousand men. Support elements for the brigade included 59 Independent Squadron, Royal Engineers, 29 Commando Regiment, Royal Artillery (with 105mm howitzers and Rapier anti-aircraft missiles), and two troops of the Blues and Royals (a cavalry regiment with Scorpion and Scimitar vehicles). The shortage of amphibious shipping resulted in the embarkation of part of the brigade in the passenger liner *Canberra,* which underwent alterations to accommodate two helicopter pads, communications equipment, and the facilities for underway replenishment-at-sea. Messing and berthing facilities existed for barely two thousand combat-laden troops. The hasty departure of the amphibious force accelerated the entire embarkation process and muddled the combat loading. But the political imperatives demanded that Commodore Michael Clapp's amphibious command depart while the British public supported the naval campaign to recapture the Falklands.[4]

The Imperial Defense Staff decided that no military units would be taken from forces assigned as part of the British Army on the Rhine or from units designated in support of NATO. Thus 5 Brigade, commanded by Brigadier Anthony Wilson, consisted of 2d Battalion Scots Guards, 1st Battalion Welch Guards, 1/7 Duke of Edinborough's Own Gurkha Rifles, and support units as a follow-on force to 3 Brigade; 5 Brigade embarked in a requisitioned luxury liner; in this case, the Admiralty took the *Queen Elizabeth II* up from trade. Barely half a year before the crisis, the Secretary of State for Defense unveiled plans to sell the *Hermes* to India and the *Invincible* to Australia, phase out Britain's amphibious force, reduce the active naval inventory by retiring nine destroyers and frigates, and reduce naval expenses by a startling 15 percent.[5]

Still, the Imperial Defense Staff and Admiral Sir John Fieldhouse (Commander-in-Chief, Fleet) harbored no illusions of defeat. The Argentine occupation force in the Falklands consisted mostly of poorly trained and unmotivated conscripts. None had received the hardened experiences of modern warfare or trained to NATO standards. Argentina's better-trained and motivated infantry units, the mountain regiments, remained at home lest Chile take advantage of the situation to settle lingering border disputes. The Argentine Marine Corps' 2d Battalion spearheaded initial capture of the islands by seizing South Georgia, but had subsequently been redeployed back to the mainland; the 5th Battalion, trained more for the defense of advance bases than in amphibious assault, replaced it in the Falklands. Argentina's Navy, while aged, consisted of the carrier *Veinticinco de Mayo,* the heavy cruiser *General Belgrano,* escort vessels, and a handful of diesel-powered submarines. The cruiser had reportedly not been armed with the naval Exocet missile (MM-38), but intelligence analysts believed that the accompanying destroyers carried the antiship weapon—as did six other ships in the Argentine Navy. Argentine Air Force pilots flew either the Pucara or the Super Etendard Mirage IIIE; ominously for the invasion force, the Etendard was equipped to carry the French-built AM39 Exocet Missile, capable of destroying or disabling a modern warship. Defense planners believed that the Argentine Air Force possessed some two thousand aircraft.[6]

On 5 April the British carrier group departed Portsmouth, flying the flag of the invasion force commander, Rear Admiral Sandy Woodward. Four days later, the amphibious force in *Canberra* departed while a third group embarked in the county-class destroyer

Antrim for the separate assault and recapture of South Georgia. The Fifth Brigade did not get underway for another five weeks.

Events moved swiftly as it became increasingly apparent that neither side in the dispute would negotiate. The United Kingdom declared a two-hundred–mile maritime exclusion zone around the Falklands, and the first British submarine took up station off Port Stanley. Meanwhile, the Argentine fleet put to sea from Puerto Belgrano even before Secretary Haig's shuttle diplomacy ended. On 15 April a British destroyer group took up a holding position in the mid-Atlantic; two days later Admiral Woodward gathered his senior commanders for a conference on tiny Ascension Island. The week before, Admiral Woodward took the opportunity to warn every member of his command—officers and ratings alike—of the difficult and dangerous days that lay ahead: "Up until now . . . you have seen fit to take the Queen's shilling. Now you must stand by to front up and earn it the hard way."[7]

Ascension is almost midway between the United Kingdom and the Falklands. The island constituted the only advance base available to the British, even though the Falklands were still 3,300 miles away. The tiny island, although a British possession, had been leased to the United States for the installation of a satellite tracking station. Ascension boasted no significant docking or repair facilities and only one small thousand-foot runway. It did provide the site for covert American support, especially vital signal intelligence. The Americans also provided the British with the AIM9L Sidewinder air-to-air missile to arm the Sea Harriers. At a conference at sea in *Glenmorgan* on 11 April, a British intelligence summary denigrated the enemy air threat. Northwood's intelligence reported that the Argentines had only one Super Etendard with the capability of launching an Exocet missile—and the Argentines had only five such missiles remaining in its inventory.

Even before the task force departed the United Kingdom, the decision had been made to recapture South Georgia as soon as was practical. This minor adjunct to the main operation—decried by some in the admiralty as an unnecessary distraction from the goal of recapturing the Falklands—was agreed upon even before 3 Commando Brigade departed Portsmouth. A company of Royal Marines embarked on the *Antrim*, steamed south to Ascension where the destroyer took on a squadron of the Special Air Service (SAS), and then continued into the South Atlantic. By then, however, most of the original Argentine invasion force on the forlorn island—700 miles east of the

Falklands and 1,100 miles from Argentina—had departed. Subsequently, as the British invasion force closed, the submarine *Santa Fe* landed approximately forty men to strengthen the tiny garrison. Operation Paraquat began with an attempt to land the SAS force on 21 April but failed because of the intolerable weather. A second attempt the following day succeeded, and the squadron ashore reported the island lightly defended. On 23 April, seventy-five Royal Marines in three groups assaulted South Georgia, landing in helicopters. Subsequently, an antisubmarine helicopter attacked the *Santa Fe,* heavily damaging the ship and forcing its crew to abandon her. In the short foray on South Georgia, neither side suffered serious casualties.[8]

By then the British public had grown increasingly restless, and the successful recapture of South Georgia served to mollify domestic criticism while the major elements of the task force in the South Atlantic prepared for the invasion of the Falklands. Some strategists had argued that the force simply bypass South Georgia, holding it to be insignificant to Operation Corporate. But to the civilian leadership, the recapture of the island would serve to galvanize the support of the electorate and parliament; moreover, the seizure would display British resolve and determination to the junta in Buenos Aires. Two days later, the Imperial Defense Staff unveiled Operation Sutton—the joint recapture of the Falklands—to the War Cabinet. On 1 May special operations forces (Special Air Service and Special Boat Squadron) landed in the Falklands; the first Vulcan bomber raid, flying from Ascension, hit Argentine positions at Port Stanley; and Sea Harrier aircraft flying from *Hermes* and naval gunfire from accompanying warships began strikes on selective targets in the Falkland Islands. By then, three British submarines were operating in the sea lanes between the Falklands and Argentina: the nuclear-powered, four-thousand-ton Valiant-class *Conqueror;* and two nuclear-powered, Swiftsure-class boats, *Spartan* and *Splendid.*[9]

On 1 May *Conqueror* sank the heavy cruiser *General Belgrano.* The major escalation of the conflict and the heavy loss of life resulted in a brief flurry of anti-British sentiment worldwide and caused senior officials in the United Kingdom to question the wisdom of its course of action. But Woodward, the Admiralty, and the War Cabinet feared that the *General Belgrano* and *Veinticinco de Mayo* were steaming on convergent courses in the direction of the British carrier group. Woodward and his staff sensed a pincer movement in the offing, with the Argentine carrier and two destroyers lying to the northwest of the battle group, and the enemy cruiser and two destroyers closing from the southwest. The potential for disaster appeared significantly possible if either the cruiser's missile-bearing escorts came within range of its Exocets or the carrier steamed within striking distance of its air armada.

The decision to sink the *Belgrano* came from Prime Minister Margaret Thatcher after cabinet approval. Woodward argued that a strike against the Argentine cruiser would prompt Buenos Aires to keep the fleet in harbor, no longer a threat to the naval task force. As Admiral Woodward noted in his memoirs, loss of his carriers would spell the end of the daring foray into the South Atlantic: "it had already been agreed between Northwood [fleet headquarters] that major damage to *Hermes* or to *Invincible* . . . would probably cause us to abandon the entire Falkland Islands operation." Admiral Sir John Fieldhouse added a postscript to the controversial decision: "It ate the heart out of the Argentinean Navy and we only had their air force to deal with then."[10]

During the next week, however, Argentina's leaders rejected a variety of peace proposals put forth by the United States, the United Nations, and several Latin American countries. On 1 May the British carrier force crossed the Argentine exclusion zone, and three days later took the first significant combat loss when an Argentine Exocet missile, fired from a Super Etendard flown from the mainland, struck and sank the destroyer *Sheffield*. In the next three days, the British lost three Harriers as it became obvious that the requisite air parity in the amphibious operating area had not been achieved.

By 9 May Admiral Woodward and his senior commanders had concluded that the main amphibious thrust—Operation Sutton—should be at San Carlos Bay, across East Falkland from Port Stanley. The conferees agreed that West Falkland was too far away, and would involve a subsequent and risky shore-to-shore amphibious landing. While Lafonia in East Falkland offered a suitable defense site against an enemy counterattack, it provided a poor position from which to mount an offensive out of the beachhead. Carlos Water contained beaches at least partially protected against air attack, two fine anchorage areas, and hydrographic reports suggested an adequate depth for the close-in amphibious craft. The nearby hill masses provided shelter from the threatening Antarctic winter weather.

The enemy disposition ashore had improved considerably since April. The initial invasion force, an estimated three thousand men, consisted mostly of marines plus two battalions of the 25th Regiment, three batteries of 155mm field guns, and an anti-aircraft artillery battery. After it became apparent that UK forces would attempt to retake the Falklands, Buenos Aires strengthened its garrison in the islands by flying in four more infantry battalions, and additional support elements. By D-day, the enemy force ashore numbered over fourteen thousand men; the UK landing force never exceeded nine thousand. Aerial surveillance and other intelligence sources revealed the main body of Argentine troops clustered in and around Port Stanley, one or two battalions occupying Goose Green on East Falkland—where, apparently, the Argentines expected the British to land, and three battalions on West Falkland (one battalion at Port Howard and two at Fox Bay). Additional detachments had been scattered throughout the islands as well. While the potential for the Argentines to repulse the landing appeared remote, no senior naval officer needed to be reminded that the United Kingdom had not landed an amphibious force of brigade size or larger in twenty years.[11]

On 12 May 5 Brigade—the follow-on force—departed the United Kingdom on the requisitioned liner *Queen Elizabeth II*. Three days later, a force from the Special Air Service (SAS) assaulted tiny Pebble Island near the northern end of West Falkland. The special operations contingent destroyed eleven aircraft, a radar site, and a small ammunition dump. The minor foray buoyed hopes of senior commanders for an easy victory ashore, when they learned that the Argentine defenders appeared to run away and had to be brought back by their officers. On 18 May the Admiralty presented the landing plan to the War Cabinet just as the landing force rendezvoused with Woodward's task group north of the Falklands. A day later, the War Cabinet signaled its approval to Woodward. On the same day, a complicated at-sea transfer commenced with assault elements of Royal Marines and Paratroops moving from the *Canberra* to amphibious assault shipping. On 21 May, 3 Commando Brigade began landing operations.

The initial assault force consisted of two groups of 650 Royal Marines, one embarked in *Fearless* and the other in *Intrepid*. Two logistic landing ships, each capable of carrying four hundred troops and 5,500 tons of cargo, followed. The initial portion of the assault force would storm ashore from landing craft in the predawn darkness. Woodward and Thompson hoped to have four battalions of infantry with combat support elements ashore by dawn. On the eve of the

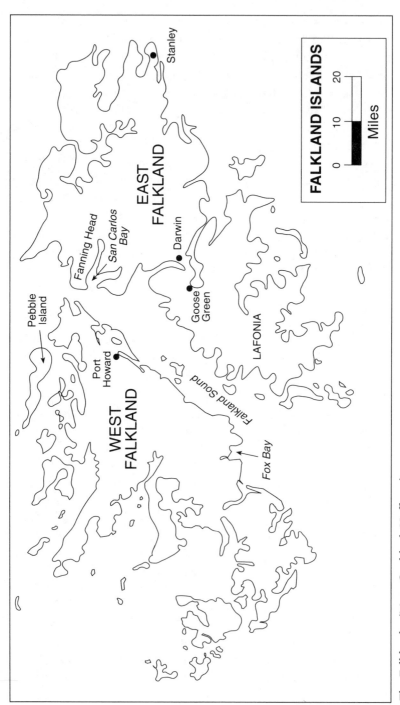

The Falklands. (Mary Craddock Hoffman)

landing, only thirty-five Harriers remained operational on the two carriers. The task force counted only seven frigates for both air defense and naval gunfire support of the amphibious force.[12]

Six frigates and one destroyer escorted the amphibious ships into the harbor. With barely 3,500 troops in the landing force, the British fell far short of the 3:1 numerical superiority assumed for a successful amphibious assault. But the additional strength of the Fifth Brigade and attachments—although it had not yet arrived in the amphibious objective area—would increase the total of the force ashore to 10,500 men, or eight battalions of infantry, more than had been sent into combat anywhere since World War II. The risks remained unconvincingly high, however, because the United Kingdom did not have the sea and air control believed to be necessary for a successful assault.[13]

H-hour came at 0300 on 21 May 1982. The initial assault waves, coming ashore in seventy-five-ton LCUs floated from *Fearless* and *Intrepid,* struck four beaches on the north side of San Carlos Bay and three landing sites on San Carlos Water. Each LCU could haul one hundred tons of cargo or 140 combat-laden troops. Within four hours, every wave was ashore. With only eight or nine hours of daylight left, it was imperative that the assaulting units be ashore by daybreak to establish a beachhead defense before darkness set in. To the astonishment of the assaulting force, complete tactical surprise was achieved, as apparently the Argentines believed the British landing at San Carlos was a diversion. Air attacks by Sea Harriers on selected targets at Goose Green and Port Stanley on East Falkland buttressed the Argentine's erroneous conclusion. By 1030 on D-day, 2,500 British troops were ashore.[14]

Air attacks against the invasion force, mostly from the mainland, did not begin until 1030 on D+1. Just as before, the enemy pilots concentrated on the combat ships rather than the amphibious assault ships. To the surprise of the invasion force, the Argentine junta waited until 25 May—Argentina's National Day—to launch a significant counterattack. The amphibious force expected some bold stroke commencing on this patriotic day, and the Argentines did not disappoint the invaders. Forty waves of Argentine aircraft struck the San Carlos area. Enemy aircraft sank four British ships with Exocet missiles (two type-21 frigates, *Ardent* and *Antelope;* one type-42 destroyer, *Coventry;* and a container ship, *Atlantic Conveyer*). Then, however, the momentum of air attacks declined sharply. Aerial combat by Sea Harriers had taken a heavy toll.

By 26 May the entire Third Brigade had moved ashore without serious mishap. An estimated 32,000 tons of ammunition and supplies had been stockpiled at San Carlos as well. As Brig. Julian Thompson maneuvered his brigade out of the beachhead, the Fifth Brigade under Brig. Anthony Wilson transferred from the *Queen Elizabeth II* to amphibious shipping positioned near South Georgia. The follow-on brigade crossed the beach at San Carlos on 1 June and struck out for Fitzroy. By then Maj. General Jeremy Moore had assumed command of the two-brigade force ashore. In less than two weeks, British forces overran Argentine positions and rolled up the flanks of the occupation force—lightly defended by dispirited conscripts. The Argentine Marines, which fought bravely and professionally throughout the conflict, never numbered more than a battalion in strength. Meanwhile, concern for the Argentine air threat continued to plague commanders. As the troops and equipment piled ashore, the troop of Rapiers was increased to a full battery of twelve antiaircraft missile launchers. Even then, Argentine aircraft struck two British Landing Ships Logistic, damaging *Sir Tristan* and sinking *Sir Galahad*.[15]

Argentine authorities attempted to stave off the pending disaster ashore by indicating a willingness to surrender to U.N. authorities, but London demurred at less than unconditional surrender and evacuation from the islands. Between 11 and 12 June, Port Stanley, Tumbledown, and Wireless Ridge fell to the forces ashore. On 14 June the Argentines surrendered. The warm glow of victory reminded most Britons of its romantic and honorable military and naval legacy. But for some observers, the entire affair appeared to "[underscore the] absurdity in a struggle so far from home for a leftover of empire."[16]

As Great Britain's stunning victory faded from the headlines, strategists of many nations dissected and analyzed the conflict. The war showed anew that the projection of sea power ashore by a determined, maritime power could succeed, even over a considerable distance. The Falklands War was unique in that the primary clash of arms took place between warships at sea and land-based air power. In this instance, considering the distances involved and the relatively meager British naval resources, the Falklands War resembled in many respects the U.S. invasion of the Solomons in 1942.[17]

Adm. Thomas H. Moorer, a former chairman of the Joint Chiefs of Staff, has argued persuasively that the conflict only underscores a greater priority on "projection forces" or rapidly deployable military capabilities. Critics of such forces have pointed scathingly to the sizable British losses in naval material at the hands of a much smaller force. The affair cost the United Kingdom an estimated $1.9 billion, and would also take the Crown twelve years to regain the naval capabilities spent in the South Atlantic.

Proponents of the modern attack aircraft carrier have found grist for their arguments in the limitations of the *Hermes* and *Invincible*. Neither ship possessed arresting gears nor catapults. Neither was capable of operating early warning or electronic warfare aircraft, a potentially fatal deficiency. Together, the two aged platforms carried only forty Sea Harriers plus helicopters, as compared with up to 160-fixed-wing, high-performance aircraft carried by a pair of *Nimitz*-class nuclear-powered carriers.[18]

The Falklands War provided a fresh endorsement of the continuing value of submarines across the spectrum of naval conflict. The nuclear-powered *Spartan* deployed 7,100 miles to the South Atlantic in twelve days. By contrast, *Onyx,* an *Oberlin*-class diesel boat, took more than a month to arrive. Once in the theater, however, diesel submarines were operationally useful. The Argentine submarine *San Luis* shadowed the British task force for thirty-six days, surviving a major ASW effort.[19]

Jeffrey Record, a prominent U.S. defense analyst, lays blame for the Argentine defeat squarely with obtuse decisions by the military junta in Buenos Aires. According to Record, Argentina's leadership displayed a gross ignorance of British history, completely misinterpreted London's intentions, and refused to believe that the Thatcher government would fight seriously until the sinking of the *General Belgrano* shocked the nation. Like other analysts, Record faults the Argentines for failing to use land-based air power from Port Stanley to disrupt the invasion.

The limitations Record decries, ironically, serve to support the U.S. Marine Corps in its perennial budgetary skirmishes with Congress and in defensive debates with critics of America's premier amphibious force. In Record's view, the war in the Falklands reaffirmed the amphibious assault as a viable option in naval warfare, reinforced the view that V/STOL aircraft such as the Harrier are the aircraft of choice for a Marine Air-Ground Task Force, and underscores the Marine Corps' contention that a force composed of long-term professionals is infinitely superior to a military body manned by short-term enlistees or conscripts.[20]

The limitations of the two aging aircraft carriers in the United

Kingdom's naval inventory emphasized the absolute and irrefutable requirement for air superiority, or at least parity, in an amphibious operation. If Great Britain's civilian leadership failed to appreciate this necessity, its senior naval officers certainly understood. During the campaign Admiral Woodward voiced his concern for air defense repeatedly:

> The Argentine Air Force must not be allowed to dominate the skies—and to stop them we do have a small number of naval interceptor aircraft . . . not many, just a couple of dozen Sea Harriers so far, with about ten more coming down in *Atlantic Conveyor,* before the country's entire inventory is fully committed.

The British Task Force commander's dispatch to Northwood was a sharp rebuke to his superiors for dispatching a naval task force in harm's way without adequate anti-air protection. For a generation, the Admiralty had placed heavy reliance on shipboard defense systems, but the salt air and corrosion from the extended deployment shorted out electrical circuits and otherwise made the systems unreliable.[21]

The material cost of Operation Corporate and Operation Sutton overwhelmed civilian decisionmakers. Before the Argentine surrender, the Crown counted fifty-one warships, twenty-one fleet auxiliaries, fifty-four merchant vessels, and thirteen air squadrons involved. From that impressive arsenal, the United Kingdom suffered the loss of two destroyers, two frigates, one container ship, one LSL, twenty-four helicopters, and ten Harriers. The war depleted the its naval assets at a furious and alarming rate. Even as the drama had barely unfolded, Admiral Sir John Fieldhouse remarked at Ascension, "I hope that people realise that this is the most difficult thing we have attempted since the Second World War."[22]

The short war in the South Atlantic took a heavy human toll as well. The United Kingdom counted 255 dead and another 777 suffered wounds. The Argentines admitted to 652 dead and missing. Besides the six British ships sunk, another ten incurred serious damage. The Argentines were believed to have lost 109 aircraft.[23]

In the final analysis, however, grave Argentine errors in tactics and strategy tipped the balance for the British. While there is no doubt that professionalism and determination by the senior officers of the UK expeditionary forces made the difference, the junta's gross lack of appreciation for the operational situation was a major contributor. During the two weeks before the first British submarines arrived in the South Atlantic, Argentina had many opportunities to resupply and reinforce its garrison in the Falklands. But after 12 April the presence of three British submarines operating in the sea lanes between Buenos Aires and Port Stanley made surface-borne reinforcements impossible. Britain quickly commanded the seas. Argentina could fly more troops to the islands, but the nation no longer had the means to deliver the requisite supplies and ammunition, heavy artillery, off-road vehicles, or helicopters. Only four resupply ships carried material to the islands during that brief period.

While both sides appreciated the importance of air superiority, the Argentines failed to lengthen the runway at Port Stanley to allow their A-4s and Super Entendards to fly from a base much closer to the British task force. Flying from bases in Argentina forced the addition of extra fuel tanks that reduced ordnance payloads and time-on-station substantially. Tactically, the Argentines provided the amphibious task force with a scenario that could not fail. The defenders chose to split their forces between the two main islands, rather than concentrate them on East Falkland—the only likely site for an invasion. After the feeble attempt to take a swipe at the British task force with two naval forces, one led by the ill-fated *General Belgrano* and the other by Argentina's lone aircraft carrier, Buenos Aires adopted an eighteenth-century strategy of a "fleet-in-being." From that date until surrender, the maritime war of attrition centered on land-based aircraft that ultimately failed to deter the invaders.[24]

U.S. support for the United Kingdom, and to a lesser extent that of Western European nations, contributed immeasurably and renewed momentarily the willingness of the West to act in concert to deter aggression. Rumors early in the conflict of Soviet submarines approaching the Falklands or Russian satellite reconnaissance information being processed and passed on to Buenos Aires by Moscow proved to be illusory. The Kremlin appeared surprised and nonplused by the specter of a presumably toothless former superpower rising up to smite an upstart invader half a world away.[25]

In the decade since the victorious landing force raised the Union Jack over Port Stanley, however, the overall amphibious capability of the United Kingdom has not increased substantially. For years, *Hermes* and *Invincible* remained the sole carriers in the Royal Navy, despite their obvious shortcoming in the South Atlantic. Recently, the Crown has approved the launching of *Ocean,* an LPH capable of embarking a full Royal Marine Commando of approximately seven hundred men; plus twelve transport helicopters and six Sea Harriers. The Admiralty also announced approval of plans to fund the construction of two LPDs to replace *Fearless* and *Intrepid.*

The Falklands conflict may have also spawned a false confidence in force projection because the United Kingdom did not encounter mines, "the poor man's anti-invasion fleet." The presence of mines in the waters of San Carlos Sound or in the harbor at Port Stanley might have proven disastrous to the amphibious invasion. The invasion force lacked information on Argentine intentions in that daunting area, and Admiral Woodward resolved the suspense by simply ordering the type-22 frigate *Alacrity* to steam into the contested waters to determine the presence or absence of mines.[26]

Deficiencies in tactical mobility were never more evident than in the South Atlantic. The naval task force and the landing force both underestimated the requirement for helicopter support. The rugged terrain, distances involved, and length of operation ashore demanded increasing use of the small number of rotary-wing aircraft in resupply missions rather than in troop lifts. Lt. Col. Andrew Whitehead, RM, 45 Commando, provided a candid assessment that underscored the difficulties of long-range force projection in the Cold War: "We had to fight and win three victories . . . against the enemy; against the appalling terrain and weather; and against our logistical inadequacies." If the reductions in British defense expenditures proposed in 1981 had taken effect, the recapture of the Falklands a year later could hardly have taken place.[27]

The case can be argued quite clearly that the United Kingdom could have won the war once the naval blockade was in effect by simply waiting for the Argentine force in the Falklands to surrender— resupply from the mainland then being impossible. But anything less than total victory and surrender would favor Buenos Aires in subsequent, protracted negotiations over the future of the disputed islands. In the end, however, everyone lost more than they gained. Argentina postponed rather than advanced any reasonable diplomatic solution to the future of the Falklands or the Malvinas; in the process of attempting to reclaim the islands by force, Buenos Aires expended untoward amounts of an already-depleted treasury. If anything, the Falklands War can only fuel anxiety concerning the colonists' future as they must ponder how long the Crown can afford the expenses for their defense.[28]

Nonetheless, many observers saw in the Falklands Conflict the revalidation of certain enduring ingredients of successful maritime power projection: the need for advanced bases; regional friends; good intelligence; early decisionmaking; ready forces of combined arms; adequate lift; operational security; local superiority of air, sea, and submarine forces; credible assault; and realistic sustainability. Each element would prove expensive—but indispensable—in the tense years of the middle 1980s.

Chapter Seven

Amphibious Warfare and Maritime Strategy in the 1980s

The superpowers observed the Falklands War as a proving ground for military strategy, doctrine, logistics, and weapons systems—the whole spectrum of conventional war in the modern age. Interpretation of the results in America differed predictably along philosophical lines. Military reformers claimed the Falklands War illustrated the need for inexpensive, less-sophisticated warships. Traditionalists argued the case for more supercarriers, high-tech aircraft, and elaborate command and control systems instead. There was at least one point of general agreement. Most analysts, Soviet as well as American, agreed that the Falklands crisis displayed the value of amphibious assault capabilities convincingly. The Falklands War, according to one analyst, "gave planners a look at amphibious warfare in the missile age under almost laboratory conditions. The data were encouraging."[1]

Indeed, the Falklands War seemed to revalidate all components of naval warfare. Even before the Royal Marines stormed ashore near San Carlos, thoughtful observers had begun to reappraise the utility of naval armed suasion. The contemporary conclusions of columnist George F. Will appear representative: "This is the moment to explode the belief that the use of naval forces for political objectives—'gunboat diplomacy' is the preferred epithet—is an anachronism. And it is time for renewed appreciation of the role of naval forces in the U.S.-Soviet balance."[2]

Such positive endorsements were good news to the Republican administration of President Ronald Reagan. Conservative Republicans, in office barely a year when the Falklands War erupted, had based much of their campaign on a return to international involvement, heightened confrontation with the Soviet Union (characterized by President Reagan as the "Evil Empire"), and a major buildup of nuclear and conventional forces. Where the preceding Carter administration sought to contain defense spending by concentrating principally on commitments to NATO's central front and the defense of South Korea, the Republicans sought to widen the areas of confrontation and invest in the means to support this strategy. The landslide Republican victory in the 1980 presidential election seemed to provide a popular mandate for this escalation in confrontation, defense spending and risk-taking.

President Reagan, a past master of popular communications, shared his personal beliefs concerning the Soviet threat with the American people. Issues of force modernization, warfare in space, strategic mobility and counterterrorism became household topics of discussion. Popular works of fiction, such as Gen. Sir John Hackett's *The Third World War: August 1985* and Tom Clancy's *Red Storm Rising* caught the public's imagination. Strategists observed, analyzed, and reported closely political and military developments within the Soviet Union. The USSR's armed presence in Afghanistan, unprecedented naval buildup in the Kola Peninsula and Pacific Northwest, and the unwelcome tension surrounding each change of top leadership concerned many Americans. Leonid Brezhnev led the Communist Party of the Soviet Union for eighteen years, but after his death in 1982 a bewildering rotation of new leaders—Yuri Andropov, Konstantin Chernenko, and Mikhail Gorbachev—followed in the next three years. Each turnover caused heightened concern in the West that superpower relations would deteriorate even further.

President Reagan made two extensive proclamations in his initial days in office that affected naval forces in general and amphibious forces in particular. First, he reaffirmed his desire to achieve "maritime superiority" over the Soviet Union. Secondly, following the release by Iran of the American hostages held throughout the 444 days preceding his inauguration, Reagan swore, "Never again!" The President's strong desire to rebuild an offensive navy and his vow to confront state-sponsored terrorism would result in a virtual naval renaissance, a costly arms race, hostile fire—and eventual tragedy for amphibious forces ashore and adrift in war-torn Lebanon.

"Though the Soviet Union is historically a land power," observed President Reagan in a speech in Long Beach on 28 December 1982, "it has created a powerful blue ocean navy that cannot be justified by any legitimate defense need." The President then compared how vital seapower was to the United States: "Freedom to use the seas is our nation's lifeblood. . . . Maritime superiority for us is a necessity. We must be able in time of emergency to venture in harm's way . . . to assure access to all the oceans of the world."[3]

This clarion call did not represent the President's first appeal for naval expansion. Reagan urged maritime superiority in a campaign speech in Chicago as early as March 1980. A plank in the Republican platform specified a six-hundred-ship Navy to achieve such superiority. The speech in Long Beach signified simply a reaffirmation, based on the encouraging reports of the Falklands War, that a navy "second to none" remained a major means toward the desired end of prevailing over the Soviet Union.

Reagan's leading spokesman for maritime superiority soon became the fiery John F. Lehman, selected by the President to serve as Secretary of the Navy. Lehman took office in early February 1981. For the next six years, he eloquently advocated President Reagan's naval renaissance. In early testimony before the appropriation committees of Congress, Lehman first articulated his strategic vision:

> The U.S. is a "continental island," tied to its allies, trading partners and resources by the great seas. The free world is an oceanic coalition. . . . Clear maritime superiority must be acquired. We must be capable— and be seen as capable—of keeping our access secure to areas of our vital interest. This is not a debatable strategy. It is a national objective— a security imperative.[4]

Lehman, an aviator in the Navy Reserve, demonstrated no reticence about his belief in the supremacy of the supercarriers. Offensive carrier warfare dominated his philosophy and became the nucleus of the controversial "maritime strategy" that followed. That concept, designed to complement the national strategy expressed by the Reagan administration, appeared in advance form in late 1981. But the Oval Office did not release it to the public in its entirety until Congressional hearings in 1983. It reflected an emerging renaissance in naval and amphibious operational thinking.

John Lehman did not originate the maritime strategy. Its roots could be traced through the preceding Chief of Naval Operations, Admiral Thomas B. Hayward, back thirty-five years to Vice Admiral Forrest B. Sherman in the immediate postwar era. The Secretary, however, became its chief spokesman and lightning rod. In its simplest form, Lehman described the maritime strategy to: "ensure use of the seas to carry the fight to the enemy and terminate the war on favorable terms."[5] The strategy, with its emphasis on "superiority in seaforce," represented unabashed Mahanian thinking. In fact, Lehman saw clear evidence of the Soviet Navy's endorsement of Alfred Thayer Mahan's theories. In a 1981 essay in *Strategic Review,* Lehman declared, "The modern Soviet naval and maritime system, fully integrated, blue-water capable and global in reach, is patently Mahanian in design." Lehman proposed a greatly expanded American navy, "visibly offensive in orientation," highly mobile, forward deployed and increasingly countervailing. "Nothing below clear maritime superiority will suffice. . . . The United States and the West must grasp the bare-knuckled truth: we are absolutely dependent on the seas for survival."[6]

The maritime strategy, as further defined by Adm. James D. Watkins, Chief of Naval Operations, and Gen. P. X. Kelley, Commandant of the Marine Corps, consisted of three major phases: deterrence or transition to war, seizing the initiative, and carrying the fight to the enemy. The latter phase evoked the most public discussion, both in praise and condemnation. Lehman proposed to exploit the Soviet Union's "inherently unfavorable maritime geography" by sending carrier battle groups and amphibious task forces "down the Baltic throat" or around Norway's North Cape to attack Russian fleet bases and facilities.

This forward philosophy frankly alarmed diplomats, continental strategists, and budget analysts alike. The Army and Air Force sensed a threat to the longstanding primacy of NATO's Central Front. Former defense intellectuals from the Carter administration took major issue with Lehman's premises. Robert Komer, Under Secretary of Defense in the previous administration, was critical. The chief flaw with the maritime strategy, as he interpreted it, "is that you can't really cope with a great Eurasian heart power like the USSR by nibbling at its flanks with carrier strikes." A retired Army colonel, John B. Keeley, warned that overemphasizing Navy and Marine forces would produce a situation akin to Europe in the early 1800s, with Britain "controlling the empty oceans while Napoleon had the land."[7] Other critics within the defense community suggested darker motives, implying that the strategy was a programmatic veil designed to achieve naval expansion at the expense of the other services. Some NATO allies expressed concern that the strategy's revolutionary emphasis on protracted conventional war might vitiate the "nuclear trigger" they depended on to deter a Soviet blitzkrieg.[8]

Lehman, however, had the full support of President Reagan and Defense Secretary Casper Weinberger, as well as many of the Navy's key commanders. Admiral Watkins endorsed the idea of countering the Soviet's missile-launching platforms, and described it in warrior's terms as "shooting the archer before he releases his arrows." Adm. Lee Baggett Jr., Supreme Allied Commander, Atlantic, stated, "If the battle for the Atlantic is fought in the Atlantic, we will lose." Nor was Lehman hesitant to strike back at his critics: "To suggest that naval support of Norway or Turkey or Japan is too dangerous because it must be done close to the Soviet Union is defeatist."[9]

Secretary Lehman also kept the maritime strategy closely aligned with the national strategy, the patchwork quilt of treaty commitments to more than forty nations and to the widely reported Soviet threat. "Unless Congress reduces our commitments or the Soviet threat weakens," he declared, "there is no way to reduce the required size of the U.S. fleet and still carry out the missions assigned to the Navy." Regarding the treaty commitments, Lehman reminded the media that the administration "didn't go looking for them; they were handed to us as the law of the land." Lehman declared that America needed a "600-ship Navy" to attain maritime superiority. Testifying before the House Subcommittee on Seapower, he argued that such a force was set "by the size of the world, the breadth of our commitments and the size of the Soviet fleet."[10]

The objective of attaining a six-hundred-ship navy (from 477 in the late 1970s, the lowest level since 1939) eventually won public and Congressional acceptance because of the popular appeal of the maritime strategy. The Reagan administration convinced Congress to appropriate huge sums of defense dollars for ship construction and conversion, resulting in an unprecedented peacetime force expansion. Lehman's fifteen carrier battle groups embodied the core of the buildup, but his master plan also called for four battleship reactivations, one hundred attack submarines, and seventy-eight amphibious ships, sufficient to lift the assault elements of a Marine Amphibious Force (MAF) and a Marine Amphibious Brigade (MAB). The Marines and the amphibious Navy welcomed the latter news, because it represented a full-cycle reversal of the anti-amphibious policies of much of the previous decade.

Renewed emphasis on amphibious warfare was an integral part of Lehman's strategy from the beginning. His 1981 *Strategic Review* article included a call for upgunning the Marines and increasing amphibious lift "to wrest important coastal land areas and chokepoints to our control." Lehman recalled in his autobiography that Reagan and Weinberger were "friends of the Corps," sharing a common interest in rebuilding amphibious credibility. "It was our firm belief that the capability to make opposed landings of MAF or MAB size anywhere in the world was an enormously valuable capability for every theater commander."[11]

The United States defense establishment proposed clearly to enter an era of widespread popular and legislative support for offensive naval power projection that had lain dormant for the previous forty years. Naturally, the Department of the Navy sought to ride the crest. The first step was to develop a joint Navy-Marine Corps amphibious warfare strategy to carry out and support the administration's maritime strategy. Admiral Watkins, General Kelley, and their respective staffs hammered out the details by 1985, providing a basis for planning and programming decisions for the rest of the decade.

In publicizing the amphibious warfare strategy, General Kelley first reflected on the bleak years (for naval forces) of the 1970s: "Making a case for an offensively oriented Navy and Marine Corps is not an easy undertaking if Europe is the primary U.S. area of interest," he noted. The turning point, according to Kelley, was the declaration of the Carter Doctrine in January 1980, which admitted that Persian Gulf oil supplies were a "vital national interest." The revised focus on global strategic commitments set the stage for the next administration's greatly enhanced defense buildup. The key ingredients for resurgent amphibious forces in the 1980s, Kelley observed, were flexibility and readiness. "Though oriented to address the phased employment of amphibious forces in a global conventional conflict, the Amphibious Warfare Strategy fully recognizes the utility of these forces in the unexpected and more likely crisis scenarios at the lower end of the conflict spectrum."[12]

General Kelley suggested a variety of amphibious operations in support of each phase of the maritime strategy, including the pre–World War I mission of seizing advanced bases in support of a naval campaign. Emphasis on a naval campaign was a critical distinction between this strategy and those that briefly floated in the immediate post-Vietnam years. The early temptation for the Marines to emulate the U.S. Army on NATO's Central Front waned and then disappeared. "We believe," observed Kelley, "that the employment of amphibious Marine Air-Ground Task Forces in a sustained land-warfare role compromises their unique capability for flexible maneuver." The Commandant matched his present and future amphibious capabilities with Secretary Lehman's controversial Phase III ("Carrying the Fight to the Enemy"), by describing potential assaults along the

North Cape, the eastern Baltic, the Black Sea, the Kuriles, or Sakhalin Island—"thereby adding a crucial measure of leverage to the successful conduct of the maritime campaign."[13]

Formulating a bold new amphibious warfare component of the maritime strategy offered one step. Providing the means to carry out such a strategy represented quite another. For once, however, an administration made abundant defense dollars available to support the strategy. In constant fiscal 1985 dollars, the U.S. Marine Corps budget grew from $5 billion in 1975 to $8.7 billion in 1985, with $1.8 billion alone earmarked for procurement. Additionally, generous Navy procurement funds were allocated to Marine aircraft. As a result, the Marine Corps was re-equipped "from stem to stern" with new or improved weapons, tactical mobility, communications, and cargo-handling equipment. Every individual and crew-served weapon in the standard infantry battalion was modernized. In addition, the administration funded training Marine Amphibious Units (MAUs) in maritime special operations, supporting the other aspect of President Reagan's outspoken counterterrorism foreign policy.[14]

The administration's willingness to invest in major overhauls and new construction to achieve the 600-ship navy represented the principal measure of growth. No less than seventy-eight ships of this total were to be amphibious warfare craft. The immediate need was to release funds to commence the long-postponed LSD-41 program, the *Whidbey Island* class. Not only would the new dock landing ships eventually replace the thirty-year-old *Thomaston*-class LSDs—aptly described by one Marine as "rode hard and put away wet"—but the enlarged well-deck capacity of the new ships permitted the embarkation of four air-cushioned landing craft (LCAC), a quantum improvement and valuable boost to the prolonged LCAC acquisition program. In another breakthrough, the Reagan administration also gained congressional approval to commence advance procurement of an entirely new class of amphibious ship, the multimission *Wasp*-class LHD, designed to replace the LPHs of the early 1960s. At 40,500 tons displacement and 844 feet in length, the new LHDs loomed even larger than the LHAs of the previous decade. Moreover, the *Wasp*-class ships possessed the capability to embark 1,900 troops, carry three LCACs in the well deck, and operate a mix of six–eight AV-8B Harriers and forty-five helicopters.[15]

The Fiscal Year 1986–1990 Shipbuilding Program included four LHDs and eight LSD-41s, including a cargo variant with a shortened well deck (two LCACs vice four) but with eight times the cargo capacity, thereby filling a need identified earlier by Congressional and Navy Department lift studies. The five-year plan also included service-life extension programs for some of the older LPDs as well as conversion of several ancillary amphibious support craft.[16]

More good news for U.S. amphibious forces came with the announcement that four World War II battleships—*Iowa* (BB 61), *New Jersey* (BB 62), *Wisconsin* (BB 64), and *Missouri* (BB 63)—would undergo modernization and return to the active fleet. The decision had its opponents, some of whom saw a reversal to 1930s-style naval warfare, and others objecting to the program cost of several billion dollars. But for a fleeting few years, the amphibians and the Marines once again enjoyed their beloved sixteen-inch naval rifles available for shore bombardment. The reactivation plan kept all three sixteen-inch turrets, then added lethal modern capabilities. Weapons design engineers replaced four of the ten twin-5 inch/38 mounts with eight quadruple Mark 143 Tomahawk cruise missile launchers. Four quadruple Harpoon antiship missile canisters were added also, along with four Phalanx 20mm mounts and Sea Sparrow launchers. The shipyards reshaped each fantail to accommodate LAMPS and other helicopters. The Navy also obtained the Israeli-made Pioneer remotely piloted vehicle system for the battleships. Given these complementary weapons systems, and the ships' fourteen-thousand-mile unrefueled steaming range, fleet commanders began to establish and deploy battleship battle groups, arguably a new "force multiplier," in troubled waters. Defending the battleship modernization program before Congress, Secretary Lehman cited each ship's ability to deliver eight hundred tons of accurate munitions on a target within a half hour, "the equivalent firepower of seventeen destroyers." Lehman responded to questions of vulnerability of the *Iowas* before the Senate Appropriations Committee by reminding the Senators that the ships' armor protection measured a foot thick, designed to stop a Japanese eighteen-inch shell.[17]

The Navy and Marine Corps at last had the support network in place: solid administration backing, reasonable congressional support, public enthusiasm, a coherent maritime strategy with supporting amphibious warfare component, and the requisite hardware in the form of new amphibious ships and naval gunfire on the way. It was time to develop jointly a new tactical plan, an amphibious scheme of maneuver in keeping with the new possibilities as well as the enduring limitations—the enemy threat and the unforgiving sea.

The Navy-Marine Corps team had long favored the "over-the-horizon" technique of launching amphibious assaults to reduce vulnerability to nuclear or conventional missile attacks. The helicopter first gave reality to that objective, but even the new heavy-lift helicopters could not deliver sufficient combat staying power ashore in the critical time needed to avoid defeat in detail. Other problems existed, however. The standard CH-46 medium helicopters, the backbone of the vertical assault, approached the outer limits of safe operational life cycles. Moreover, even with the slowly increasing number of amphibious ships, insufficient operating deck spots—the area on a flight deck required for the takeoff, landing, refueling and loading of a single helicopter—worried amphibians. This shortfall invariably meant that the first waves had to orbit indefinitely (and refuel frequently) before the entire tactical unit could be loaded and launched toward the objective. Frustrated by these problems, amphibious planners of both sea services improvised interim solutions until the *Wasp*-class LHDs joined the fleet.[18]

The arrival of the LCAC into the fleet appeared in many ways as revolutionary as that of the helicopter thirty years earlier. The LCAC's great speed, payload, sea-keeping, and beaching capabilities bolstered the spirits and expectations of amphibious commanders. Yet limitations existed still. The number of LCACs stood, at least initially, fewer; well deck space was at a premium. Technically, they were not assault craft. Planners realized the irony in the mixed capabilities of amphibious ships quickly: the most valuable ship-to-shore modes contained limitations in terms of helicopter operating deck spots and LCAC well deck spaces. Plenty of room for the slowest and most vulnerable mode, the amphibian vehicles and landing craft of the surface assault, always existed.

These paradoxes led to the "Triad" concept of amphibious assault in the 1980s. Amphibians recognized the three legs of the ship-to-shore movement as the LCAC, and the helicopters and the conventional surface assault craft. There were no problems with the LCACs, just the need for the *Whidbey Island*-class LSDs to become operational. The helicopters needed replacement soon, either by newer rotary-wing aircraft, or (as the Marine Corps increasingly requested) with the evolutionary JVX "Joint Service Advanced Vertical Lift Aircraft." The JVX became the MV-22 Osprey, and its tilt-rotor technology captured the imagination of the civilian aircraft industry. The Marines liked the

Osprey because of its versatility; among other features, it had the legs and speed to self-deploy to troubled waters, if necessary. Sufficient numbers of them could, the Marines claimed, land the landing force faster, at greater ranges and with fewer aircraft than the current inventory. Development of the MV-22, however, did not enjoy widely popular support within the Department of Defense. Its acquisition followed a tortuous and inconclusive path throughout the decade.

The third leg of the Triad concept was the high-speed amphibian, envisioned to be the spearhead of the surface assault, capable of over-the-horizon launch, surfing capacities and the ability to convert ashore to an armored fighting vehicle. The development path for the advanced assault amphibian vehicle (AAAV) proved even more tortuous than that of the Osprey. Research, development and engineering costs were frightful; acquisition had the potential to surpass even the Reagan administration's early defense budget. General Kelley terminated one overpriced, unpromising program in 1984; subsequent funds remained only for experimentation. Planners grew apprehensive that the AAAV might be prohibitively costly. The Triad, absent one full leg and with doubts about the second (MV-22), remained an unfulfilled ideal throughout the 1980s. Limitations in the ship-to-shore movement bothered amphibians. Yet it was still possible to execute maritime forcible entry with the mix of LCACs and the aging AAVs and helicopters. Meanwhile, a more serious problem, long deferred, drifted to the forefront of naval surface warfare in this decade: could the Navy truly deliver the Marines to the fight and then, once ashore, sustain them?

Writing in 1981, before the Falklands conflict, Thomas H. Etzold of the Naval War College summarized the views of several strategic analysts that "effective military power falls off in logarithmic proportion to the distance it is from national territory."[19] Great Britain's subsequent deployment of an expeditionary force over a distance of eight thousand miles seemed to undermine that assertion. Granted, the British fought a limited war for limited objectives against a modest military power. But their use of available strategic mobility assets demonstrated masterful defense planning and execution. The British pressed forty-three merchant ships and auxiliary vessels into service, including the luxury liner *Queen Elizabeth II*. These ships underwent rapid modification to enable at-sea refueling and maritime satellite communications; nineteen ships were fitted to handle helicopters.

Within three weeks of Prime Minister Margaret Thatcher's order, the British combined fleet assembled in the Falklands with 28,000 troops embarked. Both superpowers watched this development closely.[20]

A nineteenth-century military theorist, Antoine Henri Jomini, may have been the first to delineate the critical nature of strategic mobility: "Strategy decides where to act; logistics brings the troops to this point." Regardless of origin, this aspect of military science truly came into popular focus during the last years of the Cold War. The Joint Chiefs of Staff define strategic mobility as "the capability to deploy and sustain military forces worldwide in support of national strategy." The key ingredients, by definition, are deployability and sustainability; neither capability is militarily functional without the other.

In practice, strategic mobility has four main components: airlift, sealift, prepositioning (both land-based and sea-based) and host-nation support. Under the best of all worlds, a nation protects its enduring overseas interests by establishing stable, long-term alliances near the region of greatest threat that permit prepositioning ashore and a sophisticated system of host-nation support agreements to provide reception, staging and movement of reinforcing units. In this fashion, deployment is achieved largely by airlift; weapons and equipment and initial sustainability would be in place; only brief "marrying up" between airlifted men and pre-stocked equipment then follows. The United States Army enjoyed such a relationship for decades with the Federal Republic of Germany, and it worked well. The POMCUS Program ("Prepositioning of Materiel Configured to Unit Sets") solved some of America's most pressing strategic mobility problems during the heart of the Cold War. It was particularly valuable during the years when the principal focus centered on NATO's Central Front. With the coming of the Carter Doctrine and the diffusion of global warfighting responsibilities, however, the POMCUS program gave cause for concern. There were billions of dollars of U.S. arms and equipment committed to those warehouses and depots in West Germany.

In truth, no single element of strategic mobility is, by itself, the sole solution. Global commitments in the 1980s required an integrated mix of mobility systems. U.S. amphibious forces in the 1980s were committed to contingency operations along nearly 70 percent of the earth's littorals. Their general mission was to provide a forcible-entry capability to the Navy's power projection missions. In some local crises, the forward deployed MAUs aboard three–five amphibious ships could land and conduct limited military operations against light opposition for a brief time. But no one ever suggested that such a small force should serve as anything but a trip-wire obstacle in any armed confrontation with the Soviet Union. Moreover, not even amphibious sealift answered all the Marines' mobility requirements, even with President Reagan's "six-hundred-ship navy."

Unit integrity during deployment was essential for all armed forces; air-ground task force integrity for U.S. Marines was critical. Secretary Lehman promised to provide enough ships to carry the assault elements of a MAF and a MAB. That covered the forcible entry mission. The Marines still had a vital requirement for their integral aviation and combat support forces, as well as the necessary sustainability. For this, the Corps needed airlift, other forms of sealift and prepositioning—the whole works. But in so doing, they appeared in direct competition with the other services.

Logistical problems of adequate lift, reception and support made front-page headline news in America from the late 1970s on. President Carter's establishment of the Rapid Deployment Force seemed to create overnight a cottage industry of strategic analysts quick to identify every flaw in the evolving attempts to solve the problems of how best to move a credible force to the very ends of the earth with half a chance to succeed. Progress crept. Strategic mobility programs were costly and under-sponsored; the potential users, the Army and Marines, had to urge Navy and Air Force developers for higher priorities. Often these disputes had to be settled by the Joint Chiefs, Department of Defense, or Congress. Even then, some of the most promising programs became strung out indefinitely; the C-17 strategic airlifter limped on again, off again for over fifteen years.

Some longtime supporters of the Marine Corps expressed surprise to learn that the Corps could no longer deploy even brigade-size integrated fighting units overseas solely in Navy amphibious ships as they had in the Pacific during World War Two. Part of this shortfall was the failure to realize that all armed services—worldwide—now went to war equipped with an abundance of complex systems for combat and field support, everything from seismic intrusion devices to reverse osmosis water-purification units. Embarking a complete Marine air control squadron or a Hawk surface-to-air missile battery easily required an entire LST for each unit. A second factor contributed to the dilemma: the Corps' adoption of the MAGTF concept, the Marine Air Ground Task Force. Marine forces organized deliberately light in terms of tanks and heavy artillery, for example, because the MAGTF had its organic attack and fighter aircraft. But a third difference should have been obvious: even the "windfall" of seventy-eight amphibious ships hardly compared with the hundreds and hundreds of "Gators" available during the climactic assaults of the 1940s.

For strategic mobility purposes, planners divided Marine Corps amphibious brigades and larger forces unequally into three components: the assault echelon (AE) deployed by amphibious ships, configured to fight its way ashore over unimproved beaches and against sophisticated opposition; the "fly in-echelon" (FIE) consisting of those fixed-wing aircraft self-deploying (with tanker support) as the air combat element of the MAGTF; and the assault follow-on echelon (AFOE) contained the huge assortment of combat support and service support equipment, including supplies of all classes to sustain medium density combat for up to sixty days. This did not represent an inconsequential logistics tail. The AFOE for a notional MAF easily required up to thirty-two "black bottom" merchant ships from the Military Sealift Command. Moreover, the need appeared almost immediately. Most contingency plans required the AFOE to arrive in the amphibious objective area no later than five days after D-day, sometimes even earlier. The combined requirements for the AE, FIE and AFOE for a MAF deployment illustrate the dual pillars—deployability and sustainability—of strategic mobility. They also indicate the competitive stampede among the services for limited mobility assets during the critical opening days of a general conventional war.

Much of the subsequent debate during the period concerned the merits of airlift as compared to sealift. Airlift, of course, had the great advantage of rapid deployability and the untoward disadvantage of very limited sustainability. Advocates of airlift pointed out that only one American resupply ship reached Israel before the end of hostilities during the 1973 Yom Kippur War. Sealift advocates concede the point but retort that the same ship carried more tonnage than all the hundreds of sorties flown during the preceding three weeks. The promptness of airlift is valuable. So is the payload of sealift. The C-5 Galaxy, America's largest airlifter, has the capability to deliver 132 tons of cargo. A modern merchant ship chartered by the Military Sealift Command can deliver 22,700 tons. In pure economics, even excluding fuel costs, the ratio of comparative delivery cost by lift vehicle reflects a 104:1 advantage in favor of the merchant ship.[21]

Most analysts agreed that sealift, slow and rusty as it may be, remained the primary means of delivery in the 1980s. Increasing reliance on a steadily declining Merchant Marine caused considerable alarm. Would there be enough freighters, tankers and passenger ships available in time? And concerning the freighters, given the maritime industry's swing toward container ships, would there be enough of the more militarily useful break-bulk, Ro-Ro, and barge/lighter ships available in time? In March 1981 Admiral Thomas Hayward, Chief of Naval Operations, warned the House Armed Services Committee that "without adequate and reliable sealift, literally none of our military plans is executable."[22] Another source estimated that 90 percent of the Army's equipment and supplies moved into the objective area by sealift. Admiral Isaac C. Kidd testified in 1985 that "from a logistics standpoint, it was going to take six thousand shiploads every thirty days just to keep Europe alive and fighting during a war."[23] A prestigious "blue ribbon panel" appointed by Congress in 1984 to investigate maritime lift concluded that the United States possessed insufficient ships "to execute a major deployment in a contingency operation in a single distant theater such as Southwest Asia."[24] Again, sustainability should not be decoupled from deployment. Most planners agree that a single mechanized division deployed overseas needs more than one thousand tons per day delivered to sustain it in combat. Marine Corps divisions are larger; in fact, they are the largest in the military world. And a Marine division comprises only the ground combat element of a MAF.

As Navy and Marine Corps planners wrestled with these shortcomings, they concluded quickly that the problem exceeded the scope of the Department of the Navy. Indeed, interagency task forces soon sprouted with representatives from the Departments of Defense, State, Energy, Commerce and Transportation. An attractive early proposal was to obtain leases for prestocking, port access and reception airfields among America's erstwhile allies in the Middle East. The Pentagon requested $742 million in funds for fiscal years 1981-82 to build or expand facilities at Ras Banas on Egypt's Red Sea coast; Masira Island in the Gulf of Oman; and the Indian Ocean ports of Mombassa, Kenya, and Berbera, Somalia. The United States quickly accepted the political realities of the region: the stable POMCUS program in West Germany would never succeed in the shifting political sands of the Middle East.[25]

Meanwhile, the Department of the Navy took advantage of a surplus of modern merchant ships on the open market in the early 1980s to start chipping away at the strategic mobility deficit. "We picked up dead men's shoes," exclaimed John Lehman, extolling the thirty militarily useful ships obtained for sealift missions at rock-bottom prices. Eight high-speed container ships underwent conversion to Ro-Ro, then assumed a reduced operating-status (ready in four days) and were designated to transport an Army division to Europe. The Military Sealift Command leased or chartered other Ro-Ros, LASH, and Sea Bee ships. The Department of the Navy obtained two supertankers and converted them into hospital ships, commissioning the USNS *Mercy* in 1986 and the USNS *Comfort* in 1987. Each ship contained one thousand beds and twelve operating rooms.[26]

The Chief of Naval Operations' staff likewise found a practical mission for twelve "used" container ships, converting them to auxiliary crane ships capable of unloading themselves and other "non-self-sustaining" ships where port facilities might be inadequate or damaged. Navy and Marine officers developed other initiatives to improve cargo handling and discharge: elevated causeway systems, powered causeways, side-loadable warping tugs, offshore petroleum systems, astern-refueling rigs, underway replenishment consoles, "flatracks," and "seasheds" to adapt container ships to handle oversize or outsized military cargo. Long neglected specialty units in the Navy Reserve received new life and missions—for example, "NEAT" Teams and "CHAP" Groups to embark aboard chartered merchants or help cargo handling in ports. The obvious necessity for the armed services to convert their expeditionary equipment from pallets to containers caused extensive cooperation between Army and Marine Corps planners, principally with the Army's "LOTS" program (Logistics Over the Shore) and the Marine Corps "COTS" program (Container Offshore Handling Systems). The services developed or adapted lighters, cargo handling equipment, and traffic management systems. Daunting conversion problems persisted. Offloading, distributing, and recovering commercial containers over an unimproved beach in a combat zone challenged the brightest logisticians of all the armed services.[27]

A particularly vexing problem concerned how to provide immediate maintenance support for Marine Corps aviation units deploying with a MAF or MAB. The complex testing, calibration and repair equipment appeared too expensive (several billion dollars) to duplicate for prepositioning and too elaborate to set up quickly on a newly captured airstrip. The solution suggested by the logistics and aviation staffs at Marine Corps Headquarters was again to "pick up dead men's shoes." The Navy obtained a pair of *Seabridge*-class combination Ro-Ro/container ships and converted them into T-AVBs, aviation support ships. Maintained in a reduced operating status and available within five days, the ship had the capability to load quickly with repair-shop vans for avionics, ground support equipment, ordnance, and airframes. Installed helicopter platforms provided the capability of operating "in the stream."[28]

Each of these initiatives helped improve what was originally a deplorable state of strategic mobility readiness. But a proposal generated with the Department of the Navy (Headquarters Marine Corps, OPNAV Staff, Naval Sea Systems Command) to undertake a maritime prepositioning program emerged as the biggest achievement. Maritime prepositioning was an idea whose time had clearly come. The concept made good sense to just about everyone in the national security arena. While good, the POMCUS program had inherent geographical inflexibilities. With security concerns shifting from the NATO Central Front fixation to a more global consciousness, the idea of prestocking heavy equipment, fuel, and ammunition in merchant ships free to deploy anywhere was increasingly attractive. Implementation of the "Near Term Prepositioning Force" by President Carter in 1979 remained as one of the first and most enduring initiatives of the Carter Doctrine. Within two years a small flotilla of chartered Ro-Ros, tankers, and break-bulk ships embarked the heavy combat equipment of the 7th Marine Amphibious Brigade and set sail for their assigned anchorage in the remote Indian Ocean atoll Diego Garcia.

The Marine Corps was quick to seize this uncharacteristic mission. General Kelley emerged as an early, outspoken advocate. His recent experiences as the first commander of the "Rapid Deployment Joint Task Force" provided a keen appreciation for strategic mobility realities. Convincing other general and flag officers of the potential benefits of the new concept was not easy. Maritime prepositioning was hardly amphibious. The NTPF in particular limited itself to direct offload in a benign, commercial port. Planners delineated the operational concept with optimistic expectations: in times of heightened tension, the NTPF would be directed to proceed to a port nearest the trouble spot and offload; meanwhile, the troops and their more perishable cargo flew to the same port for the linkup with their equipment. The idea assumed unrestricted use of reception ports and airfields on the part of the host country, as well as early (pre-hostilities) arrival.

The potential existed for using a forward-deployed MAU for port seizure and protection should the situation deteriorate prematurely. Meanwhile, the Reagan administration and Congress accepted a Defense Department proposal to convert or construct more suitable cargo ships for the follow-on Maritime Prepositioning Program (MPS).

The NTPF program cost the Marines dearly: all the duplicate sets of combat equipment came "out of hide," drawing down the assets of other Fleet Marine Force units. But the Commandants of that era, General Robert H. Barrow and his successor, General Kelley, ensured that Congress provide the procurement costs for three full brigade sets of equipment for the MPS ships. General Barrow addressed the concerns of his more tradition-bound officers by distributing a special "White Letter" to all general officers and commanding officers in 1981. "Neither the NTPS nor MPS are substitutes for amphibious operations," he pointed out. "They are enhancements of our maritime strategic mobility. All of us take pride in being 'First to Fight.' To do so, we have to get there first, ready to fight."[29]

Far from being a threat to the amphibious mission of the Marine Corps, the maritime prepositioning programs served to enhance the feasibility of deploying Fleet Marine Forces in crisis situations. There was the added luxury of finally being able to field a truly heavy, mechanized force. The three MPS brigades, unrestricted by the availability of amphibious ships nor having to compete during mobilization for scarce "black bottoms," could afford to preposition extra tanks, armored vehicles and self-propelled artillery. The combined-arms MPS brigades loomed huge (16,500 troops in initial plans)—larger than many divisions in other armed forces.

Maritime prepositioning gave benefits to the other services as well. Airlift requirements for the troops and special equipment of the MPS brigades declined from about 4,500 C-141 equivalent sorties to less than 250, thus freeing more airlift assets for simultaneous deployment by other services. The Navy kept control of the MPS ships, providing a commodore in charge, and embarking NEAT Teams to assist the civilian crews. The potential offered by the MPS concept attracted the Army and Air Force. Soon, an "extended" NTPF flotilla existed at Diego Garcia, augmented by ammunition ships and water tankers for both services. Diego Garcia lay 2,500 miles from the Strait of Hormuz, but the British "landlord" was benevolent and security easy, and the United States for the first time had a credible military force in the Indian Ocean on a semi-permanent basis.

The Maritime Prepositioning Program, as approved by Congress, led to the conversion of eight merchant ships (five Maersk Line, three Waterman Line) and the construction of five new ships by Braintree. Even the smallest of the lot, the new Braintree ships, possessed the capability to haul the equivalent of one thousand C-141 airlifters each. Naval architects converted the ships to military specifications so as to handle wheeled and tracked vehicles, pallets, and containers, and gave them the capability of self-offloading "in the stream" to get away from the NTPF's potentially fatal requirement for existing port facilities. The thirteen ships thus completed, divided into three squadrons, loaded with their assigned combat cargo, and received assignments to operating areas and anchorages in the Indian, Pacific, and Atlantic Oceans well before the end of the decade. The political-military value of these MPS squadrons proved their worth in the initial buildup stage of Operation Desert Shield in 1991.[30]

General Kelley exuded pride for the achievement and the multi-agency teamwork that produced it. "MPS is probably one of the greatest shots in the arm not only for the Marine Corps but for the maritime industry," he told *Washington Post* military reporter George C. Wilson, adding, "what you are seeing now is the resurgence of a maritime strategy, and with that goes the U.S. Marine Corps."[31]

The maritime strategy spawned one additional strategic mobility-enhancement initiative for the United States. The lingering debates about the strategy stimulated a new interest in NATO's northern flank, specifically the country of Norway. The focus of the Carter administration on the Central Front and a "Twelve Day Conventional War" seemed to exclude the northern flank from practical consideration. Then came Navy Secretary Lehman, who spoke of the Norwegian Sea as the "principal naval battleground" of a NATO war.

Part of this was a natural extension of "carrying the war to the enemy." The unprecedented Soviet buildup along the Kola Peninsula near the 122-mile border with Norway, making the "Murmansk Oblast" one of the most heavily militarized regions in the world, added to the concerns of strategists. Rapid reinforcement of Norwegian forces in time of war thus evolved as a strategic imperative, particularly the defense of the northern airfields at Banak, Tromso, Bardufoss, Andoya, Evenes, Bodo, Orland and Vaernes. For the Marines the mission appeared as a reincarnation of the 1916 congressional mandate to seize advance naval bases in support of a naval campaign. American task forces conducted elaborate combined amphibious exercises north of the Arctic Circle, even in midwinter. The carrier *America* (CVA 66) and her battle group operated from inside Norwegian fjords in Exercise Ocean Safari 85 to reduce radar profile, taking advantage of the extended air attack early warning provided by the landing force ashore.

The requirement for American amphibious forces to deploy rapidly to defend northern Norway represented another mobility problem solved in part by prepositioning. In this case, the national authorities of Norway and the United States agreed to limited prestocking of Marine Corps combat equipment in rock-hewn storage sites in country. America promised to respect Norway's sensitive "Nordic balance." Equipment included neither nuclear arms nor other strike weapons, such as the A-6E aircraft. The U.S. government also promised not to station Marines permanently in the country. Equipment would not be stored in the north, but further south, near Trondheim. In exchange for these sensitive diplomatic concerns, Norway agreed to maintain the equipment, provide over-snow tactical vehicles, and accept responsibility for redeploying the airlifted MAB, once married with its equipment, to northern fighting positions.[32]

Despite formidable political and funding hurdles on both sides of the Atlantic, the Norway prepositioning initiative reached fruition fully in the 1980s. As a consequence, the Marine Corps announced a reduction of several thousand airlift sorties previously required in the critical first hours of a NATO crisis.. Reassuring the allies along NATO's northern flank of America's commitment to the defense of that region also produced significant political benefits.

The "confidence building measures" established in the 1986 Stockholm Agreement permitted Warsaw Pact military representatives to observe NATO exercises in progress (and vice versa). The dozens of Soviet, East German, Czech, Hungarian, and Polish officers who observed Exercise Teamwork 88 in northern Norway received a first-hand observation of NATO's enhanced capabilities for rapid reinforcement of the northern flank, including the speedy linkup of a heavy U.S. Marine Corps amphibious brigade with its prepositioned equipment and its redeployment north to the high ground protecting the key air bases.[33]

Defense strategist Francis "Bing" West, whose "Seaplan 2000" first proposed the then unpopular concept of reinforcing Norway a decade earlier, concluded by the late 1980s, "At heart, the Maritime Strategy is a firm expression of self-confidence. . . . The most remarkable metamorphosis in combat scenarios is the confidence that north-ern Norway can be reinforced and held, given the U.S. Marine prepo-sitioning and exercises begun in 1980. . . . This has troubled the Soviets as much as it has pleased the Scandinavians."[34]

"The chief characteristic of the modern era," observed Admiral Watkins in the mid-1980s, "[is] a permanent state of what I call vio-lent peace."[35] The Republican administration displayed no reluctance to employ its newly modernized naval forces in troubled waters. Fleet operating tempo increased to the stress point. By 1986 sailors and Marines were being deployed away from home ports at a rate 20 per-cent higher than during the Vietnam War.[36]

The 1980s were violent years. Curiously, much of the violence appeared unrelated to direct superpower rivalries. Cold War tensions remained high, but other nations seemed increasingly unrestrained in resorting to force to settle new or ancient disputes. The Soviet inva-sion of Afghanistan, instead of presaging further aggressive moves in either Pakistan or Iran, evolved instead into somewhat of a sideshow to an endless guerrilla war. Iraq invaded Iran; the subsequent conflict dragged on for years and spilled over into the troubled Persian Gulf. Tankers from neutral nations struck mines or suffered heavy damage from long range anti-ship missiles fired from both sides. Forward-deployed U.S. naval forces also paid a price in the Gulf: Exocet mis-siles fired from an Iraqi attack aircraft struck the *Stark* (FFG 31) in 1987; another frigate, *Samuel B. Roberts* (FFG 58), incurred heavy damage from a moored mine the following year. Bloody acts of state-sponsored terrorism against American targets were attributed to Libya; in retaliation, a night air strike against Tripoli and Benghazi in 1986 defeated the sophisticated Soviet-supplied air defense systems and inflicted avenging damage. And always there was the civil war in Lebanon, now compounded by the 1982 Israeli invasion.

U.S. amphibious forces deployed "like stormy petrels" wherever violent forces tended to threaten American interests. Amphibious ready groups steamed in endless circles on "Gonzo station" in the Indian Ocean and throughout the western Pacific. Increasingly, how-ever, amphibious deployments began to focus on two particularly troublesome spots, the Caribbean and the eastern Mediterranean Sea.

During the first week of July 1982, President Reagan announced that the United States would join a multinational force to supervise withdrawal of elements of the Palestine Liberation Organization (PLO) from Lebanon. The following month a Marine Amphibious Unit from the Sixth Fleet placed eight hundred troops ashore to work with comparable numbers of Italian, French, and British "peacekeepers." The tense evacuation of Chairman Yassir Arafat and his PLO troops from Beirut aboard U.S. landing craft without a single casualty marked one of the most successful uses of amphibious forces for political goals in the entire epoch. Amid universal acclaim for their professional achievement, the Marines and their counterparts withdrew on 10 September. Historians might have remembered the deployment as a singular diplomatic feat had it not been for the tragedy that followed.

The Lebanese civil war erupted again with a renewed fury within one week after the U.S. Marines departed Beirut with the assassination of President-elect Bashir Gemayal. Phalangist militia troops massacred Palestinian refugees in the Sabra and Shatilla camps, while occupying Israeli forces chose not to intervene. President Reagan then made the fateful decision to return the Marines ashore. On 29 September the 32d MAU landed in conjunction with returning French and Italian contingents from the original multinational force. Twelve hundred Marines took station near the Beirut International Airport. Although individual MAUs rotated regularly through Beruit, substantial numbers of Sixth Fleet Marines and sailors served ashore in that exposed position for the next sixteen months.

The history of what followed is well known. At first welcomed as "peacekeepers," dissidents began to perceive the Marines as reinforcements for the largely Christian Lebanese Army. In April 1983 terrorists detonated a car-bomb at the American embassy, destroying the building and killing sixty-three people, including seventeen Americans. The following month, the United States coordinated an Israeli agreement to withdraw from Beirut, but the Americans failed to secure Israel's promise to keep forces in the Shouf Mountains overlooking the Beirut airport. Late that summer, conditions between the Marines and the various Moslem militias deteriorated to the point of exchanging gunfire. The Marines, trying to keep peace in a land torn asunder and operating in the middle of an operational commercial airport, appeared dangerously vulnerable.

Worse, the Marines operated within a convoluted chain of command under unreasonably restrictive rules of engagement. In one nine-day period in early September, four Marines died and twenty-eight suffered wounds in sharp fighting. On 7 September, Druze militiamen fired 130 rockets into the airport compound from the Shouf Mountains. The next day naval gunfire ships of the Sixth Fleet fired

their first rounds in support of the embattled Marines. A crucial escalation occurred on 15 September when U.S. Navy ships fired hundreds of rounds in direct support of Lebanese Armed Forces under
heavy attack at Suk al Gharb. Then the newly recommissioned battleship *New Jersey* took station off Beirut on 25 September. And on 12
October President Reagan signed a congressionally approved extension of Public Law 98-119, authorizing the President to keep the
Marines deployed in Lebanon for eighteen additional months.

The payoff for this extended deployment ashore in the Lebanese
civil war came early Sunday morning, 23 October 1983, when a suicidal terrorist rammed a large truck filled with explosives into the lobby
of the airport building serving as the barracks for the battalion landing
team of the 24th MAU. The enormous explosion flattened the four-
story building and killed 241 Marines, sailors, and soldiers in their
sleep. A similar suicide attack by an explosive-laden truck on the
French barracks killed fifty-eight paratroopers.

In the outcry of grief, horror, and recrimination that followed,
people around the world expressed amazement upon learning the
extent of the joint attacks. The terrorists, whomever they represented
(the Secretary of Defense blamed the Syrians and the Iranians;
President Reagan accused the Soviet Union), had executed a masterful, diabolical plot. Subsequent investigation by the FBI of the ruins of
the building revealed the potency of the truck bombs. The Mercedes
dumptruck that leveled the Marine barracks had been loaded with six
to eight tons of TNT enhanced by bottles of pressurized propane gas
and primer cord. The FBI estimated the force of the explosion to have
been the equivalent of eleven Silkworm missiles, roughly the yield of a
small nuclear weapon. Survivors recalled finding a severed human
hand embedded in a chain link fence several hundred yards away
from the point of impact.

Critics found it difficult to accept that there would have been literally no effective defense against such a suicidal weapon, particularly
under the existing rules of engagement; an antitank trench at the compound might have stopped the vehicle, but not the slaughter. Two terrorists had effectively pole-axed the multinational forces. And
although the Marines remained on station an additional four months,
their withdrawal from Beirut seemed certain. Amphibious presence
operations, as we discussed in chapter five, may achieve temporary
objectives such as the initial "quick and dirty" Beirut landing operation in 1982; however, long-ranging political solutions are beyond the

reach of maritime expeditionary forces, particularly in the Middle East. It was a sobering lesson to relearn.[37]

The United States defense establishment worried also a lot about the Caribbean during the years of anguish in Lebanon. Soviet military supplies to the Sandinista regime in Nicaragua continued unabated throughout much of the 1980s. The Sandinistas also made covert deliveries of many of these supplies to leftist guerrillas fighting in the civil war in El Salvador. Cuban advisors appeared frequently in trouble spots. Sometimes, the "advisors" in Nicaragua were discovered to be Soviets, Palestinians, Bulgarians, and East Germans. Defense analysts observed Soviet development of major port facilities in Nicaragua at El Bluff on the Caribbean and San Juan del Sur on the Pacific with concern. The construction of a new 3,600-meter reception airfield at Punta Huete made it the largest in Central America.[38]

Other disquieting developments in the region surfaced. The American-backed Contra forces lost momentum in their guerrilla war against the Sandinistas, losing congressional support at the same time. Cuban forces demonstrated an inclination to become more adventurous and built a new reception airfield on the tiny island of Grenada, and they exchanged fire with U.S. Marines on Panama's Arraijan Fuel Farm. U.S. concern was both strategic as well as visceral. A significant percentage of American reinforcements for NATO embarked in ships from ports along the Gulf of Mexico; interdiction by Soviet-trained and equipped Cuban or Sandinista forces made them extremely vulnerable.

The United States responded to these perceived threats by increasing pressure on the Sandinistas through continued support (extralegal, as it turned out) to the Contra forces and by commencing a training and development program with Honduran armed forces. U.S. amphibious forces conducted a series of bilateral landing exercises with the Hondurans along the Caribbean coast. With permission of the Honduran government, the Marine Corps also established a temporary radar site on Tiger Island in the Gulf of Fonseca to observe Sandinista resupply efforts into El Salvador. Reports from the facilities merely confirmed the obvious; hundreds of small planes took off from Nicaragua each week, flying at low altitudes directly to Salvadoran fields. As it turned out, no call resulted for amphibious forces to intervene in either civil war in Central America. Marines and sailors served as advisors in El Salvador, but the role of the amphibious forces was to train the Hondurans while remaining ready to land on either coast of Nicaragua.[39]

The National Security Council viewed the situation in Grenada as more alarming. The overthrow of the government by the leftist New Jewel Movement, the presence of armed Cuban construction workers seeking to complete the airfield and the perceived threat to the American medical students on the island provided the Reagan administration with sufficient cause for military intervention in October 1983. The initial plan consisted simply of diverting the *Independence* (CV 62) carrier battle group and the amphibious force deploying the 22nd MAU to Lebanon. But planners knew little known about the island and its defenders. To ensure success, the Department of Defense decided to make the operation a joint affair, with all four services (plus joint unconventional forces) participating. Operation Urgent Fury thus became the first joint-service combat undertaking of significant size since the Vietnam War. Secretary Lehman, not in the operational chain, decried the Washington obsession with "jointness." He thought it absurd to waste the opportunity for a classic amphibious assault supported by carrier air with the forces at hand: "everything needed was aboard the ships of the amphibious group or the CBG [carrier battle group]."[40]

The Pentagon and Oval Office set D-day for Urgent Fury on 25 October 1983, two days after the devastating bombing of the Marine barracks in Beirut. U.S. Army units seized Point Salines airfield in the southwest corner; the Marines landed in the north to seize Pearls Airfield and the town of Grenville. When the Army encountered stiff resistance from the Cubans, the joint task force commander, Vice Admiral Joseph Metcalf III, ordered the Marines to reembark and conduct a second landing at Grand Mal Bay. Effective resistance ended by D+2 with the rescue of the medical students and the imprisoned governor, while cleanup operations required several more days. Nineteen American military men died; 115 received wounds. The Americans killed twenty-four Cubans and perhaps twice as many Grenadian troops. Urgent Fury was a victory, but not a glorious one. Helicopter losses to unsophisticated air defense weapons and casualties inflicted by "friendly fire" particularly frustrated senior officials.. "Why does every operation have to be a four-service extravaganza?" grumbled reporter George Wilson later. "Would not a Navy-Marine operation have been less complicated, more effective and less costly?" Most sea service officers would have heartily agreed, but everyone sensed a significant shift in planning for future engagements. Joint operations would be mandated increasingly in the coming eight years. In that regard, the Grenada experience, mistakes and all, provided a valuable source of lessons learned at an affordable cost.[41]

Six years after Grenada, in late December 1989, another large-scale joint intervention took place in Panama. According to the administration, Operation Just Cause was launched "to protect American lives, restore the democratic process, preserve the integrity of the Panama Canal Treaty and apprehend dictator General Manuel Noriega." The operation emerged largely as an Army show, understandable because of the existence of over ten thousand soldiers already in the Canal Zone before hostilities began. Amphibious forces played modest roles. Some Fleet Marine Forces (a Light Armored Vehicle company) had been flown into Panama six months earlier. Heli-borne Marines landed on D-day to defend the westward approaches to the Canal and secure the Bridge of the Americas. Just Cause also witnessed the first combat appearance of a Marine Corps Anti-Terrorist Security Platoon from the Atlantic Fleet. Embarked amphibious forces generally served as a ready theater reserve in case of conflict escalation by Nicaraguan or Cuban intervention. In all, the action was brief, casualties were light, and the various services seemed to work in closer synchronization than before.[42]

Except for the brief fighting in Panama, 1989 was a relatively peaceful year for U.S. amphibious forces. Evidence of some retrenchment by the Soviet Union, yet not fully understood, made for less urgency among forward deployed forces. The United States still conducted amphibious training exercises around the world: "Cold Winter" in northern Norway, "Team Spirit" in South Korea, "Solid Shield" off the East Coast, and "Thalay Thai" and "Valiant Usher" in Thailand. The Navy commissioned the *Wasp* (LHD-1), the first multi-purpose amphibious assault ship. The Commandant of the Marine Corps, Gen. Alfred N. Gray, ordered the expansion of educational programs at Quantico to include graduate-level studies in warfighting and activated the Marine Corps University. Amphibians also performed a variety of humanitarian services: cleanup operations from the *Exxon Valdez* oil spill in Alaska's Prince William Sound and disaster relief in Charleston following Hurricane Hugo and in San Francisco following the earthquake there. Some Marines began training and participating in surveillance operations with the Immigration and Naturalization

Service as part of the President's "War on Drugs." There was a sense of great changes in the wind.[43]

By 1989, President Reagan, Secretary Lehman, Admiral Watkins, and General Kelley had all left the scene. The amphibious ships, landing craft and converted merchantmen generated by their maritime strategy of the early 1980s remained either in place or well on the way. Defense strategists believed American amphibious forces as accredited and lethal as they had been since the end of World War II. Both men and ships had reached a superior state of readiness. Then something almost totally unforeseen happened to the "Evil Empire," America's mortal adversary for the previous forty-four years.

Chapter Eight

Amphibious Warfare, *Perestroika,* and Desert Storm

Western political and military leaders did not know at first what to make of Mikhail Gorbachev, who became Secretary General of the Politburo of the Central Committee of the Communist Party of the Soviet Union in March 1985. Certainly, he was a dedicated socialist and a loyal Party member. But Gorbachev differed disturbingly from the three geriatric leaders who preceded him. Younger and more energetic than they, Gorbachev appeared politically astute, accustomed to handling the media, and unafraid of reality. He recognized the sorry state of the Soviet economy and knew that his country would be doomed unless he instituted draconian reform measures.

Gorbachev's startling initiatives, *perestroika* ("restructuring") and *glasnost* ("openness"), were received with reluctance at home and with great suspicion in the West. Neither reaction surprised defense analysts or political scientists.

Gorbachev ascended to the top leadership position in the Soviet Union in less than a year and half after one of the most poisonous years in Soviet-American relations: 1983, a year that began with President Reagan's "Evil Empire" speech and "Star Wars" initiative and ended with the USSR's shooting down Korean Air Lines flight 007, the bombing of the Marine barracks in Beirut (for which many Americans blamed Soviet-backed Islamic terrorists), and the decision by the West German parliament to accept deployment of intermediate-range U.S. missiles along the Soviet border. In the aftermath, a Gallup Poll indicated American views favorable toward the Soviet Union had reached a twenty-seven-year low.[1]

Gorbachev's new policies defied immediate quantification. During the late 1980s, however, astute Western observers detected unmistakable signs of retrenchment, disengagement, and withdrawal. The political and military stakes appeared enormous. Disarmament represented an obvious, major component of *perestroika*. Gorbachev announced a one million-man reduction in the Soviet armed forces (later adjusted to three million), as well as significant reductions in defense spending and weapons production. The Soviets abandoned Afghanistan, sharply reduced their support for communist regimes in Central America and the Caribbean, cut back the operating range and tempo of their naval forces, and initiated a reluctant dialogue with resurgent nationalistic states within the monolith. Clearly, all of these initiatives signaled a major, even historic, "restructuring" underway.

Nor could any thoughtful observer deny that the Soviet Union needed major surgery critically. Richard Sharpe, a retired Royal Navy Captain, provided a representative diagnosis of the ills plaguing the Soviet Union:

> This is a Third World nation with almost 19th century standards of liv-
> ing for the vast majority of her people, major balance of payments
> problems, declining oil resources, currency nobody wants, and an
> industrial base which, with the partial exception of space and military
> programs, maintains plants and practices that are decades out of date.[2]

The Soviet Union also experienced a series of embarrassing security incidents during the 1980s that brought into question the return on investment in defense projects throughout the Cold War. The *muja-hadeen* guerrillas in Afghanistan proved no match for the front-line Soviet forces occupying that country, but—very much like the Viet Cong and North Vietnamese against the Americans in the previous decade—they demonstrated the ability to dissipate the Soviet political will in a protracted insurgency. Afghanistan had become Russia's Vietnam.

Similarly, the ease with which Israel dispatched Soviet-trained and equipped Syrian forces in Lebanon's Bekaa Valley in 1984 gained the attention of military observers worldwide. Two years later, United States naval and air forces experienced little difficulty penetrating Libya's vaunted, Soviet-equipped air defenses for the retaliatory strikes against Tripoli and Benghazi. In 1989, an experimental "Mike"-class Soviet nuclear attack submarine, the *Komsomolets,* caught fire and sank in the Norwegian Sea. Another disastrous fire at sea gutted the eight-year-old guided missile destroyer *Admiral Zakharov.* Equally disconcerting to the Kremlin, a German teenager, Mattias Rust, flew a civilian airplane through Soviet top-of-the-line air defenses and landed unharmed in Red Square. The Russian bear, it seemed, had lost at least part of its bite.

Notwithstanding the accidental loss of the *Komsomolets,* the Soviet Navy for several years appeared immune from Gorbachev's restructuring and retrenchment. While a number of older ships were sold off or scrapped, the construction of certain classes of new ships, submarines, naval aircraft and advanced landing craft continued the momentum launched earlier by Adm. Sergei Gorshkov. The visionary Soviet admiral had departed the scene (he retired in 1985 and died three years later), but many of his modernization programs persisted throughout the decade. The long-awaited full-deck carrier appeared finally on the high seas—the largest warship ever built by the Soviet Union—albeit with a ski-ramp in lieu of catapults and without nuclear propulsion. Analysts reported other major carriers, fully modernized, on the way. Indeed, 1990 represented a banner year for Soviet shipbuilding: ten new submarines and nine major combatants. And as late as August of that year, during the coalition buildup for Operation Desert Shield, Gorbachev visited the Ukraine to observe a combined amphibious and airborne landing exercise near Odessa.

U.S. Navy and Marine Corps leaders continued to watch the Soviet Navy with a wary eye. In 1987, Adm. Carlisle Trost, Chief of Naval Operations (CNO), admitted that "the Soviet Navy is getting better fast. . . . It poses a direct threat that it can back up its demands with airplanes overhead, troops on the beaches, or missiles inbound." Suspicions lingered that Gorbachev had merely paused to rebuild his technological base in order to modernize his strategic and conventional forces. As retired Marine Col. Denis J. Kiely observed in 1989, "No matter the mask the Soviets don, they are, and will remain, the premier competitors to American interests. President Gorbachev may not be reforming as much as streamlining."[3]

Adm. of the Fleet V. N. Chernavin, appointed by Gorbachev to replace Admiral Gorshkov as Commander-in-Chief in December 1985, inherited the world's largest navy. The historic mainstays of the Soviet fleet, submarines and naval aircraft, were among the best to be found in any navy. The Soviet Navy also enjoyed a significant lead in mine warfare, antiship missiles, nuclear and chemical warfare capabilities, and short-range amphibious assault. Soviet amphibious forces attained a modest high tide of their own during the last years of the USSR. Doctrinally tied to airborne forces for power projection missions, the amphibious forces appeared no longer intended for major, global deployment. On the other hand, Gorbachev's policy of withdrawing the fleet closer to the motherland served to strengthen the military value of amphibious forces. Within the short-range orbit of several hundred miles, these forces were ideally organized and equipped to execute their missions.

By 1990, the Soviet naval order of battle contained seventy-five seagoing amphibious ships, reinforced by a very large and readily available merchant marine and an impressive number of mine laying and sweeping craft. In certain scenarios, the helicopter carriers *Moskva* and *Leningrad,* as well as the V/STOL carriers *Admiral Gorshkov* (ex-*Baku*) and *Admiral Kuznetzov* (sequentially, the ex-*Leonid Brezhnev* and ex-*Tblisi*) would have been available for direct support of amphibious operations, as well. The Kremlin distributed amphibious forces among the Northern, Baltic, Black Sea, and Pacific fleets, as well as the Caspian Flotilla during this period. Northern Fleet amphibious forces trained for operations against Norway, Iceland, and the North Sea approaches to Skagarrak, the narrow waterway between Jutland and Norway. Baltic amphibians trained with their East German and Polish counterparts to gain control of the eastern approaches to the Danish Straits. Analysts on both sides realized the critical importance of the Danish island of Bornholm, "a prime target for Soviet amphibious assault." Analysts noted fewer amphibious forces in the Black Sea Fleet, but these provided components of the Mediterranean *Fifth Eskadra*, which had peaked at ninety-six ships (including eight amphibs) during the 1973 Yom Kippur War. The Pacific Fleet retained the largest amphibious assault capability. Moscow assigned the Pacific amphibians, home-ported in Vladivostok, the mission of securing the four major straits that provide egress from the Sea of Japan into the Pacific Ocean.[4]

The Soviet Navy included three special ground-combat units at the end of the Cold War: the naval infantry (*morskaya pekhota*), coastal missile artillery, and naval *spetsnaz*. All three forces grew modestly during the 1980s, although details about the naval *spetsnaz* units remained classified. The coastal missile artillery waxed and waned, drawing attention only when abruptly reinforced by four motorized rifle divisions from the Red Army, suspected to be a ruse to avoid the reductions mandated by the multilateral agreements lowering the size of conventional forces in Europe. The Soviet Naval Infantry (SNI) increased from twelve thousand to about eighteen thousand in the 1980s, the new total representing about 4 percent of all naval personnel. The mission of the SNI remained essentially unchanged: to seize important straits and waterways, either by independent amphibious landings or in conjunction with airborne forces as a spearhead for follow-on army units. The additional personnel enabled the SNI to field a division for the first time; other SNI regiments reorganized and upgraded into brigades. The Kremlin assigned the brigades to the three European fleets: at Pechenga, near Murmansk in the north; at Baltiysk with the Baltic Fleet; and at Kazachya Bukhta near Sevastopol in the Black Sea. The SNI division received orders to the Pacific Fleet and based at Vladivostok. Soviet deployment of a naval infantry regiment from this division to Cam Ranh Bay especially rankled American sea services and became a heated topic of discussion during the fiscal year 1987 defense budget hearings. Soviet Naval Infantry troops were well armed and highly trained. Moreover, they conducted their missions from capable amphibious ships and state-of-the-art assault landing craft.[5]

The Soviet amphibious fleet at this time consisted of three *Ivan Rogov*-class dock landing ships, and fourteen *Alligator*-class and twenty-three *Ropucha*-class tank landing ships. In addition, a large number of *Polnocny*-class medium landing ships served in the fleet. The Soviet LSDs were the largest amphibious warfare ships to be built in the Eastern Bloc. Closer analysis of the *Ivan Rogovs* revealed multiple capabilities: floodable well decks to carry and launch up to three *Lebed* air cushion vehicles, two helicopter decks and hangers, a large tank deck which could transport ten medium tanks or thirty armored personnel carriers, berthing capacity for over five hundred naval infantrymen, and modest naval gunfire support in the form of a 122mm barrage rocket launcher. As described in chapter 5, the appearance of *Ivan Rogov* and the new replenishment ship *Berezina* in the Indian Ocean in 1980 alarmed Western naval strategists. Curiously, the Soviets built only three *Rogovs,* and a seven-year gap existed between the second and third. No additional replenishment ships followed the *Berezina.* The Kremlin's decision to deemphasize global amphibious projection and return to short-range capabilities in the mid-1980s coincided with the ascendancy of Mikhail Gorbachev.

The Soviet Union could point with justifiable pride towards its development of the world's largest fleet of commercial and military air cushion vehicles (ACVs). A massive research and development program in the 1970s and 1980s produced six distinct classes of ACVs, which were series-produced for the Soviet Navy. At least eighty of these craft operated with amphibious forces in 1990. The *Pomornik*-class ACV, completed in 1986, measured 193 feet long and displaced 360 tons—making it the world's largest ACV. It could carry 220 troops or three medium tanks plus 100 troops at speeds up to 55 knots. Depending on the load and sea conditions, most of these craft could traverse at high speeds at ranges up to two hundred miles, generally negating the need for a mother ship. At the end of the Cold War, the Soviet Navy experimented with a new *Pelikan*-class ACV and seemed to be borrowing lessons learned by U.S. forces in the Persian Gulf concerning the value of ACVs as mine-clearance platforms.

The "Caspian Sea Monster," the experimental wing-in-ground effect vehicle, revealed another intriguing development in amphibious warfare technology. These craft, which resembled large flying boats, were designed to fly in "ground effect" over water and make landings as necessary on ice or beaches. The Soviets produced at least two military prototypes, which they called *Ekranoplans*. One variant consisted of an antiship missile platform; the other, known as *Orlan,* appeared designed for amphibious assault. The *Orlan* demonstrated a capability of transporting several hundred naval infantry troops and two light tanks at a top speed of 350 knots and a maximum height of forty feet in ground effect. *Orlan*'s most impressive characteristic was its operating range: reportedly 4,300 nautical miles with a full payload, a potential transoceanic self-deployer.[6]

Soviet amphibious forces in the late 1980s could also draw on several other elements of support from the military and intelligence establishments. The Soviet Black Sea Fleet received the potential for augmentation by twenty-six landing craft from Bulgaria and Rumania. The Baltic Fleet trained regularly with East German and Polish counterparts, whose combined fifty-four LSTs and nineteen LSMs represented a sizable force. The Polish amphibious force was, like its navy, the best trained and maintained in the Warsaw Pact aside from the Soviet Union. Polish shipyards built amphibious ships for a dozen nations around the world. The Poles had a significant amphibious lift capacity in their twenty-three *Polnocny*-class LSMs and nineteen large landing craft. In addition, the Polish Army's 7th Sea Landing Division, twelve thousand strong, conducted amphibious exercises regularly from its base in Gdansk.

Other amphibious-related assets available to the Soviet Navy consisted of helicopter-capable hospital ships, an auxiliary naval transport (the *Mikhail Kalinin*), the world's largest fleet of passenger ships readily converted to military use, the huge merchant and fishing fleets, and considerable major caliber naval gunfire support from the 130mm twin-gun mounts of the *Sovremennyy*-class guided missile destroyers or *Slava*-class cruisers. The open press reported the presence of two nuclear-powered, special-mission submarines in the Pacific and Northern Fleets. The submarines, believed capable of transporting forty troops, also contained swimmer lock-out chambers and a deck shelter for swimmer delivery vehicles—ideal platforms for naval *spetsnaz* units.[7]

Earlier in the decade the Soviets put these amphibious assets to good use in major fleet exercises and deployments. Exercise *Zapad* in 1981 was the largest naval maneuver held to date in the Baltic, over sixty Soviet vessels, including the then-new *Ivan Rogov* in its maiden Baltic appearance. Soviet amphibious and merchant ships landed six thousand naval infantry and a reinforcing motorized rifle division on the Lithuanian coast. That same year featured a major Soviet-Syrian amphibious landing exercise in the eastern Mediterranean. The Soviets also copied British amphibious tactics in the Falklands. Only months after the Royal Marines landed at San Carlos, a Warsaw Pact exercise in the Baltic featured the first use of helicopters to ferry large number of troops inland while air cushioned vehicles delivered assault vehicles and equipment well ashore. But with the Soviet fleet and its amphibious components at their most competent and lethal level in the history of the Cold War, the absolute unthinkable came to pass: first, the Baltics; then, the Warsaw Pact, finally the Soviet Union itself began to unravel in an increasingly dizzy spiral of events.[8]

The impact of these developments on the once proud Soviet Navy was startling to behold. Financial resources dissipated first. This was not simply an austere naval budget. Funds were abruptly terminated—"zeroed"—for ship and aircraft construction, overhaul and repair, operations and maintenance, and even basic payrolls and replenishment. Among other things, the sudden absence of petroleum, oils, and lubricants stopped the Black Sea Fleet as effectively as a preemptive neutron bomb. The Kremlin recalled all deployed ships to home ports. Naval strike aircraft suddenly evacuated Cam Ran Bay and other strategic sites. The elite Soviet Naval Infantry reverted yet again to an emasculated "Coastal Defense Force." Major surface combatants, including the new carrier *Admiral Kuznetsov*, appeared for sale on the world arms market. Construction of two other carriers nearing completion ended abruptly, and the ships were broken up for scrap and spare parts. Iran purchased "Kilo"-class submarines. The sprawling Nikolayev shipyard in the Ukraine launched its last *Slava*-class cruiser in September 1990, then shut down all naval construction to concentrate desperately on building floating hotels for commercial use. As the former Union of Soviet Socialist Republics dissolved into the uneasy Commonwealth of Independent States, Russia and the Ukraine began a protracted argument over ownership of the Black Sea Fleet, as much for its scrap value as for purposes of national defense.

In the last years of the USSR, the increasing toothlessness of the Soviet Navy became readily apparent. The Soviets fielded only a light force during the Tanker War in the Persian Gulf in the late 1980s. Even when raiding Iranian gunboats raked Soviet tankers with machine-gun fire, Moscow responded tepidly and cautiously. Two years later, as Operations Desert Shield and Desert Storm evolved in the Persian Gulf, the Soviet naval presence remained a mere shadow of its former self. In spite of a significant coalition war against a major arms client, the Soviet ships in the Red Sea and Gulf of Oman were fewer and remained much less visible than many of the Third World navies that participated in the maritime quarantine operation. Few doubted that an angry and overpowering Soviet flotilla like the *Fifth Eskadra* in 1973 could have changed the equation in the Gulf War significantly. As it turned out, only a single surface combatant, a lone LST, and a few support and intelligence craft represented the Soviet Union. Their lowly mission: to be available to evacuate Soviet citizens (mainly the several thousand Russian military advisors in Iraq) should such become necessary.

On Christmas Day 1991 the Soviet Union dissolved officially. Within a week, the last Soviet ships departed the Mediterranean Sea; for the first time in thirty years, that crucial body of water was devoid of warships flying the hammer and sickle.[9]

Ironically, the sudden disintegration of the Soviet Navy coincided with the rise of sizable amphibious forces within the naval establishments of a number of other nations. While few countries could afford the major capital investment of the United States in specialized ships and large air-ground task forces, many turned to the Soviet Union for a more affordable example. The model of a modest force of naval infantry and an affordable number of dedicated amphibious ships and landing craft, augmented by convertible merchant ships—all with a regional vice a global reach—seemed appealing. Other nations recognized the need for self-sustaining, rapid reaction forces to protect their national interests in distant locations. The trend in this area was to establish an airborne or air transportable unit for immediate deployment, to be followed by a small flotilla, preferably centered around a multirole amphibious ship such as an LPD or helicopter carrier with reinforcements, combat equipment and supplies. The French armed forces contain a good example of the latter model.

By 1991 there was a great variety in the range and depth of amphibious forces throughout the world. Some countries merely possessed a few short-range utility landing craft, similar to the American LCUs or the Soviet *Vydra*-class boats. Some nations formed a corps of marines even before they could afford amphibious ships or landing craft. Many smaller countries bought decommissioned amphibious ships from either or both superpowers. The Soviet Union transferred dozens of *Polnocny*-class medium landing ships in the past two decades, including ten to India, four to Iraq, and three each to Syria, Libya and Vietnam. Former U.S.-owned LSTs appeared in the navies of Peru, Indonesia, Vietnam, and Venezuela. Polish *Ropucha* and the newer *Lublin*-class LSTs were also prevalent. Should the great fire sale among the Russian Navy extend to the three *Ivan Rogov*-class LPDs, they could command high bidding.

Amphibious forces among the established NATO navies of Great Britain, France, Spain, Italy, the Netherlands, Turkey, and Greece remained at militarily significant levels. Smaller forces within the Argentine, Brazilian, Peruvian, and Venezuelan navies also remained stable. Considerable growth in the 1980s was reflected in the navies of various Southeast Asian countries. The greatest increase in size in amphibious forces occurred in the Indian Navy. Analysts predicted India would possess a full division-sized amphibious assault capability by the first decade of the twenty-first century. Observers viewed the establishment of the Pakistani Marine Corps during this period as a direct consequence.[10]

Comparing the relative size of seagoing marines or naval infantry is a useful indicator of the extent of a nation's commitment to amphibious warfare. In 1991 the United States Marine Corps numbered 201,500 (although senior officers forecast sharp reductions). The Republic of China (Taiwan) was next in size with thirty thousand. Other large forces of sea soldiers included Vietnam with 27,000; South Korea, 25,000; Thailand 20,000; Indonesia, 12,000; Great Britain 7,700; and Spain and China, 6,000 each. The Soviet Naval

Infantry peaked at 18,000 and ranked sixth in the world before the collapse of the USSR.[11]

American amphibious forces, reaping the benefits of the Reagan Administration's earlier naval expansion programs, entered the 1990s with new ships and landing craft and a fresh confidence in the value of their mission. The U.S. naval order of battle in January 1991 included sixty-one active amphibious ships, almost evenly divided between the Atlantic and Pacific fleets. In addition, the Naval Reserve force contained three *Newport*-class LSTs among the Naval Reserve Force ships; thirteen combat-loaded Maritime Prepositioning Ships (MPS) floated in several key anchorages around the world; and the Military Sealift Command had two hospital ships and two aviation logistics ships in a reduced operating status. Moreover, future amphibious ship construction plans seemed healthy in spite of drawdowns in defense spending already in evidence as the Cold War shuddered to its close. Amphibious force planners had hopes of five additional *Wasp*-class amphibious assault ships (for a total of six), two more *Whidbey Island*-class LSDs (for a total of eight), and three of the new *Harpers Ferry*-class LSDs (the cargo variant of the LSD-41s). A totally new amphibious design, temporarily designated the LX, was on the drawing board as a medium size/medium cost ship which could replace the LKAs, LSTs and older classes of LPDs and LSDs in the early twenty-first century.[12]

New technologies helped improve the execution of amphibious warfare, also. Some represented mundane efforts: barcode instrumentation for embarkation rosters and passenger manifests, computerized loading plans, reactive or ceramic armor plating for assault amphibians, and improved secure voice communications systems. Other technological innovations represented downright revolutionary breakthroughs, notably the Position Location and Reporting System (PLRS) and the NavStar Global Positioning System (GPS). PLRS helped solve a centuries-old problem for field commanders by providing the exact location of all subordinate forces instantaneously. The availability of GPS provided precision satellite navigation for even small units and platforms. The GPS system had operational implications for many aspects of land and naval warfare; the military process which seemed likeliest to gain the most benefit was the surface ship-to-shore movement. Equipped with GPS, a Navy LCAC loaded with assault troops and vehicles suddenly had the capability of hitting an unmarked break in the sand dunes or a small river mouth along an enemy coast in full darkness and at full speed.

While the U.S. Navy and Marine Corps appeared still unable to gain full funding support in this period for the two weak legs of the ship-to-shore Triad, the V-22 tilt-rotor Osprey and the advanced assault amphibian, they were at least able to make progress in tactical mobility in less controversial programs. Development of the eight-wheeled Light Armored Vehicle (LAV) provided a useful boost in small unit combat power for amphibious forces. The weight of the LAV allowed it to be transported by CH-53E helicopters; LCACs could carry several in each craft. Here was instant mobility and decent fire-power for the first landing force units ashore. The LAV's many variants also provided the landing force commander with early air defense, antitank, heavy mortar, and electronic countermeasures support.

The Navy-Marine Corps team continued to examine, discuss and refine amphibious doctrine during this period. A decade of debating the merits of maneuver warfare led to the absorption of many of the new tenets into doctrine. Most students of maritime history agreed that the sea itself seemed particularly suitable for maneuver (as opposed to attrition) warfare. The Over-the-Horizon (OTH) concept of amphibious assault, long considered an unaffordable ideal, became one focus of maneuver warfare. Even without assurances that the Osprey or AAAV would ever be fielded, amphibious planners con-ceived of ways to use the increasing number of LCACs and the new, multimission amphibious ships to make OTH operations a reality. Interestingly, the traditional wide landing beaches—uncommonly found and hence readily defended—became objectives to avoid. As explained by two officers from the Marine Corps Warfighting Center, beaches and landing zones in OTH operations "serve only as points of entry and control measures for landing forces. The point of OTH is to get mobile, combined arms teams ashore quickly, merge them into combat formations while on the move, and drive deep into the enemy's rear." Early in 1991 the Marine Corps Combat Development Command published FMFRP 14-7, an OTH amphibious-operational concept paper, a pamphlet as revolutionary in many ways as the *Tentative Manual for Landing Operations,* first published in Quantico in 1934. Other deep thinkers analyzed amphibious warfare in terms of "operational art," an emerging way of looking at warfare between tac-tics and strategy. New terms—momentum, tempo, velocity—took on new meaning in making "fundamental decisions about when and where to fight and whether to accept or decline battle."[13]

With all this analysis and reflection came a sense of change in the

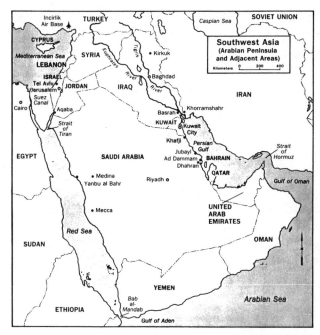

Southwest Asia.
(From Melson,
Englander, and
Dawson, *U.S.
Marines in the
Persian Gulf,
1990–1991:
Anthology and
Annotated
Bibliography*
[Washington:
GPO, 1992], 4.)

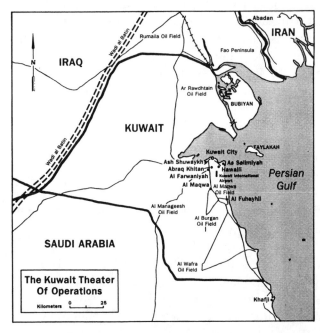

Kuwait Theater
of Operations.
(From Melson,
Englander, and
Dawson, *U.S.
Marines in the
Persian Gulf,
1990–1991:
Anthology and
Annotated
Bibliography*
[Washington:
GPO, 1992], 5.)

traditional way of waging amphibious war. The horrors of direct frontal landings by U.S. Marines against fortified Japanese defenders at bloodbaths like Tarawa, Saipan, and Peleliu in World War II cast long memories in the White House, the halls of Congress and the Pentagon. The capability of making such an assault—to "kick down the front door"—remained a requirement. But increasingly the new developments in doctrine, mobility, deception, and intelligence made such a stark requirement less critical. At the same time, the forward presence and ready mobility of amphibious forces made them ideal candidates for the less sanguinary missions of non-combatant evacuation and disaster relief operations. Amphibious forces demonstrated particular usefulness in these missions in Liberia in 1990 and Somalia, Kurdistan, and Bangladesh the following year. These events encompassed the largest deployment of amphibious forces since the Korean War, a multinational confrontation in the Persian Gulf against the Iraqi forces of Saddam Hussein in occupied Kuwait.

Hussein's masterfully executed invasion of Kuwait began on 2 August 1990. Within hours, the Iraqis overcame Kuwaiti resistance, seized the capitol, and claimed repossession of what Hussein claimed as the nineteenth province of Iraq. The news that a maverick dictator with a million-man army now controlled 20 percent of the world's oil supplies shocked most other nations. Most Americans expressed outrage. The Carter Doctrine applied: this naked aggression represented a clear threat to the nation's vital interests. The image of Iraq plundering Kuwait and threatening Saudi Arabia was unacceptable. "This will not stand!" declared a resolute President George Bush.

Hussein assumed that the western democracies would complain, wring their hands, and in the end do nothing substantial. It was a fateful miscalculation. Bush moved swiftly to establish the necessary political foundation for future military action, isolated Iraq, restrained Israel, and sought help from allies and consensus at home. The Joint Chiefs of Staff, through the Chairman, Gen. Colin L. Powell, provided the President and the National Security Council with blunt military advice to avoid the misadventures of Vietnam: "set a clear political objective, provide sufficient forces to do the job, [and then] keep out of the way." The President accepted this advice and directed implementation of the Central Command's Operation Plan 90–1002, a major deployment of over 250,000 troops to the Middle East in the next few months.

This massive deployment and the subsequent shooting war succeeded primarily because of three significant developments: first, the Saudi government offered the United States and other allies unlimited use of Arabian ports, airfields, and staging areas for the prolonged buildup of forces; second, Saddam Hussein, for whatever rationale, made no preemptive spoiling attacks across the Saudi border even when the odds were heavily in his favor; and third, the USSR, still a military superpower, did not interfere in any meaningful way with either the buildup or the war itself.

The absence of Soviet interference in the Gulf War enabled coalition success. Allied political and military leaders could only consider themselves fortunate for the timeliness of *perestroika*. The presence in the Kremlin of a hardline leader in the mold of Brezhnev, Andropov, or Chernenko might have changed the equation dramatically. The Soviet Union doubtless would have vetoed any United Nations resolution that, sequentially, condemned the invasion, established economic sanctions, created a naval blockade, and authorized the use of force.

Gorbachev's *perestroika* policy provided other strategic benefits to the Americans. The sudden absence of a Soviet threat to the Central Front enabled the Bush Administration to redeploy the entire VII Corps from Europe to the Gulf. Moreover, the U. S. Navy executed Operation Plan 90–1002 without undue concern for the *Fifth Eskadra* or Soviet naval strike aircraft formerly based in nearby Socotra Island in the Gulf of Aden or Dehalak Island in the Red Sea. By stark contrast, Gorbachev generally supported Bush, the Soviet delegation to the United Nations followed suit, and no superpower confrontation materialized. The Cold War seemed indeed to be dying fast.

American amphibious forces cannot lay claim to have been the first ground units to reach Saudi Arabia in Operation Desert Shield. That distinction went to the 2,300 men of the 82d Airborne Division's Ready Brigade, which flew directly from North Carolina. In this crisis, however, the issue was not the race of light units to arrive, but the length of time it would take to deploy heavy combat units and all their logistics train into theater to offset the hundreds of thousands of Iraqi troops now dug in along the southern Kuwaiti border. Operation Desert Shield became the ultimate test of all the mobilization and strategic mobility planning exercises of the previous two decades. Unopposed by either Soviet or Iraqi forces, the system performed remarkably well.

The Maritime Prepositioning Ship program proved to be the most successful of all the strategic mobility enhancement initiatives of the 1970s and 1980s. Ultimately, all three MPS flotillas deployed to Southwest Asia, and linked up in Saudi Arabia with airlifted troops from three heavy Marine Expeditionary Brigades. The ready availability of top-of-the-line, well maintained and plentiful combat and combat support equipment contributed invaluably to the success of Operation Desert Shield/Storm. The troops debarked from their airplanes just in time to take possession of their entire "war kit"—everything from tanks and self-propelled artillery to fuel and water, including all the necessary combat service support.[14]

The deployment of the 7th Marine Expeditionary Brigade from California in August 1991 represented a vivid example of the MPS program. The day after President Bush ordered execution of OpPlan 90–1002, the MPS-2 flotilla weighed anchor in the lagoon of Diego Garcia and steamed northwest towards the Arabian Sea. Troops of the 7th MEB began arriving at Al Jubail on 14 August. The five MPS ships dropped anchor the next day. Within five days the 7th MEB reported readiness for combat and occupied forward positions near the Kuwaiti border with 15,248 troops, 123 tanks, 425 artillery pieces, and 124 aircraft. The 7th MEB also had thirty days of initial supplies. They shared these materials, along with many of their tanks, with some of the airlifted Army units. Shortly, thirteen ships of Amphibious Group Two—with the 4th MEB embarked—arrived in the Gulf of Oman and began conducting landing exercises.

The Joint Chiefs of Staff also prevailed on the president to "push all the mobilization buttons." The rapid sealift ships for the Army's 24th Mechanized Division received activation notices early; some vessels began loading in Savannah well within five days. Other ready reserve force ships, including the two hospital ships and the aviation support ships, were activated, fully manned, and deployed promptly to the Gulf. For the first time the Defense Department activated the Civilian Reserve Air Fleet; eventually, 129 commercial aircraft flew troops and equipment to the Gulf. The president also exercised his authority to call up the reserves of each armed force.

Within two months of the President's decision to execute OpPlan 90-1002, the Pentagon counted 230,000 American troops in theater, including more than 46,000 Marines. Meanwhile, the Bush Administration worked productively to build a coalition against Hussein. Soon, ships representing nineteen different navies comprised the maritime interdiction force. In addition, sixteen nations contributed ground units or combat aircraft. President Bush decided in early November to up the ante, announcing that he would double the size of U.S. forces and call up more reserves. Clearly, a White House decision had changed the mission from defending Saudi Arabia to offensive action to liberate Kuwait, should authorization from the U.N. Security Council and the U.S. Congress follow.

The additional buildup progressed unopposed, and the authorization to use force followed. By the end of January, 1991, 430,000 American troops served in theater, the largest overseas deployment since the Vietnam War. As expected, fully 95 percent of CentCom's combat supplies and equipment came by ship—some 3,500,000 tons of dry cargo and six million tons of POL. Strategic airlift delivered 500,000 tons—a record amount. As the Gulf conflict drifted inexorably towards war that January, there was a sense of thankfulness among coalition forces that there had been time and sanctuary to get everything in place. The Pentagon counted 92,000 U.S. Marines on duty in the Gulf region; more than 17,000 were embarked aboard thirty-one amphibious ships at a peak of combat readiness: combat-loaded with 39 tanks, 112 assault amphibians, 30 light armored vehicles, 52 howitzers, 63 attack aircraft, and 96 mobile antitank missile launchers. Amphibious staffs had thoroughly developed and rehearsed landing plans. The troops and equipment assembled for the invasion of Kuwait presented a significant, lethal combat force, and they posed a legitimate threat to Iraq's Saddam Hussein.[15]

The shooting war that became known as Desert Storm evolved as a model of careful planning and violent execution. The air war essentially "put out Saddam's eyes," destroying command-and-control facilities and surveillance systems from the outset. The small Iraqi navy remained low on the target priority list, but it received enough aerial attention to render it out of action in short order. American A-6E Intruders and British Jaguars sank all three Iraqi *Polnocny*-class medium landing ships and a Winchester hovercraft. AV-8B Harriers, flying from the deck of the *Nassau* (LHA 4), conducted the first V/STOL seaborne combat bombing missions in the history of U.S. amphibious operations. When the ground war commenced on 24 February, the air-ground task forces of I Marine Expeditionary Force fought with distinction, penetrating Iraqi minefields and fixed positions along the border, then speeding northwards along the coast to Kuwait City. These combat units destroyed substantial numbers of the total Iraqi losses in tanks, armored vehicles and artillery pieces.

But coalition and U.S. forces never played the amphibious card. The amphibious task force, the largest assembled on a prolonged basis since the Inchon landing in 1950, received a great deal of media publicity during five preliminary rehearsals. With the outbreak of the ground war, the task force moved further north into the Gulf under the protection of the sixteen-inch guns of the battleship *Wisconsin* (BB 64)—but it was all a feint, an amphibious demonstration in the classic tradition of the Second Marine Division on D-day at Okinawa in 1945. Saddam Hussein bought it all the way, committing several of his best divisions to coastal defense against the landings sure to come. A thousand artillery barrels pointed out to sea, instead of south along the coast. Chinese Silkworm mobile missile launchers joined the array of defensive measures in anticipation of the assault from the sea. The Iraqis scattered Soviet anti-invasion mines along the entire Kuwaiti coast, from one to six fathoms deep. Iraq also placed anti-ship mines, both moored and bottom laid, at ranges up to fifty miles from the coast. After the liberation of Kuwait City, American forces discovered an elaborate sand table depicting Iraqi shore defenses. Hussein took the amphibious threat with deadly seriousness. Military analysts estimated that up to one fourth of Iraqi ground forces were literally pinned down along the coast awaiting the assault from the sea. This is exactly what Gen. H. Norman Schwarzkopf wanted as he swung his main attack around the unprotected western flank of the Iraqi army; it was strategic distraction at its most effective.

As the ground war unfolded, the 5th MEB landed south of Kuwait City by LCAC, LCU, and helicopter to protect the Marines' main supply route and capture by-passed Iraqi strongpoints. The 4th MEB, embarked by then for six months, made demonstrations first toward Ash Shuaybah, then toward the islands of Faylakan and Bubiyan. Public affairs officers disclosed disinformation about landings on those two key islands, "leaking" it to the press to further confuse Saddam. The Iraqis fired two Silkworms at the *Wisconsin;* one crashed into the sea while the other was shot down by a Sea Dart missile from HMS *Gloucester.* But the 4th MEB never received the long-awaited order to "land the landing force." The only real amphibious operation of the war came well after the cease fire when the 13th MEU landed on Faylakan to receive the surrender of Iraq's 440th Naval Infantry Brigade.

Postwar analysts have been tempted to suggest that the amphibious force should have been used for more than distraction and deception roles. Amphibious planners considered using the force to bypass Kuwait altogether and proceed up the Shatt-al-Arab waterway towards or past Basra, thus committing a significant force in the rear of Iraqi main force positions. The deployment issue is interesting but irrelevant. General Schwarzkopf made the theater commander's decision to fix the enemy with one hand while striking with the other. It worked; all forces contributed.[16]

The profusion of mines throughout the shallow waters inhibited large scale amphibious operations in the Gulf. Mines, the traditional nemesis of seaborne force projection, emerged as Saddam's most cost-effective weapon. The United States emptied one combat-loaded amphibious ship, the *Tripoli* (LPH-10), and configured it as a mine countermeasures vessel with a half dozen MH-53E minesweeping helicopters and sleds. The ship was accompanied by U.S. and coalition mine sweepers. Six days before the ground war commenced, *Tripoli* struck a moored contact mine which blew a 20 foot x 16 foot hole in her starboard bow. On that same day, the Aegis cruiser *Princeton* (CG-59) triggered a bottom-influence mine, damaging her so badly that she had to be towed out of the Gulf. "Mined water not only slows you up, it brings you to a dead stop," Rear Adm. John B. LaPlante, commanding the amphibious task force, remarked ruefully.[17]

In this regard, it is unfortunate that the amphibious card was not played. Otherwise, defense analysts are liable to conclude that amphibious forces are as helpless against the mine threat as critics perceived them to be against the nuclear threat in the late 1940s. Neither case is valid. Mined waters are indeed a threat. The United States still needs to get serious about addressing its decades-long deficiencies in mine countermeasures. The point remains that there were sufficient mine sweeping platforms in the Gulf to have cleared a few narrow lanes to enable the LCACs and conventional assault craft to conduct a night landing in conjunction with a heli-borne force—if the theater commander wanted it done. The capability was there.

In a larger sense, the role of American amphibious forces in the Gulf War compared quite similarly to their role in the 45-year-long Cold War. Amphibious forces were not the decisive arm of either conflict. But by existing as highly trained, forward deployed forces in readiness, amphibious forces served well as both a political deterrent and as a strategic option in conventional warfare. The Soviet

Union was hardly brought to its knees by America's amphibious forces, or its navy, or its entire defense establishment. The United States and the West won the Cold War by the sustained application of diplomatic, economic, moral, and military pressure against the Soviet Union until that system collapsed under its own misguided weight. The essential usefulness of amphibious forces played a role in this epic rivalry.

Appropriately, it remained for an Army general to put a proper perspective on the events at the end of the Cold War. Gen. Colin Powell described the impact of change in an address to the 118th annual meeting of the United States Naval Institute in the spring of 1992. Some of his remarks are well suited to this discussion:

> Yes, the Cold War has run its course—but there have been many other changes, as well, since 1990. Most important have been the changes brought about by Operation Desert Storm. . . . Perhaps Desert Storm's greatest significance to men and women in uniform has been its role as a change agent. . . . In particular it has changed forever the parameters of the Defense debates that take place in this country. . . . For example, there can be no more debate about the relative importance of sea control, power projection, or sealift—we have seen clearly that we need all three now . . . There can be no debate any longer about maritime strategy versus continental warfare, for the Sea Services have demonstrated clearly their integrated mastery of both. And there can be no more debate about the utility of amphibious warfare or maritime prepositioning ships. . . . They proved their value, once and for all.[18]

Chapter Nine

The Future of Amphibious Warfare

One vignette from antiquity may serve to illustrate both the promise and the pitfalls of future amphibious war. By 425 B.C. the Peloponnesian War between Athens and Sparta had dragged into its sixth year and reached a stalemate. The Athenians prevailed at sea, the Spartans on land, and neither could gain a strategic advantage. At this point, an Athenian field commander, Demosthenes, took the initiative and forcibly seized the small island of Pylos, directly off the Spartan coast. The landing had a galvanic effect on the deadlock. The Spartans aborted their annual invasion of Attica, brought their main army home, and, when fierce counterattacks failed to dislodge the Athenians from Pylos, sued for peace. Unfortunately for the Athenians, their great leader Pericles had died the year before, and his successor lacked political vision. The island was evacuated after a brief armistice, and the war continued for another twenty-one years. The Athenians were never again so close to victory in the war that they ultimately lost.

The political-military lessons of Pylos apply today. Amphibious capability, employed harmoniously between multiple services in consonance with national objectives, can be a valuable tool. Misused or unsupported, amphibious capability becomes an enormous waste of resources.

The Gulf War of 1991 marked the first major conflict to occur after the abrupt end of the Cold War. U.S. amphibious forces deployed in the Persian Gulf represented the sum of force modernization and expansion programs that had resulted from the height of the Soviet-American rivalry. Seventeen thousand Marines—embarked aboard thirty-one amphibious ships—deployed to the waters near Kuwait. Operation Desert Saber, the planned amphibious assault, consisted of a two-brigade night landing near Ash Shuabah to seize a beachhead, capture port facilities, and reinforce units moving northward along the coast road toward Kuwait City. The amphibious forces rehearsed their plans by conducting thirteen over-the-horizon exercises and feints off Oman, Saudi Arabia, and Kuwait in the months leading up to the shooting war. The force enjoyed the fire support of two battleships, ample close-air support from carrier task forces and nearby allied bases, as well as the combined minehunting/sweeping craft of several allies, including the *Avenger* (MCM 1), the first new American ship of its type in thirty years.

An impressive amphibious force-in-readiness resulted, the most combat-effective force assembled since the first year of the Korean War, forty-one years earlier. Presumably this was the same type of amphibious force that would have been employed against Soviet and Warsaw Pact objectives in the North Atlantic and the Baltic approaches under the Maritime Strategy—had the Cold War continued and degenerated into a general war.[1]

The amphibious force poised in the Persian Gulf in early 1991 was more than adequate to meet the needs of the joint commander, even without debarking a single troop. The question yet remains: how well would the amphibians have performed against a more sophisticated enemy? The amphibious task force in the Gulf faced several limiting factors. Chief among these was the vulnerability of the task force to the antiquated sea mines strewn in its path by the Iraqis. It is ironic to recall that the same scenario that occurred in Wonson, North Korea, at the start of the Cold War—an allied amphibious task force seriously delayed from conducting its primary mission by the presence of crude antiship mines—persisted past the end of the protracted Soviet-American rivalry.

Other limiting factors existed, such as insufficient amphibious ships to transport the entire assault echelons of the two brigades. The requirement to give up two LPH helicopter carriers to serve as Airborne Mine Countermeasures (AMCM) platforms (the second ship was required to replace the *Tripoli* [LPH 10], damaged by an Iraqi mine) compounded the untoward situation. The allies used merchant ships in the assault echelon to offset some of the shortfalls in lift, but the presence of thin-skinned merchants loaded with ammunition and fuel within the tactical formation made the amphibious task force commander extremely nervous. Because of the proximity of the modern ports, warehouses, and transportation facilities of Saudi Arabia, the amphibious force saw no need to embark the Assault Follow-on Echelons (AFOE) of the two brigades, an artificial luxury that most definitely would have been lacking in the North Atlantic.

The *Blue Ridge* (LCC 19), an amphibious force command-and-control ship, deployed to the Gulf, but a senior Navy command pre-empted its facilities for use as a flagship for higher echelons. The amphibious task force commander and the landing force commander were relegated to an LHA, a ship designed and configured to accommodate an amphibious squadron and Marine Expeditionary Unit with their small staffs. And while two battleships provided consummate naval gunfire support, periods existed when the sixteen-inch guns of these ships ranged on other support missions. The landing force commander had to make plans to heli-lift his artillery elements to a position ashore or on a nearby island (an "artillery raid") to ensure continuous fire support of the landing plans. There was precedent for this artillery tactic—Tinian and Bairiki in the Pacific during World War II, and the fire-support bases employed in Vietnam—it may not have proven successful against the Soviets in a different kind of war.[2]

For a variety of reasons, many having to do with public perception, the Department of the Navy did not emerge from the post-combat analyses of the Gulf War in as solid a position as the Army and Air Force. It did not represent an ideal way to begin the inevitable competition for roles and missions expected to follow amid severe downsizing of forces and reductions in defense spending. "The threat" persisted as the missing ingredient throughout the national security debates of the early 1990s. The time appeared prudent for new national policy directives and a supporting military strategy.

The "New World Order" forecast by the Bush administration seemed euphemistic. The Soviet Union had dissolved, but great danger existed in assuming an immediate transformation from communism to democratic, market economies among the independent nations that arose from the ashes. Russia itself, for example, remained an enormous power, hungry and ambitious, a nation with a centuries-old history of competition with the West for influence and markets. Meanwhile, the ongoing "fire sale" of former Soviet planes, ships, and weapons systems continued. The hammer-and-sickle flag may have been replaced by the traditional Tsarist naval flag of the Cross of Saint Andrew, but the first time that ensign fluttered over a Russian ship in the Mediterranean it flew aboard a *Kilo*-class diesel submarine being delivered to its new owners, Iran. The world, no longer constrained by bipolar superpowers, grew more, not less, dangerous. By 1992, analysts counted 250 submarines in the inventories of Third World Countries. Intelligence agencies identified thirteen countries believed to have (or to be in the process of acquiring) chemical-warfare capabilities. And every maritime state, it seemed, had sea mines on hand.

The allies at Wonson in 1950 knew they faced a daunting task in clearing the antiquated Soviet mines laid by the North Koreans. But they had a respectable force of minesweepers from the United States, South Korea, and Japan. Nine full days were allotted to the sweeping process. Instead, it took sixteen days. Three minesweepers were sunk, and by the time the landing force came ashore, the opportunity to interdict retreating North Korean forces had been squandered. Rear Admiral Allan E. Smith, commanding the amphibious task force, reported angrily that "we have lost control of the seas to a nation without a navy, using pre–World War I weapons, laid by vessels that were utilized at the time of the birth of Christ."[3]

Four decades later, Chief of Naval Operations (CNO) Admiral Frank B. Kelso, admitted a similar sense of futility concerning mines in the Persian Gulf: "We recently relearned some hard lessons—how mines can frustrate even the most powerful of naval forces." He described mines as "the true stealth weapon of the 1990s and beyond." The CNO also identified mine countermeasures as one of the fundamental building blocks of naval power in the coming years.[4]

The Gulf War demonstrated, again, how a nation with almost no navy could still pose a serious threat to amphibious forces. The Iraqis spread a complex network of more than 1,200 mines, a mixture of contact and influence types. Seventy-five percent of these were the old LUGM-145, a three-horned chemical contact mine with a three-hundred-pound explosive charge, based on the vintage Soviet M-04 mine. One of these antiquated explosive devices likely damaged the *Tripoli*.[5]

The naval services expressed frustration on two accounts: first, they were chagrined that mine/countermine warfare had been allowed to atrophy for decade after decade, in spite of repeated warnings from top level officers in both services; second, they reflected disappointment that many promises from industries involved in MCM research and development failed to reach fruition. The services pursued fuel-air explosives for thirty years in the vain hope that over-pressure created by such weapons would create the kind of chain reaction needed to detonate enemy mines along beaches and in shallow water. More recently, while helicopter-borne lasers showed promise in detecting mines along landing beaches, the requirement for neutralizing the weapons—once detected—remained to vex seaborne commanders.

Currently, forty-six nations possess naval mines similar to or better than those used by Iraq to threaten coalition naval forces in the Gulf. Of particular concern are the hundreds of thousands of naval mines available in Russia and other former Soviet states, presumably for sale to the highest bidder. The United States critically needs a consistent, top-level focus on needs of mine warfare, as advocated earlier by Admiral Kelso. Years ago, before the Cold War, the United States possessed this capability. The Allies mustered three hundred minesweepers for the Normandy landings in June 1944, and the American fleet included 116 minesweepers for the invasion of Okinawa in April 1945.

The U.S. fleet also needs to include dedicated platforms for AMCM operations and a mother ship capable of deploying the small MSOs on board. These platforms should not be taken from already scarce amphibious lift assets; a retiring aircraft carrier or amphib maintained in reduced operational status (ready to sail in four to five days) could suffice.

Developing a viable mine/countermine warfare capability has always proved crucial to amphibious operations; it remains critical in the post–Cold War world. No nation can seriously undertake littoral, expeditionary warfare without first building a true, independent capability to detect and clear mines rapidly. Amphibious forces now possess the speed and navigational skills to conduct surprise landings in darkness along very narrow axes of advance. The capability will not be seen as credible without a deployable, swift, and effective mine hunting/clearing force.[6]

Nor should national security strategists in the 1990s lose heart at the persistent risk of mine warfare. As military historian Theodore L. Gatchel reminds us, "during World War II, amphibious assaults prevailed over a wide range of defensive measures including massive, reinforced concrete fortifications, large-caliber seacoast artillery, naval mines of many types, mobile armored forces, beach minefields with literally millions of mines, miniature submarines, smart bombs, and suicide attacks."[7]

President George Bush set the tone for maritime operations in the post–Cold War age in his address to the Aspen Institute on 2 August 1990: "No amount of political change will alter the geographic fact that we are separated from many of our most important allies and interests by thousands of miles of water." In fact, forty of our forty-two treaty allies are overseas. More importantly, most of our important trading partners and suppliers of critical resources are overseas.

Political emphases at home and abroad may wax and wane, but it is difficult to imagine any lessening of the nation's fundamental requirement for maritime security to protect its most basic interests in the future.

Given that assertion, it is likely as well that American political leaders will continue to find it important to maintain a maritime expeditionary capability of some description. Amphibious warfare is prone to remain a desirable option within that context. Consequently, future naval strategists may benefit from the following summary of the enduring principles of amphibious warfare—some derived from antiquity, others from experience gained in the protracted Cold War.

- *Amphibious operations, by definition, involve a forcible assault launched from the sea against a hostile shore.* The element of *forcible entry* is integral to this form of warfare. Any hybrid "amphibious" capability that does not include the distinguishing assault feature is not an amphibious operation but merely reinforcement-by-invitation, an administrative lift.
- *Amphibious warfare requires local, temporary command of the sea,* to include effective superiority over enemy air, surface, sub-surface, and mine warfare capabilities.
- *Although forcible entry is the central feature of amphibious operations, this does not mean that direct, frontal assaults against fortified positions in the Tarawa model are the inevitable products.* At Tarawa in 1943, the landing force commander had no options other than a direct, frontal, daylight attack, which cost 35 percent casualties in the assault waves and a loss of 72 percent of the LVTs. The current state of amphibious art is such that speed, mobility, darkness, and surprise are used to land assault forces at the soft spots, enabling quick penetration and exploitation. Amphibious forces should nevertheless be capable of fighting their way ashore against opposition, or extracting themselves from an unpromising position once ashore.
- *Amphibious assaults, the most difficult of all military operations, are inherently risky.* Lt. Gen. Bernard E. Trainor, USMC (Ret.), director of the National Security Program at Harvard University's John F. Kennedy School of Government, has observed that "a full-scale amphibious operation is a high-stakes enterprise. It either succeeds dramatically or fails dramatically. There is nothing in between." An experienced amphibious sailor, Capt. John P. Kelly, USN, reached a similar conclusion: "It is not the nature of naval warfare, particularly amphibious war, to be bloodless."[8]
- *Amphibious forces are vulnerable to a wide range of enemy weapons through-*

out all phases of an amphibious operation. Amphibious task forces pose particularly attractive targets. They are subject to interdiction at any point—staging, embarkation, initial sortie, rehearsal and rendezvous area, movement to the objective area, and the ship-to-shore movement itself. Amphibious ships can be sunk or disabled by enemy submarines, antiship missiles, mines, chemical or biological weapons, and frogmen with limpet explosives. They require protection throughout the cycle.

- *Amphibious operations require unity of command.* This hoary and fundamental principle is still challenged from time to time. Only one officer can be in command at any given time, and this command must be painstakingly phased from naval commander to landing force commander as the operation progresses through prearranged milestones. Violation of this principle throughout the Gallipoli campaign of 1915 contributed to that spectacular failure. The U.S. Navy must resolve or otherwise clarify its Composite Warfare Concept, a defensive doctrine that has yet to recognize the extent of authority required by the naval amphibious task force commander engaged in offensive amphibious operations.

- *The most effective amphibious forces are those comprising combined arms,* both within the landing force and within the amphibious task force. Therefore, a landing force deployed with task-organized artillery, armor, antiaircraft weapons, command-and-control, and close air support is a "force multiplier," most especially if deployed with a task force that includes naval aviation, mine warfare, command and control, naval gunfire, and special operations forces. The Soviet Navy realized this principle and put it into practice whenever practical.

- *Amphibious warfare provides national command authorities the option of combining a strategic offense with a tactical defense.* The Chinese theoretician Sun Tzu recognized this operational initiative and he believed the combination offered the best features of both military perspectives. Examples include Gen. Alexander A. Vandegrift and Adm. Richmond Kelly Turner at Guadalcanal in 1942, as well as Demosthenes at Pylos in 425 B.C.

- *Amphibious operations, by themselves, rarely win wars.* There are major exceptions—the Norman invasion of Britain in 1066, arguably the Allied defeat of Japan in World War II—but in most historic cases, amphibious warfare has best been employed as a supporting operation to open a new front, relieve a defensive position, divert enemy attention and resources, or recapture the initiative. Gallipoli represented an attempt to accomplish all these. The Inchon and Normandy landings best exemplify this principle: massive, risky, surprise landings that successfully altered the fighting, but did not on their own end either conflict directly.

- *Forward-deployed amphibious forces can represent a credible threat-in-being with disproportionate influence on the enemy.* Operation Desert Storm best exemplifies this principle. To a lesser degree, the small Soviet amphibious force in the eastern Mediterranean during the October War of 1973 created disproportionate influence. So it was in the Napoleonic Wars. "With 30,000 men in transports at the Downs," complained Napoleon, "the English can paralyze 300,000 of my army, and that will reduce us to a second-class power."[9]
- *Forward-deployed amphibious forces are capable of conducting political-military missions far beyond force projection.* These capabilities cover most of the spectrum of conflict, from rising tensions to limited nuclear war. The U.S. diverted amphibious forces en route to, or returning from, the 1991 Gulf War, for meaningful humanitarian assistance, disaster relief, inter-positioning and noncombatant evacuation missions in four countries. These trends are expected to intensify in the post–Cold War world. In addition, Marine Expeditionary Units are routinely trained and qualified for such maritime special operations missions as hostage rescue, boarding parties during quarantine or blockade operations, and landing parties to seize and protect (or neutralize) offshore oil-well platforms.
- *Amphibious forces are undeniably expensive.* Specialized ships, helicopters, assault craft and attack aircraft represent significant capital investments with long lead times. Amphibious training is expensive. Personnel costs are also significant. Providing sufficient Marines and sailors to form an equitable manpower pool to meet extended deployments and high operating tempos is a major consideration.
- *Any major amphibious deployment will always require additional sealift and airlift assets to transport the assault follow-on echelon (AFOE).* Even in the best of times, sufficient amphibious ships to lift the assault echelon rarely exist; there will never be enough "grey-bottoms" to lift the AFOE. Planners should never consider the AFOE as "miscellaneous sustainment supplies." Typically, the AFOE contains personnel, weapons, and equipment needed to round-out the expeditionary force's combat capability. General war plans and contingency plans must account for lifting the AFOE directly behind the amphibious force.
- *Forward-deployed amphibious forces offer a useful alternative to political vacuums created in distant spots by overseas troop reductions and preemptive loss of foreign bases.* In Harlan K. Ullman's analysis, "maritime forces are self-contained and automatically transport a cultural and living environment over international waters that is not subject to the same thorny questions of sovereignty and access and bases ashore. There are clearly political savings to this type of sea deployment."[10]

- *Maritime prepositioning ships are now a proven enhancement of some of the nation's strategic mobility requirements.*
- *An often overlooked capability of amphibious forces is extraction of embattled forces under fire.* The Soviets prepared to use their limited amphibious forces to extract their "military advisors" in the Mideast during the 1973 War and the 1991 Gulf War. Other examples abound in history: the final evacuation of Japanese forces from Guadalcanal and Kiska in 1943, the bloodless evacuation of 35,000 surviving Allied troops from Gallipoli in 1916, and the spectacular evacuation of Dunkirk in 1940 are among them.
- *The advent of the Global Positioning System (GPS) has revolutionized control of the ship-to-shore movement.* The common availability of this small device among the crew chiefs of every LCAC, AAV, and assault boat should mark the end of the time-consuming, momentum-robbing control measures of the surface assault by the primary control ship. It should also mark the end of the traditional, parade-ground formations that lumber, wave after wave, fitfully toward a broad beach in daylight behind an open control boat. The use of GPS with new night vision devices aboard high speed landing craft will permit transit along narrow, cleared lanes through minefields toward and across an unexpected landing point. The initial GPS systems have proven accurate within fifty feet. By contrast, some of the landing craft in Operation Torch, the night Allied landings in North Africa in 1942, missed their assigned beaches by as much as ten miles. Many Cold War landings came to similar grief before the advent of GPS.
- *Amphibious forces are offensive and "interventionist" by nature.* These attributes may well appear out of fashion within some political circles of the 1990s, but it is important to recognize both the nature of the beast and the sensitivity of some politicians to such characteristics.

The Joint Chiefs of Staff, looking ahead several decades past the end of the Cold War, concluded in 1991 that a valid requirement for amphibious capability will persist, since it "directly supports our national military strategy of force projection and forward presence throughout the foreseeable future." The sea services, after a few false starts, gradually produced a new departmental doctrine to reflect the new economic and political realities of the 1990s. A panel led by admirals and generals generated a document in April 1991 entitled "The Department of the Navy Integrated Amphibious Operations and Marine Corps Air Support Requirements Study." The following eighteen months brimmed with soul-searching and compromise as the two services worked with the Navy Department staff to consolidate their collective roles for the future.[11]

In late September 1992, the services signed a Navy and Marine Corps White Paper entitled ". . . From the Sea: A New Direction for the Naval Services." It was as revolutionary a document as has ever been produced by the sea services. The new doctrine identified a major change in operational focus, from open ocean warfighting toward joint operations conducted *from* the sea. The emphasis shifted to regional, expeditionary, littoral warfare. In changing operational art, from blue water independence to green water "battlespace dominance of the seaward littoral," the U.S. Navy seemed to be reverting to the Soviet or Napoleonic models, where navies existed primarily to support objectives of the land campaign. Emphasis on jointness resulted in a forced modification of the Army/Air Force "Air-Land" doctrine into an expanded "Sea-Air-Land" concept.

Like any new doctrine, ". . . From the Sea" appeared to offer opportunities, especially for amphibious forces. Emphasis on littoral, expeditionary warfare suggests a greater role for the amphibians. Accent on forward deployment, maritime prepositioning, strategic sea lift, and "operational maneuver from the sea" likewise implied continued usefulness of amphibious forces. The doctrine paper identified a typical littoral expeditionary mission as seizing and defending ports, naval bases, and coastal airfields to "enable" reinforcement by larger, follow-on Army and Air Force units; and there was nothing particularly new in that. The major changes seemed to be the elevating of some heretofore "orphans" like mine warfare, maritime patrol aircraft, amphibious ships, naval gunfire, and attack submarines at the likely expense of the more traditional warfighting communities in the Navy.[12]

Considering these developments, it appears that the amphibious capability of at least one of the superpowers survived the Cold War intact and in fact enhanced. Practitioners of the amphibious art should be reassured by these indicators. There are nevertheless some lingering concerns. The new doctrine speaks boldly of a major shift in operational focus to littoral, expeditionary warfare. But will subsequent naval program objectives and congressional funding in fact be directed toward acquiring and maintaining improved mine warfare, naval gunfire, strategic sealift, and amphibious capabilities? Will there be sufficient funds programmed and appropriated year after year to   build enough "LX" ships to offset the pending block obsolescence of the twenty-six LSTs, LKAs, LPDS, and LSDs scheduled for the dustbin?

Will there be sufficient resources—troops, ships, planes, heavy weapons, funding, operating areas, and firing ranges to permit realistic, joint training? Where will U.S. and allied amphibious forces conduct future, large-scale landing exercises when coastal training areas around the world are being closed by development or environmental concerns? And what will become of the former Soviet Union's old sea-control and power-projection hardware—the cruisers, submarines, long range naval aircraft, antiship missiles, mines, transport airlift, amphibious ships, and air-cushioned landing craft? (Where do former naval *spetsnaz* officers go for transition training and future employment?)

The Cold War is history. The forty-five-year competition between the superpowers for influence and hegemony ended with a whimper instead of the long anticipated bang. Throughout all those years, the Soviet Navy deployed around the world in one crisis situation after the other without ever firing a shot in anger. Similarly, the Soviet Naval Infantry never made an opposed landing across a "hot beach." Yet the presence of these forces, together with other elements of the massive Soviet military establishment, invariably caused a reactive and matching deployment of American forces. Both sides measured themselves by comparison to the each other in terms of ships, aggregate firepower, rapid deployability, operational security, or political credibility.

The abrupt disintegration of the Soviet Union created a power vacuum in which a witch's brew of ethnic, sectarian, and religious animosities boiled over into deadly conflicts. There is a dangerous proliferation of nuclear and chemical weapons and the long-range means of delivery. In many respects, the world is a riskier place than during much of the Cold War. The national defense policy of the United States will be greatly influenced by new domestic and international forces, many only dimly perceived in advance. Whatever new strategic focus that emerges from these influences is likely to include the continuing requirement for amphibious expeditionary forces at some level.

A military analyst, Jeffrey Record, provided a useful and interesting forecast in a recent editorial in *The Baltimore Sun:*

> The Marines have traditionally been "first to fight" for U.S. interests in the Third World, most of which, because it is logistically barren, requires self-sustaining expeditionary forces as well as a capacity to enter territory forcibly, if need be. At a time when aspiring Third World hegemonies like Saddam Hussein's Iraq are surfacing as greater threats to our interests than the recently vanished Soviet Union, such forces are needed more than ever.[13]

Amphibious warfare's essential usefulness across the spectrum of conflict, as embodied by the readiness and flexibility of forward deployed expeditionary forces, should ensure its survival as one enduring instrument of national security policy. "You are Athenians," cried Demosthenes to his troops waiting for the Spartan counterlandings on Pylos Island, "and you know by experience the difficulty of disembarking in the presence of the enemy."

Notes

Introduction
1. General Bradley quoted in U.S. Congress, House, 81st Cong., 1st sess., Hearing Before the House Armed Services Committee, 25–26 March 1949, 525; Liddell Hart quoted in Frank, *Guadalcanal*, 58.
2. Weigley, *Eisenhower's Lieutenants*, 38–40, 43–49, 71–76, and 77–187. For the most recent discussion of amphibious doctrinal development in the interwar period, see Allan R. Millett, "Assault from the Sea: The Development of Amphibious Warfare Between the Wars," unpublished MS, The Mershon Center, The Ohio State University. The Japanese amphibious experience is covered in a variety of materials: Lehman, "Japanese Landing Operations in World War II"; Dull, *The Imperial Japanese Navy*, 21–29; Hayashi and Coox, *Kogun*, 29–46; and Sakurai, *Historical Review of Landing Operations of the Japanese Forces*. Any understanding of the Japanese Army must begin with a reading of Coox, *The Anatomy of a Small War: The Soviet-Japanese Struggle for Changkufeng/Khasan, 1938*, and Coox, *Nomonhan: Japan Against Russia, 1939*. Accounts based on the British experience include Ladd, *Assault from the Sea, 1939–1945*, Fergusson, *The Watery Maze*, and Clifford, *Amphibious Warfare Development*. For Soviet amphibious history, see Daly, "Soviet Naval Infantry"; Atschkassov, "Landing Operations of the Soviet Fleet During World War II," 299–307; Constance, "A New Role for Soviet Marines," 20–21; Panteleyev, "The Soviet Navy After Three Years of War," 22–23; and Gartoff, "Soviet Doctrine on Amphibious Operations," 54–60. While there is no shortage of material on the American experience, Isley and Crowl, *The U.S. Marines and Amphibious War*, remains the seminal work.
3. Definitions from Alexander, "Amphibious Warfare," 145–50.
4. Oral histories, Marine Corps Historical Center (hereafter MCHC): General Robert E. Cushman, Jr.; and General Louis B. Wilson; see also Admiral Frank W. Vannoy, "Where Do the Gators Go from Here?"; Robert S. Salzer, "The Navy's Clouded Amphibious Mission"; Norman Polmar, "Landing Their Landing Force"; and Soviet Naval Infantry (Defense Intelligence Agency, 1980).
5. Sir Julian Corbett, *Some Principles of Maritime Strategy*, 59.
6. Mundy, "Getting It Right . . . From the Sea," 69–71.

Chapter One

1. Sherry, *Preparing for the Next War: American Plans for Postwar Defense, 1941–45,* 16–18, 26, 195–98, 207–8, 218–22, and 224–29; Davis, *The Admirals Lobby,* 135; and Halperin, *Limited War in the Nuclear Age,* passim. For the most recent scholarly study, see Love, *History of the U.S. Navy,* 2:311–28.

2. Quoted in Davis, *Post-War Defense Policy and the U.S. Navy, 1943–1946,* 157–58; see also Coraley, *The Politics of Military Unification.*

3. Hoopes and Brinkley, *Driven Patriot: The Life and Times of James Forrestal,* 394–99.

4. Quoted in Albion and Connolly, *Forrestal and the Navy,* 269–70.

5. Head, "Amphibious Operations," 6.

6. Quoted in Heinl, "Inchon, 1950," in *Assault from the Sea* (hereafter *AS*), 337. For additional views of Marine Corps observers of the drama, see Vandegrift with Asprey, *Once a Marine* 311–320; Heinl, "The Right to Fight," 23–29; and Krulak, *First to Fight,* 120–40. The best study of the brouhaha is Keiser, *The U.S. Marine Corps and Defense Unification.*

7. Heinl, *Victory at High Tide: The Inchon-Seoul Campaign,* 16.

8. Oral history, Victor H. Krulak, MCHC; see also Schnabel, *United States Army in the Korean War,* vol. 1, *Policy and Direction: the First Year,* 1: 139. See also, Karig, *Battle History of the War in Korea,* 166–67.

9. CinCFE to DA for JCS, 23 July 1950, quoted in Schnabel, *United States Army in the Korean War,* 1:142.

10. Heinl, *Victory at High Tide,* 24–25; 33.

11. Hoyt, *On to the Yalu,* 26.

12. Quoted in Manchester, *American Caesar,* 559.

13. Oral histories, Oliver P. Smith and James H. Doyle, MCHC.

14. Montross and Canzona, *U.S. Marine Corps Operations in Korea,* 2:40–51. The complete Army version is in Schnable, *United States Army in the Korean War,* 1: 139–72; the Navy's account may be found in Field, *History of Naval Operations: Korea,* 171–218.

15. The most recent account of this conference, of which no recording was made, is found in Love, *History of the U.S. Navy,* 2: 329–38.

16. JCS to CinCFE, 28 August 1950, quoted in Schnabel, *United States Army in the Korean War,* 1:151.

17. Montross and Canzona, *U.S. Marine Corps Operations in Korea,* 2: 53–71.

18. Schnabel, *United States Army in the Korean War,* 1: 155–56.

19. Heinl, "Inchon, 1950," in *AS,* 350.

20. CinCFE to JCS, 6 September 1950 and JCS to CinCFE, 8 September 1950, quoted in Schnable, *United States Army in the Korean War,* 1: 154.

21. Oral histories at the MCHC: Edward A. Craig and Alpha L. Bowser; see also Krulak, *First to Fight,* 134 and Heinl, *Victory at High Tide,* 62–63.

22. Guttman, *Korea and the Theory of Limited War: Cold War and Limited War,* passim.
23. Heinl, "Inchon, 1950," 337–38.
24. MacArthur, *Reminiscences,* 351–52.
25. Heinl, *Victory at High Tide,* 37; see also, Cagle, "Inchon—Analysis of a Gamble," 47–51; H. Pat Townsend, "Inchon: The General's Decision," 28–34; and Heinl, "The Nucleus of Victory at High Tide," 1:70–78, 2: 45–50.
26. Quoted in Heinl, *Victory at High Tide,* 79.

Chapter Two
1. Commanding General, Fleet Marine Force (Pacific) to Commandant of the Marine Corps, 21 August 1946, ser. 0265-46, container 11, Record Group 127, Federal Records Center, Suitland, National Archives and Records Administration.
2. Clifford, *Progress and Purpose: A Developmental History of the United States Marine Corps,* 71–78; and Mersky, *U.S. Marine Corps Aviation: 1912 to the Present,* 125–26.
3. Rawlins, *Marines and Helicopters,* 1946–1962, 30.
4. Heinl, *Soldiers of the Sea,* 514, 523; Krulak quoted in Rawlins, *Marines and Helicopters,* 1946–1962, 26.
5. Mersky, *U.S. Marine Corps Aviation,* 125–28; and Kirschner, "Helicopters with the U.S. Marine Corps," 30–31.
6. Griffith, "Amphibious Warfare: Yesterday and Tomorrow," 871; see also Weller, "Firepower and the Amphibious Assault," 54–61.
7. Hogaboom Report, 7 January 1957, serial AD 2513-req, VE 23.2N121312\1, archives, MCHC; Deputy Chief of Naval Operations (Fleet Operations and Readiness) to Chief of Naval Operations, 21 September 1955, serial OP-343/at, archives, MCHC; and Clifford, *Progress and Purpose,* 86–88. The recommendations of the Hogaboom Board appeared in a series published in the *MCG* 4 (April 1957): 26-30; (May 1957): 10–12; and (July 1957): 20–24.
8. Mataxis, "The Marines' New Look," 11–17; see also Cushman, "Amphibious Warfare Tomorrow," 30–34, and Schofield, "The Need to Develop Sea-borne Forces," 36–63.
9. Burgess, "Amphibious Warfare in the Nuclear Age," 68–73; see also, Liddell Hart, "Marines and Strategy," 10–17 and "The Value of Flexibility and Force," 483–92; Tobin, "United States Amphibious Warfare Capability," 392–99; and Michel, "Planning Amphibious Operations for Atomic Warfare: The Beach Viability Diagram," 116–18.
10. Rosenburg, "Arleigh Albert Burke," in Love, ed. *The Chiefs of Naval Operations,* 263–319; Wadleigh, "Charles Sparks Thomas," 2: 857–74,

and "Thomas Sovereign Gates," 2: 877–93, in Coletta, ed., *American Secretaries of the Navy.*

11. Hittle, "The Rise of Russian Seapower," 12–19; Neuski, "Soviet Amphibious Analysis," 22; Neuski, "Soviet Amphibious Teaching," 26; and Pritchard, "The Soviet Marines," 19-30.

12. Whitehead, "Britain's Sea Soldiers," 57-61; Willasey-Wilsey, "The Royal Marines," 64-70; Evans, *Amphibious Operations: The Projection of Sea Power Ashore,* 37-41; Smith, *Per Mare Per Terram: A History of the Royal Marines,* 140-49; Strandberg, "Royal Marines," 56-57; Gourlay, "Commando Carrier [*HMS Bulwark*]," 18-21; Rankin, "Per Mare Per Terram," 40-45; Crockett, "Action in Malaya," 28-38; Ladd, *The Royal Marines,* 291-96; West, "Operation Musketeer," 34-39; Young, *Four-Five,* 250-69; and Barker, *Suez,* 197.

13. Edwards, "Netherlands Korps mariniers," 48-52; Strandberg, "Netherlands Marines," 54-55; Hopkins, "Korps Komando," 42-51; Hartmo, "Indonesian Marine Corps," 37-40; Rempel, "The Missing German Naval Infantry," 82-84; "All American Marines," 36-38; Bonsignore, "Italy's Marines," 41-45; Hahn, "The Chinese Marine Corps," 121-27; Branan, "Asian Amphibians: The Royal Thai Marine Corps," 33-41; Kester, "Marines . . . in the Americas," 44-53; W. T. Alexander, "The Royal Netherlands Marines," 20-25; Sharfen, "Het Korps Marines," 12-16; Besch, "PRC [People's Republic of China] Display Amphibious Arm," 6; Thibault, "The French Marines," 136-38; Altman, "ROK Marines," 44-45; Berundez, "The Philippine Marines," 37-39; and Skaarup, "The Danish Marine Regiment," 50.

14. Bodron, "U.S. Intervention in Lebanon," 66-76.

15. Shulimson, *Marines in Lebanon,* passim; Potter, *Arleigh Burke,* 426-27; Rosenberg, "Arleigh Albert Burke," 288-90; Wade, "Operation Bluebat," 10-23; McClintock, "The American Landing in Lebanon," 71-76; and McClintock, *The Meaning of Limited War,* 98-123.

16. Pate, "How Can We Cope with Limited War?" 16-17.

17. Whitlow, *U.S. Marines in Vietnam: The Advisory and Combat Assistance Era, 1954-1964,* 86-95; Simpson, "Thailand," 87-89

18. Nathan, ed., *Cuban Missile Crisis Revisited;* Young, *When the Russians Blinked: The U.S. Maritime Response to the Cuban Missile Crisis,* passim. See also Allison, *Essence of Decision: Explaining the Cuban Missile Crisis;* Robert A. Divine, ed., *The Cuban Missile Crisis;* Kennedy, *Thirteen Days: A Memoir of the Cuban Missile Crisis;* and Yarmolinsky, "Department of Defense Operations During the Cuban Crisis," 83-99.

19. Shoup, "The New American Militarism," 54. See also Fulbright, *The Arrogance of Power,* 84; Kruger and Shaw, *U.S. Marine Corps Operations in the Dominican Republic,* April-June 1965; and Tompkins, "Ubique," 32-39.

20. Bartlett, *Lejeune: A Marine's Life, 1867-1942*, 197-98.

21. Soper, "Observations: Steel Pike and Silver Lance," 46-53; see also the after-action reports of Operations Steel Pike and Silver Lance, reference section, Marine Corps Historical Center; and Price, "The (USS) *Blue Ridge (AGV-19),*" 133-35.

22. Ibid.; Robert D. Heinl, Jr., "The Gun-Gap and How to Close It," *USNIP* 90 (September 1965): 25-32; and Bartlett, *Lejeune,* 197-98.

23. Soper, "Observations," 55; see also "Exercise Ligtas," 114-120.

24. McCain, "The New Role of Amphibious Power," 28-33; and McCain, "Amphibious Warfare During the Next Decade," 104-11.

Chapter Three

1. For useful materials on the origins of the Second Indochina War, see The Pentagon Papers: *The Defense Department History of United States Decisionmaking on Vietnam. Senator Gravel Edition,* 3:242–321; Turner, *Vietnamese Communism: Its Origins and Development,* 168–82; Cf. Herring, *America's Longest War: The United States and Vietnam, 1953–1975,* 1–44 with Lewy, *America in Vietnam,* 3–41; McAlister and Mus, *The Vietnamese and Their Revolution;* McAlister, *Vietnam: The Origins of Revolution;* Harrison, *The Endless War: Fifty Years of Struggle in Vietnam,* 207–239; Smith, *Viet-Nam and the West,* 1–135; Nguyen, *The Long Resistance, 1858–1975,* 145–66; Hooper, Allard, and Fitzgerald, *The United States Navy and the Vietnam Conflict,* vol. 1, *The Setting of the Stage to 1959;* and Davidson, *Vietnam at War: The History, 1946–1975,* 283–333.

2. Cf. Marolda, "Tonkin Gulf: Fact and Fiction," 281–303 with Moise, "Tonkin Gulf Reconsidered," 304–22 in Cogar, ed., *New Interpretations in Naval History: Selected Papers from the Eighth Naval History Symposium.*

3. Westmoreland, *A Soldier Reports,* 156–60. See also Palmer, *Summons of the Trumpet: U.S.-Vietnam in Perspective,* 80–90.

4. Shulimson and Johnson, *U.S. Marines in Vietnam: The Landing and the Buildup, 1965.* See also Simmons, "Marine Operations in Vietnam, 1965–1966," 27–35.

5. Alexander, "An Amphibious Operation in Viet-Nam," 37–40.

6. Shulimson and Johnson, *U.S. Marines in Vietnam, 1965,* 193–203.

7. Peatross, "Victory at Van Tuong Village," 2–13.

8. Ibid., 238–40.

9. Shulimson and Johnson, *U.S. Marines in Vietnam: The Landing and the Buildup, 1965,* 202–203.

10. Mumford, "Jackstay: New Dimensions in Amphibious Warfare," 371–85.

11. Shulimson, *U.S. Marines in Vietnam: An Expanding War, 1966,* 297–306.

12. Telfer, Rogers, and Fleming, *U.S. Marines in Vietnam: Fighting the North Vietnamese, 1967,* 150–81.

13. General Robert E. Cushman, Jr., interview, 1 November 1982, Marine Corps Historical Center, quoted in Shulimson, *U.S. Marines in Vietnam, 1968* (draft copy), chapter 31, p. 8.

14. Interview of General Robert H. Barrow by *Armed Forces Journal International* (November 1980), cited in Besch, "Amphibious Operation at Vinh," 54–60.

15. Shulimson, *U.S. Marines in Vietnam, 1968* (draft), chapter 31, pp. 1–17.

16. Smith, *U.S. Marines in Vietnam: High Mobility and Standdown, 1969,* 297–310.

17. Miller and Toole, "Amphibious Forces: The Turning Point," 26–32; for the possibility of an amphibious assault in Vinh, north of the Demilitarized Zone, see Besch, f.n. 14 above.

18. Dunham and Quinlan, *U.S. Marines in Vietnam: The Bitter End, 1973–1975,* 177–215 and 238–65.

19. Meyer, "The Ground-Sea Team in River Warfare," 54–61; Baker and Dickson, "Army Forces in Riverine Warfare," 64–74; Black and Murphy, "The South Vietnamese Navy," 52–61; and Harrigan, "River Warfare in Vietnam," 317–24.

20. Hilgartner, "Amphibious Doctrine in Vietnam," 28–31.

21. Chaisson is quoted in Shulimson, *U.S. Marines in Vietnam, 1966,* 303; see also oral histories at the MCHC: Victor H. Krulak and Robert H. Barrow.

22. Oral history, Ormond R. Simpson, MCHC.

23. Quoted in Simmons, *The United States Marine Corps, 1775–1975,* 299; see also Millett, *Semper Fidelis: The History of the United States Marine Corps,* 559–606.

Chapter Four

1. Next to electronic warfare, amphibious warfare may be the most acronym-laden military specialty in the U.S. defense establishment. LVT was the acronym used in World War II, the Korean War, and the Vietnam War to denote a Landing Vehicle Tracked, or amphibious tractor ("amtrac"). This designation changed in the mid-1970s to AAV, for Assault Amphibian Vehicle.

2. The differential in surfing capabilities between the LVTP-5 and the rest of the ship-to-shore assault craft was graphically demonstrated during Exercise Dull Knife in Papohaku Bay, Molokai, Hawaii, on 30 September 1963. The first two waves, comprised of infantry embarked in LVTP-5s, landed at H-hour without incident. The following three assault waves, consisting of twenty-one LCVP landing craft loaded with infantry, broached in the surf, spilling most of the troops and demolishing fifteen boats. In some cases, the largest surviving piece of the damaged boats was

the engine block; incredibly, there were no fatalities. Colonel Alexander was an eye-witness. See also *The Honolulu Advertiser,* 1 October 1963, p. 1.

3. For an excellent history of the Yom Kippur War and its impact, see O'Ballance, *No Victor, No Vanquished: The Yom Kippur War.*

4. *Facts on File, 1970*; item dated 26 August 1970.

5. West, "The Case for Amphibious Capability," 18–24. West concluded that while amphibious capability still had its utility, the mission itself was "not integral to the existence of the Marine Corps."

6. Binkin and Record, *Where Does the Marine Corps Go From Here?*; see also Mel Jones, "Where Does the Corps Go From Here?" *Navy Times,* 9 February 1976.

7. Lind and Record, "Twilight for the Corps," 38–43; see also Taft and Lind, *White Paper on Defense:* "A Modern Military Strategy for the United States," March 1976.

8. Salzer, "The Navy's Clouded Amphibious Mission," 24–33.

9. Vannoy, "Where Do the Gators Go From Here?" 88–95.

10. Uhlig, "Assault by Sea," 18–20.

11. "USMC: Hitting the Beach in Grey Line Tour Buses?" 33–34.

12. Moskin, *The U.S. Marine Corps Story,* 2d Rev. General Wilson's testimony is quoted on page 701; General Haynes's report is summarized on pages 708–9.

13. Wilson, "Ready-Amphibious-Marine," 18–25.

14. General Wilson quoted in Moskin, *The U.S. Marine Corps Story,* 705.

15. Soper, letter in "Comment and Discussion" section, *USNIP* 107 (October 1981): 21. Colonel Soper was credited with being the architect for the Marine Corps in forging a joint consensus for the 1963–65 ship construction program.

16. Ibid. See also Salzer, "The Navy's Clouded Amphibious Mission," 31. Miller, "Amphibious Warfare: The Decade of Decision," 77; Alexander, "Combined Amphibious Operations in Northern Europe," 30; and Alexander, "Amphibious Warfare: What Sort of Future?" 67.

17. Col. Alexander was Senior Marine Officer for Commander Amphibious Group Two aboard *Mount Whitney* (LCC 20) during 1977–1979; See also A. S. Miller, "USS *Mount Whitney* (LCC-20)", in "Professional Notes," *USNIP* 103 (November 1977): 106–8.

18. An additional LPD was assigned a non-amphibious mission and reconfigured as the flagship for Commander, Naval Forces Middle East, in the Persian Gulf. See Miller, "Amphibious Warfare: Decade of Decision," 75.

19. General Cushman was quoted in the article "New Amphib Tactic Bared by Cushman," *Navy Times,* 15 March 1972; see also Millett, *Semper Fidelis: The History of the United States Marine Corps,* 610.

20. Miller, "Amphibious Warfare: Decade of Decision," 75.

21. Miller and Petterson, "Guns vs Butter—Without the Guns," 32.
22. Ibid., pp. 32–37; see also McCain, "Amphibious Warfare During the Next Decade," 108–9; Soper, "Naval Gunfire Today and Tomorrow," 52–59; and Heinl, "The Gun Gap and How to Close It," 27–36.
23. Millett, *Semper Fidelis,* 612.
24. Wilson, "Ready-Amphibious-Marine," 24.
25. Walt, "Landing Techniques—A Look to the Future," 20–27.
26. Bill, "The Amphibious Assault—Fast, Flexible and Powerful," 46–57; and Kenneth W. Estes, "Ground Mobility for Marines," contained in "Professional Notes," *USNIP* 103 (November 1977): 106.
27. Alexander, "The Next Assault Amphibian," 38–43.
28. Hanley, "A 60-Knot Landing Force," 45–55.
29. Miller, "LCAC and the Lift Dilemma," 49; see also Alexander, "Amphibious Warfare: What Sort of Future?" 65–67.
30. General Wallace M. Greene, Jr., 9 June 1965, quoted in Clifford, *Progress and Purpose: A Developmental History of the United States Marine Corps, 1900–1970,* 113.
31. Alexander, "The LVTP-7 and the Surface Assault," 35–36; and Caldwell, "The Role of the Tracked Amphibian in Modern Amphibious Warfare," 80–82.
32. Alexander, "The LVTP-7 and the Surface Assault," 36; Alexander, "Amphibious Warfare: What Sort of Future?" 67.
33. Alexander, "Combined Amphibious Operations in Northern Europe," 26–32; Commandant of the Marine Corps White Letter 1–80, 17 January 1980, subject: Flexibility in MAGTF Operations. The Commandant urged his subordinate commanders to be flexible in dealing with requests for non-amphibious use of Marine Corps assets by other services. Two examples are a willingness to use embarked AV-8 assets to assist in the emergency defense of naval forces and a willingness to use USMC helicopters in mine clearing and anti-submarine warfare "on a case-by-case/not-to-interfere basis with Marine operations."

Chapter Five

1. On the Yom Kippur War of 1973 see O'Ballance, *No Victor, No Vanquished,* 8, 170, 260–261, 270, and 307; Blechman and Hart, "The Political Utility of Nuclear Weapons," based on direct interviews with the 1973 WSAG principals (Kissinger, Schlesinger, CIA Director William E. Colby, and Chairman of the Joint Chiefs of Staff Admiral Thomas Moorer), 136–150; Dismukes and McConnell, *Soviet Naval Diplomacy,* 146, 193, 198 and 203; and Parks, "Foreign Policy and the Marine Corps," 20. Colonel Alexander was Officer-in-Charge of the second echelon of 32d Marine Amphibious Unit in 1973, from which the JCS directed Company L, 3d

Battalion, 6th Marines to be airlifted to Sigonella the morning following DEFCON III.

2. Gorshkov, "Certain Questions Concerning the Development of the Naval Art," 28, quoted in Dismukes and McConnell, *Soviet Naval Diplomacy,* 302.

3. Luttwak, *The Political Uses of Sea Power,* 6–13. See also Cable, *Gunboat Diplomacy: Political Applications of Limited Naval Force*; and Mellin, "The Amphibious Force: A Ready Political Instrument," 40–45. Cable (49) described the "catalytic" use of naval forces. Mellin (44) discussed the negotiating advantage to the power demonstrating the greatest resolve, possessing the greater credibility and dealing diplomatically from military strength on the scene.

4. Schelling, *Arms and Influence,* 2–3, 71. Emphasis in the original.

5. Turner, "The Naval Balance: Not Just a Numbers Game," 344–45.

6. John K. Cooley, "Navy's Task: Three-Ocean Strength," *The Christian Science Monitor,* 29 April 1980, 6.

7. Williams, "U.S. Navy Missions and Force Structure: A Critical Reappraisal," 508–10.

8. Gormley, "The Direction and Pace of Soviet Force Projection Capabilities," 262, 268.

9. Defense Intelligence Agency report, *The Soviet Naval Infantry,* (Washington: DIA, 1980) (hereafter DIA, *Soviet Naval Infantry*), 1. Turbiville, "Warsaw Pact Amphibious Operations in Northern Europe," 22.

10. Cliff, "Paloondra!" 19, 26; and Barry M. Blechman, "The Role of Force in Soviet Diplomacy," lecture, Georgetown University Graduate School, 17 February 1982.

11. Whelan, "The Soviet Baltic Fleet: An Amphibious Force in Being," 123; and Gormley, "The Direction and Pace of Soviet Force Projection Capabilities," 268.

12. Hansen, "Soviet Projection Forces—Their Status and Outlook," 76, 78, and 80; DIA, *Soviet Naval Infantry,* 75; and Gormley, "The Direction and Pace of Soviet Projection Force Capabilities," 268.

13. Hansen, "Soviet Projection Forces—Their Status and Outlook,", 81–82; and Clark, "The Soviet Merchant Fleet Wins by Losing," 70–74.

14. Simmons, "The Marines and Crisis Control," 35.

15. Hansen, "Soviet Projection Forces," 78.

16. Kulish, ed., *Military Force and International Relations,* 137.

17. Kotsch, "The Six-Day War," 79–80; O'Ballance, *No Victor, No Vanquished,* 310, 315, and 321; "Israel Strikes at the PLO," *Time,* 21 June 1982, 17; and Townsend, "Vertical Assault: The Proof is in the Doing," 117–19.

18. Blechman and Kaplan, *Force Without War: U.S. Armed Forces as a Political Instrument,* 16, 38–39, 43–45, 71, and 102.

19. Kaplan, *Diplomacy of Power: Soviet Armed Forces as a Political Instrument,* 45, 689–93; Gormley, "The Direction and Pace of Soviet Force Projection Capabilities," 267; and Shulsky, "Coercive Diplomacy," 115 in Dismukes and Connell.

20. On the *Eisenhower* deployment, see Sweetman, *American Naval History: An Illustrated Chronology,* 271.

21. Robinson, "Soviet Moves Spark Defense Support," 81.

22. Dismukes and McConnell, *Soviet Naval Diplomacy,* viii.

23. O'Ballance, *No Victor, No Vanquished,* 317–18.

24. Regarding the 1973 war, see O'Ballance, *No Victor, No Vanquished,* 180 and 332; and Parks, "Foreign Policy and the Marine Corps," endnote 9, 25. On the Soviet airlift to Angola, see Gormley, "The Direction and Pace of Soviet Force Projection Capabilities," 272. For the F-15 deployment, see Williams, "U.S. Navy Missions and Force Structure," 519.

25. Etzold, *Defense or Delusion: America's Military in the 1980s,* 220.

Chapter Six

1. McGruther, "When Deterrence Fails: The Nasty Little War for the Falkland Islands," 47–49.

2. Hastings and Jenkins, *The Battle for the Falklands,* 1–44.

3. Woodward with Robinson, *One Hundred Days: The Memoirs of the Falklands Battle Group Commander,* 72.

4. Hastings and Jenkins, *The Battle for the Falklands,* 83–87.

5. Woodward with Robinson, *One Hundred Days,* 61–62.

6. Middlebrook, *Operation Corporate: The Story of the Falklands War, 1982,* 87–88; Scheina, "The Malvinas Campaign," 104.

7. Woodward with Robinson, *One Hundred Days,* 80; see also Freedman, *Britain and the Falklands War,* 45–65.

8. Freedman and Gamba-Stonehouse, *Signals of War: The Falklands Conflict of 1982,* 218–24.

9. Woodward with Robinson, *One Hundred Days,* 122–23; Nott, "The Falklands Campaign," 118–29; Hastings and Jenkins, *The Battle for the Falklands,* 125; and Middlebrook, *Operation Corporate,* 102–103.

10. Woodward with Robinson, *One Hundred Days,* 5; and Middlebrook, *Operation Corporate,* 151, 185; and Evans, *Amphibious Operations: The Projection of Sea Power Ashore,* 69.

11. Woodward with Robinson, *One Hundred Days,* 188–90; and Middlebrook, *Operation Corporate,* 195–205.

12. Hastings and Jenkins, *The Battle for the Falklands,* 189.

13. Middlebrook, *Operation Corporate,* 185.

14. Woodward with Robinson, *One Hundred Days,* 234–49. For the perspective of the Royal Marines in Third Brigade, see Thompson, *No Picnic: 3*

Commando Brigade in the South Atlantic, 54–78; and Vaux, *Take That Hill,* 81–100.

15. Moore and Woodward, "The Falklands Experience," 25–32; see also Freedman and Gamba-Stonehouse, *Signals of War: The Falklands Conflict of 1982,* 357–76.

16. Hastings and Jenkins, *The Battle for the Falklands,* 315.

17. Baker, "Sealift, British Style," 111–18; Goldrick, "Reflections on the Falklands," 102–104; and Kemmey, "The Fascinating Falklands Campaign," 100–101.

18. Moorer and Cottress, "In the Wake of the Falklands Battle," 23–28.

19. Peppe, "Submarines in the Littorals, " 47; and Carlson, "How Many SSNs Do We Need?" 49.

20. Record, "On the Lessons of Military History," 26–39; and Bailey, "Training for War: The Falklands," 58–70; see also Dutwell, "Postscript: The Falklands War," 82–83, and Summers, "Strategy Lessons Learned: The Falklands Island Campaign," 91–112.

21. Woodward with Robinson, *One Hundred Days,* 99.

22. Hastings and Jenkins, *The Battle for the Falklands,* 123.

23. Franks Report (London: HMSO, 1983), ch. 4; reprinted in Hastings and Jenkins, *The Battle for the Falklands,* 361–72.

24. Cf. Train, "An Analysis of the Falkland/Malvinas Island Campaign," 33–50 with Zakheim, "The South Atlantic Conflict: Strategic, Military, and Technological Lessons," 159–88 in Coll and Armand, *The Falklands War: Lessons for Strategy, Diplomacy, and International Law.* See also O'Ballance, "The Other Falklands Campaign," 9–16.

25. Mastny, "The Soviet Union and the Falklands War," 46–54.

26. Woodward with Robinson, *One Hundred Days,* 202–206; Menaul, "British Defense Perceptions After the Falklands War," 43–50; and Mason, "Hay for the Hobby Horses," 34–41.

27. Hastings and Jenkins, *The Battle for the Falklands,* 232; see also Hobkisk, "The Haseltine Reorganization of Defense: Kill or Cure?" 45–50, and Williamson, "The Future of Air Power," 33–36.

28. Cf. Turner, "The Unobvious Lessons of the Falklands War," 50–57 with Cordesman, "The Falklands Campaign: The Lessons of British Defense Planning," 22–24; see also Cable, "Surprise and the Single Scenario," 33–38. For the Argentine perspective, see Scheina, "The Malvinas Campaign," 98–117.

Chapter Seven

1. Lind, "Simple Tanks Would Suffice," 22–24; and Moore, "Is the Doctrine Viable?" 32.

2. George F. Will, "The Uses of Gunboat Diplomacy," *Washington Post,* 25 April 1982, C–7.

3. President Reagan quoted in Lehman, *Command of the Seas,* 120–21.

4. Lehman, *Command of the Seas,* 119.

5. Ibid, 126. Vice Admiral Sherman was Deputy CNO for Operations (OP-03) when he formulated his strategic vision for the postwar Navy in a hypothetical, general war against the Soviet Union. His top-secret presentation to President Harry S. Truman on 14 January 1947 emphasized forward, offensive operations, including amphibious assaults to "reinforce threatened forward positions, seize new ones, and eventually open the Dardanelles." Subsequent iterations of such an offensive naval concept include the prize-winning essay "On Maritime Strategy" (*Proceedings* 79 [May 1953]: 467–77) by Adm. J. C. Wylie, and congressional testimony in 1979 by Admiral Hayward, CNO during the Carter Administration. The best account of the early days of this strategic concept is contained in Palmer, *The Origins of the Maritime Strategy.* Palmer provides the complete text of Sherman's pre-sentation to President Truman in an appendix (95–101). An excellent source for the more recent history of the maritime strategy is Hattendorf, "The Evolution of the Maritime Strategy, 1977–1987," 7–38.

6. Lehman, "Rebirth of U.S. Naval Strategy," 9–15.

7. Komer and Keeley are quoted in George C. Wilson, "In Policy Shift, Pentagon Seeks Naval Superiority," *Washington Post,* 14 December 1981, A–1; for a definitive account of Komer's opposition to the Maritime Strategy, see Komer, *Maritime Strategy or Coalition Defense.*

8. West, "The Maritime Strategy: The Next Step," 45.

9. Watkins, "The Maritime Strategy," 12. The supplement contained integrated essays by Admiral Watkins, General Kelley, and Secretary Lehman; the Naval Institute published 150,000 copies. Quotes by Admiral Baggett and Secretary Lehman are from Lehman, *Command of the Seas,* 138, 147.

10. Lehman, "The 600-ship Navy," 36; and Hartmann, *Naval Renaissance: The U.S. Navy in the 1980s,* 232. See also Will, "The Uses of Gunboat Diplomacy," C–7.

11. Lehman, "Rebirth of a U.S. Naval Strategy," 13; and Lehman, *Command of the Seas,* 158.

12. Kelley and O'Donnell, "The Amphibious Warfare Strategy," 23–25.

13. Ibid., p. 26.

14. Wilson, "Marines: A Young, Quality Force, Menaced by a New Peril," *The Almanac of Sea Power, 1985,* 18.

15. Polmar, "The U. S. Navy: Amphibious Lift," 123–25; *Almanac, 1985,* 135–36. The LHD was initially identified as LHDX; the seven *Iwo Jima*-class LPHs were commissioned during 1961–70.

16. Information provided by Eugene Shoultz, Program Manager for Amphibious Warfare and Strategic Sealift at Naval Sea Systems Command, quoted in Walsh, "Amphibious Sealift Plans Face New Realities," 61.

17. Truver and Polmar, "Naval Surface Fire Support and the *Iowas*," 131; and Lehman, *Command of the Seas*, 177. Secretary Lehman's testimony before the Senate Appropriations Committee is described in Hartmann, *Naval Renaissance*, 151.

18. Jennings, "MAF Heliborne Assaults: Trump or Joker?" 115.

19. Etzold, *Defense or Delusion: America's Military in the 1980s*, 16.

20. Lehman, *Command of the Seas*, 271, 284.

21. Vlahos, "Strategy and Status of Sealift," 20; See also Meyer, "Airlift/Sealift: You Can't Be There Until You Get There," 88. Contemporary studies indicated airlift used six times more fuel per ton delivered than sealift.

22. Manning, "Sealift Readiness: You Don't Get What You Don't Pay For," 40.

23. Hartmann, *Naval Renaissance*, 209.

24. Cameron, "Facing Up to America's Strategic Sealift Shortfall," 71. The comparative success of the subsequent massive deployment of Desert Shield reflected certain mobility initiatives and improvements, as well as an arguably less urgent process: it was Iraq, not the Soviet Union, who had invaded Kuwait.

25. George C. Wilson, "U. S. Looks to Sea for Mideast Staging Area," *Washington Post*, 9 December 1981, 7.

26. Lehman, *Command of the Seas*, 181–82.

27. Truver, "Sealift for the Overseas Connection," 58; and Hartmann, *Naval Renaissance*, 227.

28. Wilcox, "T-AVB: Mobile IMA for the MAB," 117–18. Should the situation ashore stabilize, the vans could be offloaded and the ships would then be useful for other deployability missions. Lt. Col. H. Wayne Whitton's research paper at the Marine Corps Command and Staff College in 1979 provided the impetus for this initiative.

29. Commandant of the Marine Corps White Letter No. 2–81, Subject: "Amphibious Operations and Maritime/Near Term Prepositioning Ships," 17 February 1981.

30. George C. Wilson, "Marines," 21.

31. Ibid.

32. Linn, "Marines in the Naval Campaign: Integrating Land/Sea Operations," 82; and Alexander, "The Role of U.S. Marines in the Defense of North Norway," 180–93.

33. Grove, *Battle for the Fiords*, 115.

34. West, "Maritime Strategy: The Next Step," 47–48.

35. Watkins, "The Maritime Strategy," 5.

36. Hartmann, *Naval Renaissance*, 157.

37. Hartmann, *Naval Renaissance*, 233; and Moskin, *The U.S. Marine Corps Story*, 736–42. The *New Jersey* (BB 62) fired its sixteen-inch guns in support of Marines ashore on 14 December 1983, then participated in the

largest naval bombardment since the Korean War in early February 1984. It was all to little avail. The U. S. "Peacekeeping Forces" were evacuated to their ships on 27 February. For an excellent account of the Lebanon deployment, see Frank, *Marines in Lebanon, 1982–1984.*

38. Ashby, "Nicaragua: Soviet Satrapy," 51–54.
39. Lehman, *Command of the Seas,* 333; "Once More onto the Beach," *Time,* 28 November 1983, 42–44; and Spector, *U.S. Marines in Grenada, 1983.*
40. Lehman, *Command of the Seas,* 291–303; and Hartmann, *Naval Renaissance,* 240–42.
41. Wilson, "Marines: A Young Quality Force," 22.
42. Simpson, "Reconnaissance in Force," 72–73.
43. Ferante, "Chronology of the United States Marine Corps—1989," 11.

Chapter Eight
1. Bundy, "A Portentous Year," 485–96. The all-time low in favorable American views toward the Soviet Union occurred in 1956 following the crushing of the Hungarian uprising. The Soviet invasion of Afghanistan in 1980 resulted in a 13 percent favorable rating; this shrank to 9 percent in late 1983.
2. Sharpe, "Despite *Perestroika,* Soviet Naval Capability Continues to be Formidable." Sharpe was then editor of *Jane's Fighting Ships.*
3. Trost, "Looking Beyond the Maritime Strategy," 13. The CNO also stated that the Soviet Navy "does its level best to influence the decisions of any government with maritime interests." Kiely, "Gorbymania," 99.
4. Polmar, *The Naval Institute Guide to the Soviet Navy,* 5th Ed., 19 (hereinafter Polmar, *Soviet Navy).*
5. Ibid., 55–57. Hartmann, *Naval Renaissance,* 162; and Polmar, "Landing Their Landing Force," 101–103.
6. Polmar, *Soviet Navy,* 56–61, 215–16, 223–30. "Periscope," U.S. Naval Institute Military Data Base, 1990; and Sommer, "*Ekranoplan:* The Soviet Sea Monster," 144–45.
7. Polmar, *Soviet Navy,* 57, 130, 259, 263, 431, 446–51; and P. A. Petersen and J.G. Hines, "The Soviet Conventional Offensive in Europe." (Defense Intelligence Report DIA–DDB–2622–4–83).
8. Polmar, *Soviet Navy,* 38–39; Bruner, "Soviet Military Science and the Falklands Conflict," 93–95; V. Engel, "Control of the Assault Landing," 80–82; and Jensen, "Shield 82."
9. Thanks in part to Gorbachev's policy of *glasnost,* the rapid disintegration of the Soviet Navy at the end of the Cold War was well documented. The following accounts track this progress: Polmar, "The Soviet Navy: Not What It Used to Be," 121–22; Manthorpe, "The Final Soviet View," 101–102; Polmar, "World Navies in 1992," 104–106; Ranger and Wiencek, "Watching the Old Enemy," and Friedman, "Russia Stages a Fire

Sale," both in *USNIP* 118 (March 1992): 48–51, 123; Pocalyko, "Future of Force in Maritime Europe," 42. Commander Pocalyko described the withdrawal of the Soviet Fleet from the Mediterranean as "the maritime equivalent of the fall of the Berlin Wall."

10. Vlahos, "Middle East, North Africa and South Asia," ("Annual International Navies Review"), 124–25; see also Dunn, "Iran's Amphibious Maneuver Adds to Gulf Neighbor's Jitters," 23.

11. Polmar, *Soviet Navy,* 56; and "Periscope," United States Naval Institute Military Data Base, 1990. Other sizable forces of marines below the 6,000 level or maritime rapid-reaction forces (such as the French) are not included in this list.

12. "Periscope," United States Naval Institute Military Data Base, 1991; and O'Neil and Hankins, "Picking the Latest Gator," 91–93.

13. Bierly and Seal, "Over-the-Horizon Amphibious Operations"; and Pugh, "Operational Art and Amphibious Warfare," both contained in *MCG* 75 (July 1991): 41–42 and 81–85. See also, FMFRP 14–7, *Over-the-Horizon (OTH) Amphibious Operations Operational Concept* (Quantico, Virginia: Marine Corps Combat Development Command, 1991).

14. General Alfred N. Gray, 29th Commandant of the Marine Corps, changed the designation of Marine air-ground task forces in 1987. He replaced the middle adjective "amphibious" with "expeditionary." Hence, Marine Amphibious Units (MAUs) became Marine Expeditionary Units (MEUs); MABs became MEBs; MAFs became MEFs. The basic organization of these forces (ground combat element, air combat element, and service support element) remained essentially the same.

15. Details of force deployments to the Gulf during Operation Desert Shield are extracted from the following unclassified accounts. Friedman, *Desert Victory: The War for Kuwait;* Allen, Berry, and Polmar, *War in the Gulf;* "Periscope," United States Naval Institute Military Data Base, 1990, 1991; and Woodward, *The Commanders.* See also Palmer, *On Course to Desert Storm: The United States Navy and the Persian Gulf,* passim.

16. Information on Operation Desert Storm extracted primarily from the following unclassified sources: Friedman, *Desert Storm,* cited above; Van Riper, "Observations During Operation Desert Storm," 55–61; Pope, "U.S. Marines in Operation Desert Storm," 63–69; Friedman, "The Seaward Flank," 81–83; Hopgood, "Experience: Handle With Care," 81–82; "Desert Storm: Interview with Major General Harry W. Jenkins, Jr., USMC," *USNIP* 118(May 1992): 120–22; Kelly, LaPlante, and Jenkins, "Amphibious Warfare: A Roundtable Discussion," 36–38; and Brown, "Marine Forces Afloat in Southwest Asia, 1990–1991," 60–63. See also Schwarzkopf with Petre, *It Doesn't Take a Hero,* passim; Pleasant, "Amphibious Lessons from the Gulf," 24; and Kitfield, "Send in the Marines . . . But Where?" 16–19.

17. Rear Admiral John B. LaPlante quoted in Evans, "Desert Storm: With the Army and Air Force," 64.
18. Powell, "Dealing With the Changes," 11.

Chapter Nine
1. Brown, "Marine Forces Afloat in Southwest Asia, 1990–1991," 61-62; and Trainor, "Still Go-ing . . . Amphibious Warfare," 32.
2. LaPlante, "The Path Ahead for 'Gators and Marines," 34–38.
3. Fortin, "Those Damn Mines," 30–34.
4. Kelso, "Building Blocks of Naval Power," 39–44.
5. Nagle, "Having a Blast in the Persian Gulf," 104–107.
6. Other sources of mine warfare information include Gatchel, "A Matter of Style: Varying Approaches to the Challenges of Amphibious War," 56–57, and Blickensderfer, "Amphibious Mines: Silent Enemy of the Landing Force," 84–87.
7. Gatchel, "Beetles, Alligators, and Flying Bananas: Revalidating the Concept of the Amphibious Assault," 62; see also White, "Supply and Sustainment: The Gator Navy–an Endangered Species," 18. For a detailed analysis of the problems faced by forces defending *against* a potential amphibious assault, see Theodore L. Gatchel, *At the Water's Edge* (Naval Institute Press, forthcoming).
8. Trainor, "Still Go-ing . . . Amphibious Warfare," 33; and Kelly, "The Achilles Heel," 43.
9. As quoted in Corbett, *Some Principles of Maritime Strategy,* 59.
10. Ullman, *In Harm's Way: American Seapower and the 21st Century,* 231; see also Kelly, "Beyond the Cold War: the Future of U. S. Amphibious Operations," 36–38.
11. O'Neil and Hankins, "Picking the Latest 'Gator," 91.
12. O'Keefe, Kelso, and Mundy, ". . . From the Sea: A New Direction for the Naval Services," 18–22; and Toti, "Sea-Air-Land Battle Doctrine," 70–74; see also Oswald, "Reacting Rapidly . . . From Ocean to Beachhead," 73–76; and Jordan, "Littoral Warfare–the Shape of Things to Come," 140–43.
13. Record, "No More Iwo Jimas?" *The Baltimore Sun,* 15 February 1992, A–6; see also Biggs, "Utility of Amphibious Warfare in Conventional Deterrence," 40–45; and Tailyour, "Future of Amphibious Warfare," 33–37.

Bibliography

Books

Albion, Robert G., and Robert H. Connolly. *Forrestal and the Navy.* New York and London: Columbia University Press, 1962.

Allison, Graham T. *Essence of Decision: Explaining the Cuban Missile Crisis.* Boston: Little, Brown, 1981.

The Almanac of Sea Power, 1985. Arlington: Navy League, 1985.

Ammond, G. A. *Soviet Navy in War and Peace.* Moscow: Progress, 1981.

Armand, Anthony R. *The Falklands War: Lessons for Strategy, Diplomacy, and International Law.* Boston and London: Allan Unwin, 1985.

Barker, A. J. *Suez: The Seven Day War.* New York: Praeger, 1965.

Bartlett, Merrill L. *Assault from the Sea: Essays on the History of Amphibious Warfare.* Annapolis: Naval Institute Press, 1983, 1985.

———. *Lejeune: A Marine's Life, 1967–1942.* Columbia: University of South Carolina Press, 1991.

Binkin, Martin, and Jeffrey Record. *Where Does the Marine Corps Go From Here?* Washington: The Brookings Institute, 1976.

Blair, Arthur H. *At War in the Gulf: a Chronology.* College Station: Texas A&M University Press, 1992.

Blechman, Barry M., and Stephen S. Kaplan. *Force Without War: U.S. Armed Forces as a Political Instrument.* Washington: Brookings Institution, 1978.

Cable, James. *Gunboat Diplomacy: Political Applications of Limited Naval Forces.* New York: Praeger, 1970.

Clifford, Kenneth J. *Progress and Purpose: A Developmental History of the U.S. Marine Corps, 1900–1970.* Washington: GPO, 1973.

———. *Amphibious Warfare Developments in Britain and America from 1920–1940.* Laurens, N.Y.: Edgewood, 1983.

Coox, Alvin D. *The Anatomy of a Small War: The Soviet-Japanese Struggle for Changkufeng/Khasan, 1938.* Westport and London: Greenwood, 1977.

———. *Nomonhan: Japan Against Russia, 1939.* Stanford: Stanford University Press, 1985.

Coraley, Demetrius, *The Politics of Military Unification.* New York: Columbia University Press, 1966.

Corbett, Julian. *Some Principles of Maritime Strategy.* London: Longmans, Green, 1991.

Davidson, Phillip B. *Vietnam at War: The History, 1946–1975.* Novato, Calif.: Presidio, 1988.

Davis, Vincent. *Post-War Defense Policy and the U.S. Navy, 1943–1946.* Chapel Hill: University of North Carolina Press, 1962.

Dickens, Peter. *Narvik: Battles in the Fjords.* Annapolis: Naval Institute Press, 1974.

Dismukes, Bradford, and James McConnel. *Soviet Naval Diplomacy.* New York: Pergamon Press, 1979.

Divine, Robert A., ed. *The Cuban Missile Crisis.* Chicago: Quadrangle Books, 1971.

Dunham, George R., and David A. Quinlan. *U.S. Marines in Vietnam: The Bitter End, 1973–1975.* Washington: GPO, 1990.

Etzold, Thomas H. *Defense or Delusion: America's Military in the 1980s.* New York: Harper & Row, 1982.

Evans, M. H. H. *Amphibious Operations: The Projection of Sea Power Ashore.* London: Brassey, 1990.

Fergusson, Bernard. *The Watery Maze.* New York: Holt, Rinehart, and Winston, 1961.

Field, James F., Jr. *History of Naval Operations: Korea.* Washington: GPO, 1962.

Frank, Benis M. *Marines in Lebanon, 1982–1984.* Washington: GPO, 1987.

Frank, Richard B. *Guadalcanal.* New York: Random House, 1990.

Freedman, Lawrence. *Britain and the Falklands War.* London: Basil Blackwell, 1988.

———. and Virginia Gamba-Stonehouse. *Signals of War: The Falklands Conflict of 1982.* Princeton: Princeton University Press, 1991.

Friedman, Norman. *Desert Victory: The War for Kuwait.* Annapolis: Naval Institute Press, 1991.

Gray, Colin S. *The Leverage of Sea Power: The Strategic Advantages of Navies in War.* New York: Free Press, 1992.

———, and Roger W. Barnett, eds. *Seapower and Strategy.* Annapolis: Naval Institute Press, 1989.

Grechko, Andrei A. *Vooruzhennye Sily Sovietskogo gosundarstva* [Armed Forces of the Soviet State: A Soviet View]. Washington: GPO, 1975.

Grove, Eric. *Battle for the Fiords.* Annapolis: Naval Institute Press, 1991.

———. *The Future of Sea Power.* Annapolis: Naval Institute Press, 1990.

Guttman, Allen. *Korea and the Theory of Limited War.* Boston: Heath, 1972.

Halperin, Martin H. *Limited War in the Nuclear Age.* New York: Wiley, 1963.

Harrison, John Pinckney. *The Endless War: Fifty Years of Struggle in Vietnam.* New York: Free Press, 1982.

Hartmann, Frederick H. *Naval Renaissance: The U.S. Navy in the 1980s.* Annapolis: Naval Institute Press, 1990.

Hastings, Max, and Simon Jenkins. *The Battle for the Falklands.* New York: Norton, 1983.

Heinl, Robert D., Jr. *Victory at High Tide: The Inchon-Seoul Campaign.* Philadelphia and New York: Lippincott, 1968.

Herring, George C. *America's Longest War: The United States and Vietnam, 1953–1975.* New York: Wiley, 1975.

Hooper, Edwin Bickford, Dean C. Allard, and Oscar P. Fitzgerald. *The United States Navy and the Vietnam Conflict. Vol. 1, The Setting of the Stage to 1959.* Washington: GPO, 1976.

Hoopes, Townsend, and Douglas Brinkley. *Driven Patriot: The Life and Times of James Forrestal.* New York: Knopf, 1992.

Hoyt, Edwin P. *On to the Yalu.* New York: Military Heritage Press, 1984.

Isely, Jeter A., and Philip A. Crowl. *The U.S. Marines and Amphibious War: Its Theory, and Its Practice in the Pacific.* Princeton: Princeton University Press, 1951; reprint ed., Quantico: Marine Corps Association, 1979.

Kaplan, Stephen S. *Diplomacy of Power: Soviet Armed Forces as a Political Instrument.* Washington: Brookings Institution, 1981.

Karig, Walter M. *Battle History of the War in Korea.* New York: Rinehart, 1952.

Keiser, Gordon W. *The U.S. Marine Corps and Defense Unification.* Washington: National Defense University Press, 1982.

Komer, Robert W. *Maritime Strategy or Coalition Defense.* Cambridge, Mass.: Abt Books, 1984.

Kruger, Jack, and Henry I. Shaw, Jr. *U.S. Marine Corps Operations in the Dominican Republic, April–June 1965.* Washington: GPO, 1976.

Krulak, Victor H. *First to Fight.* Annapolis: Naval Institute Press, 1984.

Kulish, V. M., ed. *Military Force and International Relations.* Moscow: International Relations Publishing House, 1972.

Ladd, James D. *Assault from the Sea, 1939–45.* New York: Hippocrene, 1976.

———. *The Royal Marines, 1919–1980.* London: Jane's, 1980.

Lee, William T. *Soviet Military Policy Since World War II.* Stanford: Hoover Institution Press, 1986.

Lehman, John F., Jr. *Command of the Seas.* New York: Scribners, 1988.

Lewy, Guenter. *America in Vietnam.* New York: Oxford University Press, 1978.

Love, Robert W., Jr., ed. *Changing Interpretations and New Sources in Naval History: Papers from the Third Naval History Symposium.* New York and London: Garland, 1980.

————. *History of the U.S. Navy.* 2 vols. Harrisburg, Penn.: Stackpole, 1992.

Luttwak, Edward N. *The Political Uses of Sea Power.* Baltimore: The Johns Hopkins University Press, 1974.

Lynn-Jones, Stephen, Sean M. Shaw, and Steven E. Van Evera. *Soviet Military Policy: An International Security Reader.* Cambridge: MIT Press, 1984.

Manchester, William. *American Caesar.* Boston: Little, Brown, 1978.

Marolda, Edward J., and Oscar P. Fitzgerald. *The United States Navy and the Vietnam Conflict.* Vol. 2, *From Military Assistance to Combat, 1959–1965.* (Washington: Naval Historical Center, 1986).

McAlister, John T., Jr. *Vietnam: The Origins of Revolution.* New York: Doubleday, 1971.

McClintock, Robert. *The Meaning of Limited War.* Boston: Houghton Mifflin, 1967.

Mersky, Peter B. *U.S. Marine Corps Aviation: 1912 to the Present.* Annapolis: Nautical & Aviation Press, 1983.

Middlebrook, Martin. *Operation Corporate: The Story of the Falklands War, 1982.* New York: Viking, 1985.

Millett, Allan R. *In Many a Strife: General Gerald C. Thomas and the U.S. Marine Corps, 1917–1956.* Annapolis: Naval Institute Press, 1993.

————. *Semper Fidelis: The History of the United States Marine Corps.* New York: Macmillan, 1980.

Montross, Lynn, and Nicholas A. Canzona. *U.S. Marine Corps Operations in Korea.* 5 vols. Washington: GPO, 1955.

Moorehead, Alan. *Gallipoli.* New York: Harper & Row, 1956.

Moskin, J. Robert. *The U.S. Marine Corps Story,* 2nd ed. New York: McGraw-Hill, 1987.

Moulton, J. L. *The Royal Marines.* London: Cooper, 1972.

Nguyen Khan Vien. *The Long Resistance, 1858–1975.* Hanoi: Foreign Languages Publishing House, 1975.

O'Ballance, Edgar. *No Victor, No Vanquished: The Yom Kippur War.* San Rafael, Calif.: Presidio, 1978.

Palmer, Dave Richard. *Summons of the Trumpet: U.S.-Vietnam in Perspective.* San Rafael, Calif.: Presidio, 1978.

Palmer, Michael A. *On Course to Desert Storm: The United States Navy and the Persian Gulf.* Washington: Naval Historical Center, 1992.

————. *Origins of the Maritime Strategy: The Development of American Naval Strategy, 1945–1955.* Annapolis: Naval Institute Press, 1990.

Polmar, Norman. *The Naval Institute Guide to the Soviet Navy.* 5th ed. Annapolis: Naval Institute Press, 1991.

Rawlins, Eugene W., and William J. Sambito. *Marines and Helicopters, 1946–1962.* Washington: GPO, 1976.

Sakurai, Shozo. *Historical Review of Landing Operations of the Japanese Forces.* Washington: Center for Military History, 1952.

Schelling, Thomas C. *Arms and Influence.* New Haven: Yale University Press, 1966.

Schnabel, James F. *United States Army in the Korean War.* Vol. 1, *Policy and Direction: The First Year.* Washington: Center for Military History, 1972.

Schwarzkopf, Norman H., with Peter Petre. *It Doesn't Take a Hero.* New York: Bantam, 1992.

Shulimson, Jack. *U.S. Marines in Lebanon, 1958.* Washington, D.C.: HQMC, 1966.

————. *U.S. Marines in Vietnam: An Expanding War, 1966.* Washington: GPO, 1987.

————. *U.S. Marines in Vietnam, 1968.* Manuscript.

————, and Charles M. Johnson. *U.S. Marines in Vietnam: The Landing and the Buildup, 1965.* Washington: GPO, 1978.

Simmons, Edwin H. *The United States Marine Corps, 1775–1975.* New York: Viking, 1974.

The Soviet Naval Infantry. Washington: Defense Intelligence Agency, 1980.

Smith, Charles R. *U.S. Marines in Vietnam: High Mobility and Standdown, 1969.* Washington: GPO, 1988.

Smith, Ralph. *Viet-Nam and the West.* Ithaca: Cornell University Press, 1968.

Spector, Ronald H. *U.S. Marines in Grenada, 1983.* Washington, D.C.: GPO, 1987.

Sweetman, Jack. *American Naval History: An Illustrated Chronology.* Annapolis: Naval Institute Press, 1984.

Telfer, Gary L., Lane Rogers, and V. Keith Fleming, Jr. *U.S. Marines in Vietnam: Fighting the North Vietnamese, 1967.* Washington: GPO, 1984.

Thompson, Julian. *No Picnic: 3 Commando Brigade in the South Atlantic.* New York: Hippocrene, 1985.

Turner, Robert F. *Vietnamese Communism: Its Origins and Development.* Stanford: Hoover Institution, 1975.

Ullman, Harlan K. *In Harm's Way: American Seapower and the 21st Century.* Silver Spring: Bartleby, 1991.

Vandegrift, A. A., with Robert B. Asprey. *Once a Marine.* New York: Norton, 1964.

Vaux, Nick. *Take That Hill.* London: Brassey, 1990.

Weigley, Russell F. *Eisenhower's Lieutenants: The Campaign of France and Germany, 1944–1945.* Bloomington: Indiana University Press, 1981.

Westmoreland, William C. *A Soldier Reports.* New York: Doubleday, 1976.

Whitlow, Robert H. *U.S. Marines in Vietnam: The Advisory and Combat Assistance Era, 1954–1964.* Washington: GPO, 1977.

Woodward, Bob. *The Commanders.* New York: Simon and Schuster, 1991.

Woodward, Sandy, with Patrick Robinson. *One Hundred Days: The Memoirs of the Falklands Battle Group Commander.* Annapolis: Naval Institute Press, 1992.

Young, David. *Four-Five: The Story of 45 Commando, Royal Marines, 1943–1971.* London: Leo Cooper, 1972.

Young, John M. *When the Russians Blinked: The U.S. Maritime Response to the Cuban Missile Crisis.* Washington: MCHC, 1990.

Articles

List of Abbreviations

AFJI   *Armed Forces Journal International*
MA   *Military Affairs*
MCG   *Marine Corps Gazette*
MR   *Military Review*
NWCR   *Naval War College Review*
RUSJDS *Royal United Services Journal for Defense Studies*
USNIP *United States Naval Institute Proceedings*

Alaez, Octavio. "Evolución orgánica de la Infanteria de Marina [Organic Evolution of the Marine Corps]," *General de Marina* 186 (March 1974): 307–24.

Alexander, D. G. "The Royal Marines," *MCG* 50 (November 1966): 45.

Alexander, Joseph H. "An Amphibious Operation in Viet-Nam," *MCG* 50 (January 1966): 37–40.

———. "Amphibious Warfare," in *International Military and Defense Encyclopedia* (New York: Macmillan-Brassey's, 1992), 145–150.

———. "Amphibious Warfare: What Sort of Future?" *USNIP* 108 (February 1982): 62–68.

———. "Combined Amphibious Operations in Northern Europe," *USNIP* 106 (November 1980): 27–32.

———. "The LVTP-7 and the Surface Assault." *MCG* 56 (June 1972): 31–36.

———. "The Next Assault Amphibian," *USNIP* 115 (November 1989): 38–43.

———. "Role of U.S. Marines in the Defense of North Norway," *Naval Review, 1984,* 180–193.

———. "Tarawa's Lasting Legacy: The Assault Amphibious Vehicle," *Amphibious Warfare Review* (Summer-Fall 1993): 60–64.

Alexander, W. T. "The Royal Netherlands Marines," *Leatherneck* 49 (December 1986): 20–25.

"All America Marines," *MCG* 47 (June 1963): 36–38.

Altman, S. J. "ROK Marines," *MCG* 46 (May 1962): 44–45.

Armstrong, Charles L. "Early Observations on Desert Shield," *MCG* 75 January 1991): 34–36.

Arthur, Stanley R. "Desert Storm at Sea," *USNIP* 117 (May 1991): 82–87.

Ashby, Timothy. "Nicaragua: Soviet Satrapy," *USNIP* 110 (July 1984): 51–54.

Atschkassov , W. I. "Landing Operations of the Soviet Fleet During World War Two," Michael C. Halbig, trans., in Bartlett, ed., *Assault from the Sea,* 299–307.

Bailey, Jonathon. "Training for War: The Falklands," *MR* 63 (September 1983): 58–70.

Baker, A. B., III. "Sealift, British Style," *USNIP* 109 (June 1983): 11–118.

Baker, John W., and Lee C. Dickson. "Army Forces in Riverine Warfare," *MR* 45 (August 1967): 64–74.

Baldwin, Hanson. "The Amphibious Aspects of Normandy," in Bartlett, ed., *Assault from the Sea,* 320–25.

Balev, B. "Seaborne Landing at Novorossissk," *Soviet Military Review* (July 1972): 40–42.

Barna, Tom S. "MPF Offload: No Longer a Paper Tiger," *MCG* 75 (November 1991): 40–41.

Berundez, Joseph J., Jr. "The Philippine Marines," *Leatherneck* 35 (April 1978): 37–39.

Besch, Edwin W. "Amphibious Operation at Vinh," *MCG* 66 (December 1982): 54–60.

———. "PRC [People's Republic of China] Display Amphibious Arm," *MCG* 68 (April 1984): 6.

Bien, Lyle G. "From the Strike Cell," *USNIP* 117 (June 1991): 38–60.

Bierly, Jerome F., and Thomas E. Seal. "Over-the-Horizon Amphibious Operations," *MCG* 75 (July 1991): 41–42.

Biggs, Geoffrey. "Utility of Amphibious Forces in Conventional Deterrence," *RUSJDS* 138 (April 1993): 40–45.

Bill, David S. "The Amphibious Assault—Fast, Flexible, and Powerful," *USNIP* 88 (October 1962): 46–57.

Black, Edwin F., and R.P.W. Murphy. "The South Vietnamese Navy," *USNIP* 90 (January 1964): 52–61.

Blechman, Barry M., and Douglas M. Hart. "The Political Utility of Nuclear Weapons," *International Security* 7 (Summer 1982): 132–56.

Blickensderfer, Thomas L. "Amphibious Mines: Silent Enemy of the Landing Force," *MCG* 76 (November 1992): 56–57.

Bodron, Margaret M. "U.S. Intervention in Lebanon," *MR* (February 1976): 66–76.

Bonsignore, Ezio. "Italy's Marines," *Armies and Weapons* 3 (n.d.): 41–45. (Foreign Marines file, reference section, MCHC.)

Branan, Barry M. "Asian Amphibians: The Royal Thai Marine Corps," *USNIP* 106 (November 1980): 33–41.

Brodie, Bernard. "New Tactics in Naval Warfare, *Foreign Affairs* 24 (January 1946): 210–23.

Brown, Ronald J. "Marine Forces Afloat in Southwest Asia, 1990–1991," *MCG* 76 (November 1992): 60–63.

Bruner, Ralph M. "Soviet Military Science and the Falklands Conflict," *USNIP* 111 (November 1985): 90–95.

Bundy, William P. "A Portentous Year," *Foreign Affairs: America and the World, 1983,* (New York: Council on Foreign Affairs, 1984), 485–96.

Burgess, J. C. "Amphibious Warfare in the Nuclear Age," *Army Infantry Digest* 16 (July 1961): 68–73.

Cable, James. "Surprise and the Single Scenario," *RUSJDS* 128 (March 1983): 33–38.

Cagle, Malcolm W. "Inchon—Analysis of a Gamble," *USNIP* 80 (January 1954): 47–51.

Caldwell, Robert C. "The Role of the Tracked Vehicle in Modern Amphibious Warfare," *NWCR* 23 (January 1970): 70–75.

Cameron, Allan W. "Facing Up to America's Strategic Sealift Shortfall," *AFJI* 126 (July 1989): 70–75.

Carlson, Christopher P. "How Many SSNs Do We Need?" *USNIP* 119 (July 1993): 49–54.

Clark, J. W. "The Soviet Merchant Fleet Wins by Losing," *USNIP* 107 (December 1981): 70–74.

Cliff, D. K. "Paloondra!" *MCG* 56 (January 1972): 19–27.

Cliff, Donald F. "Soviet Naval Infantry: A New Capability," *NWCR* 24 (June 1971): 90–101.

Collins, John M. "Options in the Middle East," *USNIP* 116 (October 1990): 119–22.

Constance, George. "A New Role for Soviet Marines," *MCG* 65 (December 1981): 20–21.

Cordesman, Anthony J. "The Falklands Campaign: The Lessons of British Defense Planning," *AFJI* 120 (February 1983): 22–24.

Crockett, Anthony. "Action in Malaya," *MCG* 39 (January 1955): 28–39.

Cushman, John H. "Maneuver from the Sea," *USNIP* 119 (April 1993): 47–48.

Cushman, Robert E., Jr. "Amphibious Warfare Tomorrow," *MCG* 39 (April 1955): 30–34.

Daly, Robert W. "Russian Combat Landings," *MCG* 54 (July 1969): 39–42.

———. "Soviet Naval Infantry." Manuscript.

Dunn, Michael Collins. "Iran's Amphibious Maneuvers Add to Gulf Neighbors' Jitters," *AFJI* 129 (July 1992): 23.

Dutwell, Robert M. "Postscript: The Falklands War," *USNIP* 109 (January 1983): 82–83.

Dyer, George C. "Naval Amphibious Landmarks," *USNIP* 92 (August 1966): 51–60.

Edwards, H. W. "Netherlands Korps mariniers," *MCG* 37 (September 1953): 48–52.

Estes, Kenneth W. "Ground Mobility for Marines," *USNIP* 103 (November 1977): 106.

Evans, David. "Desert Storm: With the Army and Air Force," *USNIP* 117 (June 1991): 62–64.

"Exercise Ligtas," *Journal of the Royal Artillery* 92 (September 1965): 114–20.

Ferrante, Ann A. "Chronology of the United States Marine Corps—1989." *Fortitudine* 20 (Summer 1990): 11.

Fortin, Ernest. "Those Damn Mines," *USNIP* 118 (July 1992): 30–34.

Frank, W. F. "The Soviet Landing at Novorossiisk," *MR* 39 (March 1960): 12–16.

Friedman, Norman. "Russia Stages a Fire Sale," *USNIP* 118 (April 1992): 123.

———. "The Seaward Flank," *USNIP* 117 (July 1991): 81–83.

Gartoff, Raymond L. "Soviet Doctrine on Amphibious Operations," *MCG* 28 (September 1944): 22–23.

Gatchel, Theodore L. "A Matter of Style: Varying Approaches to the Challenges of Amphibious Warfare," *MCG* 76 (November 1992): 56–57.

———. "Beetles, Alligators, and Flying Bananas: Revalidating the Concept of the Amphibious Assault," *MCG* 77 (September 1993): 59–63.

Gebhardt, James F. "The Evolution of Soviet Concepts for Amphibious Warfare in the 1930s." Paper presented at the annual meeting of the Society for Military History, Durham, North Carolina, April 1989.

Gibson, T. A. "Gallipoli," in Bartlett, ed., *Assault from the Sea,* 142–53.

Godson, Susan. "Preparation for the Amphibious Invasion of Normandy, 1944," in Bartlett, ed., *Assault from the Sea,* 308–19.

Goldrick, J. V. P. "Reflections on the Falklands," *USNIP* 109 (June 1983): 102–104.

Gordon, John W. "General Thomas Holcomb and 'the Golden Age of Amphibious Warfare,'" *Delaware History* 21 (Fall–Winter 1985): 256–70.

Gormley, Dennis M. "The Direction and Pace of Soviet Force Projection Capabilities," *Survival* 24 (November–December 1982): 266–76.

Gourlay, B. I. S. "Commando Carrier [*HMS Bulwark*]," *MCG* 44 (November 1960): 18–21.

Graybar, Lloyd J. "Bikini Revisited," *Military Affairs* 44 (Fall 1980): 118–23.

Griffith, Samuel B. "Amphibious Warfare: Yesterday and Tomorrow," *USNIP* 76 (August 1950): 871–75.

Hahn, Bradley. "The Chinese Marine Corps," *USNIP* 110 (March 1984): 121–27.

Hanley, M. J. "A 60-Knot Landing Force," *USNIP* 93 (March 1967): 45–55.

Hansen, James H. "Soviet Projection Forces—Their Status and Outlook," *AFJI* (October 1981): 76.

Harrigan, Anthony. "River Warfare in Vietnam," *Marine Rundschau* 63 (June 1966): 317–24.

Hattendorf, John B. "The Evolution of the Maritime Strategy: 1977 to 1987," *NWCR* 41 (Summer 1988): 7–38.

Head, A. H. "Amphibious Operations," *Canadian Army Journal* 11 (March 1950): 6.

Heinl, Robert D., Jr. "The Gun Gap and How to Close It," *USNIP* 91 (September 1965): 27–36.

———. "The Nucleus of Victory at High Tide," *MCG* 51 (September 1967): 20–28 and (October 1967): 45–50.

———. "The Right to Fight," *USNIP* 88 (September 1962): 23–29.

———. "The U.S. Marine Corps: Father of Modern Amphibious Doctrine," in Bartlett, ed., *Assault from the Sea,* 185–94.

Hilgartner, P. L. "Amphibious Doctrine in Vietnam," *MCG* 54 (January 1969): 28–31.

Hittle, J. D. "The Rise of Russian Seapower," *MCG* 39 (September 1955): 12–19.

Hobkisk, Michael. "The Haseltine Reorganization of Defense: Kill or Cure?" *RUSJDS* 130 (March 1985): 45–50.

Hopgood, M. T. "Experience: Handle With Care," *USNIP* 117 (October 1991): 81–82.

Hopkins, Frederick W. "Korps Commando," *MCG* 50 (November 1966): 37–40.

Hull, Andrew W. "Soviet Naval Infantry," *MCG* 64 (July 1980): 67–70.

Isby, David C. "Island War: The U.S. Amphibious Offensive Against Imperial Japan, 1942 to 1945," *Strategy and Tactics* 52 (September–October 1975): 21–36.

Jaroch, Roger M. "Amphibious Forces: Theirs and Ours," *USNIP* 108 (November 1982): 41–48.

Jennings, Joseph F. "MAF Heliborne Assaults: Trump or Joker?" *USNIP* 111 (November 1985): 114–17.

Jordan, John. "Littoral Warfare . . . the Shape of Things to Come?" *Jane's Intelligence Review* 5 (March 1993): 140–43.

Kelley, P. X. "Rapid Deployment: A Vital Trump," *Parameters* 11 (Spring 1981): 50–53.

———, and Hugh O'Donnell. "The Amphibious Warfare Strategy," *USNIP,* Maritime Strategy Supplement, January 1986): 18–29.

Kelly, John J. "Beyond the Cold War: The Future of U.S. Amphibious Operations," *Sea Power* 35 (May 1992): 36–38.

Kelly, John J., John B. LaPlante, and Harry W. Jenkins, Jr. "Amphibious Warfare: A Roundtable Discussion," *MCG* 76 (August 1992): 36–38.

Kelly, John P. "The Achilles Heel," *USNIP* 111 (November 1985): 41–45.

Kelso, Frank B. "Building Blocks of Naval Power," *USNIP* 118 (November 1992): 39–44.

Kemmey, David J. "The Fascinating Falklands Campaign," *USNIP* 109 (June 1983): 100–101.

Kester, Charles. "Marines . . . in the Americas," *Leatherneck* 46 (November 1963): 44–53.

Kiely, Denis J. "Gorbymania," *Amphibious Warfare Review* 7 (Summer 1989): 99.

Kitfield, James. "Send in the Marines . . . But Where?," *Government Executive* 24 (March 1992): 16–19.

Kirschner, Edwin J. "Helicopters with the U.S. Marine Corps," *NATO Journal* 1 (December 1961): 30–31.

Klein, Edwin. "Red Marines," *MCG* 30 (May 1946): 9–14.

Kotsch, W. J. "The Six-Day War," *USNIP* 94 (June 1968): 72–81.

Lamers, A. C. "The Royal Netherlands Marine Corps," *MCG* 50 (November 1966): 44–52.

LaPlante, John B. "The Path Ahead for 'Gators and Marines," *USNIP* 118 (November 1992): 34–38.

———. "It's Time for the 'Gators," *Naval Review,* 1993: 49–52.

Lehman, John F., Jr. "Once More Onto the Beach," *Time,* 28 November 1983: 42–44.

———. "Rebirth of U.S. Naval Strategy," *Strategic Review,* Summer 1981: 9–15.

———. "The 600-Ship Navy," *USNIP* (Maritime Strategy Supplement), January 1986: 30–40.

Liddell Hart, B. H. "Marines and Strategy," *MCG* 44 ((July 1960): 101–107.

———. "The Value of Flexibility and Force," *RUSIJ* 105 (November 1960): 483–92.

Lind, William S. "Simple Tanks Would Suffice," *Harper's,* September 1992: 22–24.

———. and Robert Taft. "A Modern Military Strategy for the United States," *White Paper on Defense,* March 1976.

———. and Jeffrey Record. "Twilight for the Corps," *USNIP* 104 (July 1978): 38–43.

Linn, Thomas C. "Marines in the Naval Campaign: Integrating Land/Sea Operations," *AFJI* 125 (April 1988): 80–82.

Manning, Larry C. "Sealift Readiness: You Don't Get What You Don't Pay For," *USNIP* 107 (October 1981): 34–43.

Manthorpe, William H. J. "The Final Soviet View," *USNIP* 118 (February 1992): 101–103.

Marini, Alfred J. "The Royal Marines," *British History Illustrated* 3 (March 1977): 18–33.

Marolda, Edward J. "Tonkin Gulf: Fact and Fiction," in William B. Cogar, ed., *New Interpretations in Naval History: Selected Papers from the Eighth Naval History Symposium* (Annapolis: Naval Institute Press, 1989), 281–303.

Mason, R. A. "Hay for the Hobby Horses," *RUSJDS* 127 (December 1982): 34–41.

Mataxis, Theodore C. "The Marines' New Look," *MR* 38 (February–March 1959): 11–17.

McCain, John S., Jr. "Amphibious Warfare During the Next Decade," *USNIP* 89 (January 1963): 104–11.

———. "The New Role of Amphibious Power," *Army Infantry Digest* 16 (July 1961): 28–33.

McClintock, Robert. "The American Landing in Lebanon," *USNIP* 88 (October 1962): 64–79.

McGruther, Kenneth R. "When Deterrence Fails: The Nasty Little War for the Falkland Islands," *NWCR* 36 (March–April 1983): 47–49.

Mellin, William F., Jr. "The Amphibious Force: A Ready Political Instrument," *USNIP* 103 (August 1977): 40–45.

Menaul, Stewart. "British Defense Perceptions After the Falklands War," *Strategic Review* 12 (Winter 1984): 43–50.

Meyer, Deborah G. "Airlift/Sealift: You Can't Be There Until You Get There," *AFJI* 121 (July 1984): 76–91.

Meyer, Richard M. "The Ground-Sea Team in River Warfare," *MR* 44 (September 1966): 54–61.

Michel, John F. "Planning Amphibious Operations for Atomic Warfare: The Beach Viability Diagram," *Military Engineer* 50 (March–April 1958): 116–18.

Miller, A. S. "USS *Mount Whitney* (LCC 20)," *USNIP* 103 (November 1977): 106–108.

Miller, E. J. "Amphibious Forces: The Turning Point," *USNIP* 100 (November 1974): 26–32.

Miller, John G. "Amphibious Warfare: The Decade of Decision," *USNIP* 107 (September 1981): 74–79.

———. "LCAC and the Lift Dilemma," *MCG* 65 (December 1981): 47–50.

———, and H. W. Petterson. "Guns vs Butter—Without the Guns," *USNIP* 108 (January 1982): 32–37.

Moise, Edwin E. "Tonkin Gulf Reconsidered," in William B. Cogar, ed., *New Interpretations in Naval History: Selected Papers from the Eighth Naval History Symposium* (Annapolis: Naval Institute Press, 1989), 304–22.

Moore, Jeremy, and John Woodward. "The Falklands Experience," *RUSJDS* 128 (March 1983): 25–32.

Moore, Richard S. "Is the Doctrine Viable?" *USNIP* 111 (November 1985): 32–36.

Moorer, Thomas H., and Alvin J. Cottress. "In the Wake of the Falklands Battle," *Strategic Review* (Summer 1982): 23–28.

Mumford, Robert E. "Jackstay: New Dimensions in Amphibious Warfare," *Naval Review,* 1968, 371–85.

Mundy, Carl E. ". . . From the Sea: A New Direction for the Naval Services," *MCG* 76 (November 1992): 18–22.

———. "Getting It Right . . . From the Sea," *USNIP* 120 (January 1994): 69–71.

———. "Naval Expeditionary Forces: Stepping Lightly," *MCG* 77 (February 1993): 14–15.

Nagle, R. J. "Having a Blast in the Persian Gulf," *USNIP* 118 (October 1992): 104–107.

Neuski, N. A. "Soviet Amphibious Analysis," *MCG* 44 (February 1960): 22.

———. "Soviet Amphibious Teaching," *MCG* 44 (March 1960): 26.

Nott, John. "The Falklands Campaign," *USNIP* 109 (May 1983): 118–29.

O'Ballance, Edgar. "The Other Falklands Campaign," *MR* 63 (January 1983): 9–16.

O'Connor, Raymond G. "The U.S. Marine Corps in the 20th Century," *MA* 38 (Summer 1974): 97–103.

O'Neil, John E., and James D. Hankins, Jr. "Picking the Latest Gator," *USNIP* 118 (August 1992): 91–93.

"Operation Musketeer," *An Cosantoir* 17 (August 1957): 387–94.

Oswald, Julian. "Reacting Rapidly . . . from Ocean to Beachhead," *NATO's Fifteen Nations* 37 (1992): 73–76.

Panteleyev, Teni Phildervich. "The Soviet Navy After Three Years of War," *MCG* 28 (September 1944): 22–23.

Parks, W. Hays. "Foreign Policy and the Marine Corps," *USNIP* 102 (November 1976): 19–25.

Pate, Randolf McC. "How Can We Cope With Limited War," *Army-Navy-Air Force Register,* 28 November 1959: 16–17.

Peatross, Oscar F. "Victory at Van Tuong Village," *Naval Review, 1968:* 2–13.

Peppe, P. Kevin. "Submarines in the Littorals," *USNIP* 119 (July 1993): 46–48.

Pleasant, Timothy W. "Amphibious Lessons from the Gulf," *MCG* 77 (June 1993): 24.

Pocalyko, Michael N. "Future of Force in Maritime Europe," *USNIP* 118 (August 1992): 42–47.

Polmar, Norman. "Landing Their Landing Force," *USNIP* 113 (January 1987): 101–103.

———. "The Soviet Navy: Not What It Used to Be," *USNIP* 118 (January 1992): 121–22.

———. "The U.S. Navy: Amphibious Lift," *USNIP* 107 (November 1981): 123–25.

————. "World Navies in 1992," *USNIP* 118 (March 1992): 104–106.

Pope, John R. "U.S. Marines in Operation Desert Storm," *MCG* 75 (July 1991): 63–69.

Powell, Colin. "Dealing With the Changes," *USNIP* 118 (July 1992): 11–15.

Preston, Anthony. "Amphibious Warfare in the 1990s," *Naval Forces* 13 (1992): 12–14.

Price, Harold B. "The (USS) *Blue Ridge* (AGV 19)," *USNIP* 94 (June 1968): 133–35.

Pritchard, Charles G. "The Soviet Marines," *USNIP* 98 (March 1972): 19–130.

Pugh, Paul F. "Operational Art and Amphibious Warfare," *MCG* 75 (July 1991): 81–85.

Quinlan, David A. "Naval Forces Are Rapid Deployment Forces," *USNIP* 107 (November 1981): 32–35.

Ranger, Robin and Wiencek, David G. "Watching the Old Enemy," *USNIP* 118 (April 1992): 48–53.

Rankin, R. H. "Per Mare Per Terram," *MCG* 37 (April 1953): 40–45.

Record, Jeffrey. "On the Lessons of Military History," *MR* 65 (August 1985): 26–39.

————. "No More Iwo Jimas?" *Baltimore Sun,* 15 February 1992, A6.

Rempel, W. "The Missing German Naval Infantry," *MR* 31 (July 1956): 82–84.

Robinson, Clarence A., Jr. "Soviet Moves Spark Defense Support," *Aviation Week and Space Technology,* 21 January 1980: 81.

Rosenberg, David Alan. "Arleigh Albert Burke," in Robert W. Love, Jr., ed. *The Chiefs of Naval Operations* (Annapolis: Naval Institute Press, 1984), 263–319.

Rothenberg, Gunther. "From Gallipoli to Guadalcanal," , in Bartlett, ed., *Assault from the Sea,* 175–82.

Royce, Randolf B. "The Father of Forcible Entry," *USNIP* 111 (November 1985): 63–70.

Salzer, Robert S. "The Navy's Clouded Amphibious Mission," *USNIP* 104 (February 1978): 24–33.

Scheina, Robert L. "The Malvinas Campaign," *USNIP* 109 (May 1983): 98–117.

Schofield, B. B. "The Need to Develop Sea-borne Forces," *Army Quarterly* 84 (April 1962): 36–63.

Sharfen, John C. "Het Korps Marines," *MCG* 71 (October 1987): 12–16.

Sharpe, Richard. "Despite *Perestroika,* Soviet Naval Capability Continues to be Formidable," *Almanac of Seapower, 1990* 33 (January 1990): 37–40.

Shoults, Eugene E. "Maritime Prepositioning: Long Term Solution," *MCG* 64 (August 1980): 57–59.

Shoup, David M. "The New American Militarism," *Atlantic,* April 1969: 54.

Simmons, Edwin H. "The Marines and Crisis Control," *USNIP* 91 (November 1965): 26–35.

Simpson, Ross W. "Reconnaissance in Force," *Amphibious Warfare Review* 8 (Summer 1990): 72–73.

Skaarup, H. E. "The Danish Marine Regiment," *MCG* 51 (August 1967): 50.

Sommer, Geoffrey S., "Ekranoplan: The Soviet Sea Monster," *USNIP* 113 (January 1987): 101–103.

Soper, James B. "Comment and Discussion," *USNIP* 107 (October 1981): 21.

———. "Naval Gunfire Today and Tomorrow," *USNIP* 92 (September 1966): 52–59.

———. "Observations: Steel Pike and Silver Lance," *USNIP* 91 (November 1965): 46–53.

Strandberg, Carl H. "Royal Marines," *MCG* 45 (October 1961): 56–57.

Summers, Harry G., Jr. "Strategy Lessons Learned: The Falklands Island Campaign," *Art of War Quarterly* (September 1983): 91–112.

Tailyour, R. S. "Future of Amphibious Warfare," *RUSJDS* 136 (Spring 1991): 33–37.

Thibault, G. E. "The French Marines," *USNIP* 94 (March 1968): 136–38.

Tobin, John L. "United States Amphibious Warfare Capability," *RUSIJ* 106 (August 1961): 392–99.

Tompkins, Rathvon Mc. "Ubique," *MCG* 49 (August 1965): 32–39.

Toti, William J. "Sea-Air-Land Battle Doctrine," *USNIP* 118 (September 1992): 70–74.

Townsend, H. Pat. "Inchon: The General's Decision," *MR* 47 (April 1967): 28–34.

Townsend, Patrick L. "Vertical Assault: The Proof is in the Doing," *USNIP* 97 (November 1971): 117–19.

Train, Harry D. "An Analysis of the Falkland/Malvinas Island Campaign," *NWCR* 41 (Winter 1988): 33–50.

Trainor, Bernard E. "Still Go-ing . . . Amphibious Warfare," *USNIP* 118 (November 1992): 30–32.

Trost, Carlisle A. H. "Looking Beyond the Maritime Strategy," *USNIP* 113 (January 1987: 13–16.

Truver, Scott C. "Sealift for the Overseas Connection," *AFJI* 124 (August 1986): 54–60.

———, and Norman Polmar. "Naval Surface Fire Support and the *Iowas*," *USNIP* 111 (November 1985): 130–33.

Turbiville, Graham H. "Warsaw Pact Amphibious Operations in Northern Europe," *MCG* 76 (October 1976): 20–26.

Turner, Frederick C. "The Resurgent Soviet Marines," *MCG* 54 (June 1969): 29–31.

Turner, Stansfield. "The Naval Balance: Not Just a Numbers Game," *Foreign Affairs* 55 (January 1977): 344–45.

————. "The Unobvious Lessons of the Falklands War," *USNIP* 109 (April 1983): 50–57.

Uhlig, Frank Jr. "Assault by Sea," *MCG* 60 (June 1976): 18–20.

"USMC: Hitting the Beach in Grey Line Tour Buses?" *AFJI* 116 (March 1979): 33–34.

Van Riper, Paul K. "Observations During Operation Desert Storm," *MCG* 75 (June 1991): 55–61.

Vannoy, Frank W. "Where Do the Gators Go From Here?" *USNIP* 104 (March 1978): 88–95.

Vlahos, Michael. "Middle East, North Africa, and South Asia," *USNIP* 117 (March 1991): 124–25.

————. "Strategy and Status of Sealift," *Journal of Defense and Diplomacy* (March 1984): 18–23.

Wade, Sidney S. "Operation Bluebat," *MCG* 43 (July 1959): 10–23.

Wadleigh, John R. "Charles Sparks Thomas," in Paolo E. Coletta, ed., *American Secretaries of the Navy* (Annapolis: Naval Institute Press, 1980), 2: 857–74.

————. "Thomas Sovereign Gates," in Paolo E. Coletta, ed., *American Secretaries of the Navy* (Annapolis: Naval Institute Press, 1980), 877–93.

Walsh, Edward J. "Amphibious Sealift Plans Face New Realities," *AFJI* 127 (April 1990): 60–64.

Walt, Lewis W. "Landing Techniques—A Look to the Future," *MCG* 35 (February 1951): 20–27.

Watkins, James D. "The Maritime Strategy," *USNIP* (Maritime Strategy Supplement), January 1986: 12.

Weller, Donald F. "Firepower and the Amphibious Assault," *MCG* 36 (March 1952): 54–61.

West, Francis J. "The Case for Amphibious Capability," *MCG* 58 (October 1974): 18–24.

————. "The Maritime Strategy: The Next Step," *USNIP* 113 (January 1987): 40–49.

————. "Limited U.S.-Soviet Conflict and the RDF," *MCG* 64 (August 1980): 39–46.

West, Gordon. "Operation Musketeer," *MCG* 41 (July 1957): 34–39.

Whelan, Matthew J. "The Soviet Baltic Fleet: An Amphibious Force in Being," *USNIP* 107 (November 1981): 122–25.

White, Carl. "Supply and Sustainment: The Gator Navy—An Endangered Species?" *Sea Power* 34 (February 1991): 18.

Whitehead, A. F. "Britain's Sea Soldiers," *USNIP* 107 (November 1981): 57–61.

Wilcox, Wayne P. "T-AVB: Mobile IMA for the MAB," *USNIP* 111 (November 1985): 117–18.

Will, George F. "The Uses of Gunboat Diplomacy," *Washington Post,* 25 April 1982, C7.

Willasey-Wilsey, A. P. "The Royal Marines," *USNIP* 91 (November 1965): 64–70.

Williams, John A. "U.S. Navy Missions and Force Structure: A Critical Reappraisal," *Armed Forces and Society,* Summer 1981: 508–10.

Williamson, Keith. "The Future of Air Power," *RUSJDS* 130 (March 1985): 33–36.

Wilson, George C. "In Policy Shift, Pentagon Seeks Naval Superiority," *Washington Post,* 14 December 1981, A1.

———. "U.S. Looks to Sea for Mideast Staging Area," *Washington Post,* 9 December 1981, A7.

———. "Marines: A Young, Quality Force, Menaced by a New Peril," *The Almanac of Sea Power* 1985: 18.

Wilson, Louis H., Jr. "Ready-Amphibious-Marine," *USNIP* 103 (November 1977): 18–25.

Wylie, J. C. "On Maritime Strategy," *USNIP* 79 (May 1953) 467–477.

Yarmolinsky, Adam. "Department of Defense Operations During the Cuban Crisis," *NWCR* 32 (July–August 1979): 38–46.

Zakheim, Dov S. "The South Atlantic Conflict: Strategic, Military, and Technological Lessons," in Alberto L. Coll and Anthony R. Armand, eds., *The Falklands War: Lessons for Strategy, Diplomacy, and International Law* (Boston and London: Allan and Unwin, 1985), 159–88.

Oral Histories

All from the Marine Corps Historical Center in Washington, D.C.

Gen. Robert H. Barrow, USMC
Lt. Gen. Alpha L. Bowser, USMC
Lt. Gen. Edward A. Craig, USMC
Gen. Robert E. Cushman, Jr., USMC
Vice Adm. James H. Doyle, USN
Lt. Gen. Victor H. Krulak, USMC
Lt. Gen. Ormond R. Simpson, USMC
Gen. Oliver P. Smith, USMC
Gen. Louis H. Wilson, USMC

Index

ABOUT THE AUTHORS

Col. Joseph Alexander served for twenty-nine years as an assault amphibian officer in the Marine Corps. He commanded a company in Vietnam and a battalion in Okinawa and served for five years at sea aboard amphibious ships. As a colonel he was chief of the Strategic Mobility Branch, HQMC; Military Secretary to the twenty-eighth Commandant; Chief of Staff, 3d Marine Division; and Director of the Marine Corps Development Center.

Colonel Alexander holds an AB degree in history from the University of North Carolina, masters degrees in history and government from Georgetown and Jacksonville, and he is a distinguished graduate of the Naval War College. He is a member of the Society for Military History and a Life Member of the Naval Institute and the Marine Corps Historical Foundation.

An independent historian, Colonel Alexander is the author of *Across the Reef,* the fiftieth-anniversary commemorative history of the Battle of Tarawa, and *Utmost Savagery: The Amphibious Seizure of Tarawa* (NIP, upcoming). He has written several dozen feature essays for *Proceedings, Naval History, Marine Corps Gazette, Leatherneck, Amphibious Warfare Review, World War II, Fortitudine,* and *Officer Review.* On several occasions he has participated as a guest historian in military documentaries produced by Lou Reda Productions for the Arts and Entertainment TV network.

Colonel Alexander lives in Asheville, North Carolina, with his wife, Gale, and serves as a volunteer home builder and member of the board of Habitat for Humanity.

Lt. Col. Merrill L. Bartlett was commissioned a second lieutenant in 1963 following graduation from Washington State University and served until being placed on the disability retired list in 1983. He completed his graduate studies at San Diego State University and the University of Maryland, College Park. From 1977 until his retirement Lieutenant Colonel Bartlett taught history at the U.S. Naval Academy. In 1979 he received the William C. Clements Award as the outstanding military educator at the Naval Academy, and in 1981 and 1987 the Robert D. Heinl, Jr., Prize for the best published essay on the history of the Marine Corps. At his retirement ceremony, the Naval Academy announced the creation of the Merrill Bartlett Prize in History.

Lieutenant Colonel Bartlett is the editor of *Assault from the Sea: Essays on the History of Amphibious Warfare* (Naval Institute Press, 1983, paperback 1985) and the author of *Lejeune: A Marine's Life, 1867–1942* (University of South Carolina Press, 1993). His essays and book reviews have appeared in the Marine Corps *Gazette,* U.S. Naval Institute *Proceedings, Naval History, American Neptune,* Naval War College *Review,* and *Journal of Military History.*

The **Naval Institute Press** is the book-publishing arm of the U.S. Naval Institute, a private, nonprofit society for sea service professionals and others who share an interest in naval and maritime affairs. Established in 1873 at the U.S. Naval Academy in Annapolis, Maryland, where its offices remain, today the Naval Institute has more than 100,000 members worldwide.

Members of the Naval Institute receive the influential monthly magazine *Proceedings* and discounts on fine nautical prints and on ship and aircraft photos. They also have access to the transcripts of the Institute's Oral History Program and get discounted admission to any of the Institute-sponsored seminars offered around the country.

The Naval Institute also publishes *Naval History* magazine. This colorful bimonthly is filled with entertaining and thought-provoking articles, first-person reminiscences, and dramatic art and photography. Members receive a discount on *Naval History* subscriptions.

The Naval Institute's book-publishing program, begun in 1898 with basic guides to naval practices, has broadened its scope in recent years to include books of more general interest. Now the Naval Institute Press publishes more than seventy titles each year, ranging from how-to books on boating and navigation to battle histories, biographies, ship and aircraft guides, and novels. Institute members receive discounts on the Press's nearly 400 books in print.

For a free catalog describing Naval Institute Press books currently available, and for further information about subscribing to *Naval History* magazine or about joining the U.S. Naval Institute, please write to:

Membership & Communications Department
U.S. Naval Institute
118 Maryland Avenue
Annapolis, Maryland 21402-5035

Or call, toll-free, (800) 233-USNI.